NEWMAN AND THE MODERNISTS

Edited by Mary Jo Weaver

COLLEGE THEOLOGY SOCIETY
RESOURCES IN RELIGION • 1

UNIVERSITY
PRESS OF
AMERICA

LANHAM • NEW YORK • LONDON

Typeset at Saint Joseph's University Press,
Philadelphia. Cover design and illustration
by Susan M. Wilks.

Library of Congress Cataloging in Publication Data
Main entry under title:

Newman and the modernists.

  (Resources in religion ; 1-   )
  Bibliography: v. 1, p.
  Includes index.
    1. Modernism—Catholic Church—History of doctrines—
19th century—Addresses, essays, lectures.
2. Modernism—Catholic Church—History of doctrines—
20th century—Addresses, essays, lectures.   3. Newman,
John Henry, 1801-1890—Influence—Addresses, essays,
lectures.   4. Catholic Church—Doctrines—History—
19th century—Addresses, essays, lectures.   5. Catholic
Church—Doctrines—History—20th century—Addresses,
essays, lectures. I. Weaver, Mary Jo. II. Series:
Resources in religion ; 1, etc.
BX1396.N48   1985   230'.2'0924   85-22589
ISBN 0-8191-4687-0 (v. 1 : alk. paper)
ISBN 0-8191-4688-9 (pbk. : v. 1 : alk. paper)

TABLE OF CONTENTS

SERIES EDITORS' PREFACE

The College Theology Society co-publishes **CTS RESOURCES IN RELIGION** with University Press of America as part of its commitment to scholarship and effective teaching. This series makes available important resources which reflect the traditional interests and focus of the Society including Catholic theology and life, the broader Christian tradition, and universal religious experience as well as creative teaching in college and university settings.

The Research and Publications Committee of the CTS has sole editorial responsibility for the selection, design and production of **CTS RESOURCES IN RELIGION, CTS STUDIES IN RELIGION,** and **CTS REPRINTS IN RELIGION.** Further information regarding these series can be found in the October 1983 number of the *CSR BULLETIN* and any changes will be announced there in future issues. The sale and distribution of the volumes in these three series are the responsibility of University Press of America.

The editors are grateful to the members of the Research and Publications Committee, to the officers and board of the CTS, and to the others who contributed to the editorial and production process. We acknowledge the leadership provided by the former president of the Society, Rodger Van Allen. We also express our thanks for the personal support given by our colleagues at Marquette University and Saint Joseph's University. Special acknowledgment is made of the services rendered by Susan Wilks and Carmen Croce of Saint Joseph's University Press and by Terri Boddorff and Jed Lyons of UPA.

Managing Editor
Joseph F. Gower
Saint Joseph's University
Philadelphia, PA 19131

Chair, Publications Committee
Robert Masson
Marquette University
Milwaukee, WI 53233

PREFACE

NEWMAN AND THE MODERNISTS

John Henry Newman's preeminence among Roman Catholics in the nineteenth century secured him a following among those who hoped that the Roman Catholic church would finally enter into dialogue with the modern world. They hoped to find in Newman a new method. As George Tyrrell said in his first letter to Wilfrid Ward on 12 December 1893, "I cannot but think that if Newman were studied and assimilated it would tend to unbarbarise us and enable us to pour Catholic truth from the scholastic to the modern mould without losing a drop in the transfer." (M.J. Weaver, *Letters from a "Modernist": The Letters of George Tyrrell to Wilfrid Ward 1893-1908* [Shepherdstown, WV: Patmos Press, 1981], 3). I always imagine Newman looking like Jean-Antoine Houdon's statue of Voltaire, sitting with an enigmatic smile and an impish delight in his own elusiveness. No matter what scholars try to do to systematize or discover Newman he remains decidely free, not caught up in or bound by any single interpretation. This richness of thought helps to explain the fascination Newman has had for religious thinkers for the last hundred and fifty years, and it may also explain how it was that various Modernists understood him differently, and proffered disparate analyses of Newman and his thought.

Nineteenth century religious thinkers—Catholic and Protestant—were drawn to Newman. Their various appraisals of his work and the implications of his thought form a fascinating composite portrait. When one looks at the work of Roman Catholic Modernists, especially, one finds several Newmans pressed into the service of one cause or another, understood from radically diverse points of view. The purpose of this book is to display and interpret the various faces of Newman as drawn by the Modernists and their antagonists. By the end of the book we will have a better understanding of Newman's attractiveness for a number of late nineteenth-century European Catholics, but we will not have managed to capture Newman. We can imagine him, at the end of this volume, still smiling.

The contributors to this volume are, for the most part, members of the Roman Catholic Modernism seminar in the American Academy of Religion.

We have noticed, over the last several years, that Newman's name and work insinuated themselves into many of our debates and discussions. Accordingly, in 1980, as we looked to the agenda for future meetings, we proposed to study the various "Newmans" of the Modernists: clearly, Tyrrell's Newman differed from that of Loisy, and both of them interpreted Newman in a way that made Newman's biographer, Wilfrid Ward, quite nervous. We hoped to gather together most of the major Modernist thinkers and to draw compositely a picture of the suggestive complexity of Newman's thought. The essays that follow were all written with publication in mind, but no essayist working on a particular person's though can write in such a way that his or her contribution perfectly dovetails with other contributions. Nevertheless, we have made a determined effort to write a book about Newman and the Modernists rather than simply to collect essays that might or might not fit together. To that end we have added an epilogical conclusion that summarizes the theological implications of our work. Readers will notice differences in perspective: some of the essayists are predominantly historians and some are theologians. We hope, however, that the total effect is richer for these differences. Readers will also notice some omissions, and it must be admitted at the outset that we simply were not able to get an essay on Baron von Hügel's relationship to Newman's work, nor were we able to find a willing interpreter of Newman's influence on the Italian Modernists. No book like this one can be complete, but we believe we have covered most of the major Modernist thinkers and Newman interpreters of the period, though not without some surprises: we include an essay on the relatively unknown William J. Williams, but do not include one on Blondel or on Laberthonnière. Readers may know that the whole question of Newman and Modernism is a lively one at the moment. The Modernism seminar held its meeting in December 1982 and presented the papers you find printed here. In the summer of 1983, a similar conference was held in England, at Birmingham, where a rather different set of papers was presented on Newman and Modernism. Access to both sets of papers should provide as nearly a complete a picture as can be formed at the moment; access to either one or the other set of papers will probably be incomplete.

This collection begins with an essay on Newman himself and his attractiveness to nineteenth-century thinkers. Paul Misner (Marquette University) introduces Newman and the book by showing how and why Newman was a source of ideas and a model for some of the Modernists and their friends. The book then lingers over England, moves on to France and Germany, and ends up where Roman Catholic religious controversies usually end up, at the Vatican. Newman's influence in England was, as one can imagine, widespread: he attracted essentially conservative interpreters like Wilfrid Ward, Modernist thinkers like George Tyrrell, and thoughtful but not well-known thinkers like William John Williams. Wilfrid Ward is the subject of two essays in this volume because he plays two distinct roles in relation to Newman. Mary Jo Weaver (Indiana University) discusses Ward's interpretation of Newman and his uses of Newman in his own work; Ward's claim to have been virtually the only person in the late nineteenth century to have really understood Newman is examined in the light of his essays. Nadia Lahutsky (Texas Christian University) concentrates on Ward's biography of Newman and on his attempts to be both faithful and fair; the technical problems and personal intrigues surrounding Ward's writing of the "official" biography of the cardinal deserve, we believe, a chapter in themselves. John Root (Illinois Institute of Technology) presents the case for Mr. Williams, a member in good standing of the English Modernist party, strongly influenced by the work and writings of Tyrrell. Root's essay has the advantage of rescuing an important figure from obscurity; Williams, as can be seen in this essay, was a fascinating thinker, and one who can provide yet another perspective on the wide-ranging influence of Newman. Nicholas Sagovsky (Theological College, Edinburgh) writes about the most important of the English Modernists, George Tyrrell, who was attracted to Newman and constrained finally to part company with "Newmanism" because, he said, "Newman cannot help us anymore." Tyrrell's relationship with other English intellectuals and his friendship with Bremond were all touched by his love/hate relationship with Newman.

Roger Haight (Regis College, Toronto) and Ronald Burke (University of Nebraska at Omaha) give two sides of French Modernist interpretation of Newman. Haight focuses on Henri Bremond's interpretation of Newman as an experientialist, what one might today call an existentialist thinker, while Burke analyzes the relationship between Newman's *Essay on the Development of Christian Doctrine* and Alfred Loisy's exegetical work. The French interpretations of Newman differ from each other and from English interpretations. Accordingly, they reflect not only differences in Newmanian influence and interpretation, but also the diversity of Modernist concerns.

All roads lead to Rome, and the penultimate essay by Gary Lease (University of California, Santa Cruz) gives us the Vatican interpretation of Newman, a study in ambiguity: Vatican officals were disturbed by the seeming oxymoron "controversial Cardinal." Finally, in order to summarize and interpret these interpretations and to place them in a theological context, Gabriel Daly (Augustinian House of Studies, Dublin) presents an epilogical conclusion, a theological reflection on Newman and Modernism.

Hopeful that Newman smiles kindly both on this work and on that of his interpreters, the Modernists, we dedicate this volume to the Modernists and to those religious thinkers in contemporary Catholicism whose brilliant work sometimes puts them under a cloud of suspicion.

Mary Jo Weaver
Indiana University
Bloomington, IN 47405

ACKNOWLEDGMENTS

We wish to add a word of thanks to librarians: we are indebted to the research librarians at our home institutions and abroad, and especially to Mr. Robert Smart at University Library, St. Andrews who has been so generous to so many of us. We also thank our colleagues both in our departments and in the Roman Catholic Modernism seminar in the AAR. Their encouragement, criticism and questions have helped us to shape our essays into their present form. Where we would be without our typists, secretaries, graduate assistants and friends is a thought too bleak to entertain and so we thank them warmly and readily acknowledge their excellent skills. Finally, we owe many thanks to our copy editor and indexer, Louise Martin, without whom consistency would have been only a dream. Bouyant with the memory of all the help we have received, we must also take responsibility for our mistakes: individual authors therefore claim any and all errors in their essays or omissions in the bibliography and apologize for them.

The Contributors

Part One

NEWMAN HIMSELF

1

The "Liberal" Legacy of Newman

Paul Misner

To take Newman at his word is always advisable, provided in turn that his word is taken in its context. To take Newman at his word, then, he was the early and unwavering defender of revealed truth against the assaults of rationalism or, as he put it, "liberalism in religion."[1] Roman Catholic Modernism, on the other hand, when it emerged within a decade of Newman's passing *ex umbris et imaginibus in veritatem,* was extremely liberal in its biblical criticism, whatever else it may have been.

Such are the opening positions from which one may approach a consideration of Newman and the Modernists. As far as Newman is concerned, it is not my intention to turn the conventional wisdom on its head, but merely, as hinted, to put it in context.

It may be noted first that Newman shared a "tradition of discourse" with a distinct group of English men of letters and affairs of his age, a tradition named after Samuel Taylor Coleridge by some students of Romanticism.[2] There is a sense in which the word *conservative* retains its consistency and its place in nineteenth-century intellectual and social history, as distinct from and opposed to the distinctively liberal tradition of discourse and view of language, reason, and society. In this sense, to be explained immediately, Newman was and remained thoroughly conservative and anti-liberal.

In the conservative or Coleridgian "tradition of discourse," language conveyed a communication with the existing world in the measure in which it was learned and trusted. Reason was a participation in a higher knowledge imparted by tradition. Society or community was regarded as prior to its individual members. The community mediated to its members the language and the reason with which they functioned as human beings.

By contrast, in the liberal or Benthamite "tradition of discourse," language was a purely instrumental faculty of the human (individual) mind, best used only to denote distinctly such objects of knowledge as could be made useful to satisfy wants. Reason was the tool enabling one to proceed from the known to the unknown by verifiable steps. Society was merely the aggregate of individuals. Its main problem consisted in reducing

3

to a minimum the unavoidable friction arising from numbers of human beings seeking to meet their individual needs in proximity to one another.

If this account of the conservative-liberal difference can be granted for the sake of historical classification, then it is clear that Newman remained a conservative all his life. The various softenings and nuances that we shall notice in his later, Roman Catholic, years (by comparison with his earlier years, 1801-1845, in the Church of England) do not, even cumulatively, suffice to indicate a change in traditon of discourse from Coleridgian to Benthamite.

Most religious writers of Newman's time who are still known today, and many Victorian doubters or agnostics too, are more conservative than liberal in this understanding of the decisive differences. Conservatives as here understood did not repudiate the Enlightenment as to the decisive principle that reason and critical judgment were to be applied in all matters of human interest, including religious traditions. Among churchmen, therefore, frictions commonly arose between such conservatives and elements to their right: reactionaries or traditionalists, standpatters with no rationale of discourse beyond the way things were before. As to Liberal Catholicism, its typical protagonists throughout the nineteenth century all owe more to such a conservative tradition of discourse than to the typically liberal one. A characteristic shift of designation occurs in churchly settings and other situations in which conservatives form the relatively more open wing. It is principally because traditionalists were called "conservatives" in church circles that the appellation of "liberal" came to be applied to their more progressive coreligionists.

Newman, Liberal Catholicism, and Ultramontanism
up to the First Vatican Council

The promulgation of Rome's Syllabus of Errors at the end of 1864 was the beginning of the end of the Liberal Catholic movement. Before this, however, there had been a significant flowering of a sensibility and outlook in which Catholic loyalties were wedded with contemporary values such as self-determination and a scientific spirit in various degrees and combinations. By way of a general description, one can say that "Liberal Catholics" were prompted by a desire to bridge the gap between the intellectual, social, and political challenges of the day and an outmoded ecclesiastical culture that no longer served effectively the church's mission in the world. The chief bearers of that culture, however, strove with remarkable success to hold the nineteenth century at bay. The discomfiture of the Liberal Catholic movement, taking place as quickly and as thoroughly as it did, has to be explained by connecting it with the development of Ultramontanism.

As an upshot of the nearly total subjugation of the church attempted in the course of the French Revolution and by Napoleon, the new Ultramontanism (or papalism) of nineteenth-century Catholicism was at root an anti-*Gallican* movement, parallel to Newman's own anti-Erastian stance underlying the Oxford Movement in the Church of England. Freedom of the church from state control was the common element. But from the moment when Félicité de Lamennais forced Pope Gregory XVI to choose between the liberationist and the papal elements in French Ultramontanism, these elements began to diverge. Catholics who sought some accommodation with the modern age (the Tübingen School, Antonio Rosmini, Henri-Dominique Lacordaire, the abbé Maret, Charles Montalembert, Lord Acton) began to be considered not Ultramontane but "Liberal."

From the 1860s on, those English Catholics who prized freedom of opinion and open discussion of issues looked to Newman for leadership, and from time to time he managed to strike a blow for liberty in the church. This in itself would to some extent explain the use of his name in a subsequent generation among progressive Catholics dissatisfied with papal policy. But there is more to the story. There is a broad *fundamentum in re* for the symbolic use of Newman as a figurehead of reform-minded Catholics in the early twentieth century.

To begin to place Newman in this context, it is important to remember that his antecedents were Anglican, that nothing in recent French history had any appeal for or claim on him, and that he had never entertained the dream of a papacy reconciled with what we may call, for brevity's sake, democracy. Were it not for its counterproductive aspects, he would have supported not only the authority of the pope in the modern church (all Liberal Catholics accepted that), but even papal authority exercised in an authoritarian mode. Eventually, however, he dropped for practical purposes the original conservative affirmation of the role that the church ought by rights to play in the public life of the nation. His Tractarian "opposition to Erastianism" became, in his later Catholic period, a "preference for the tolerant and even neutral State."[3]

Could Newman, then, given his decidedly conservative general posture, properly be called a "Liberal Catholic?" In most contexts, yes. He might not qualify on a doctrinaire reading of Acton's definition: Liberal Catholics as those who wanted freedom not only *for* the church by also *in* the church.[4] But certainly from 1864 (the year of the *Apologia pro Vita Sua* as well as, several months later, Pius IX's Syllabus of Errors), he does qualify in a generally more applicable characterization: one was a Liberal Catholic to the extent that one preferred, out of concern for religion, open discussion of issues and doctrines—and deplored authoritarian ways with their apparatus of censorship, delations, isolation from society at large, and what Newman called "narrowing the lines of communion" (*Letters and Diaries* 22:314).

He was always careful, like Félix Dupanloup, not to attack the abstract "thesis" that the Roman Catholic church should have acknowledged authority in the public sphere. But he was at one with the predominantly pragmatic preference of prominent Liberal Catholics for open rather than authoritarian approaches in the church's dealings with the nineteenth century (e.g., *Letters and Diaries* 28:71-72). Since this may strike some readers of Newman as overstated, it would be well to warrant it by making a rapid survey of the pertinent periods of Newman's life. How and to what extent he allied himself with the hard-pressed cause of Liberal Catholicism will thus become apparent.

Newman and the Oxford Movement

The portrait that Newman drew of this Anglican self and his "religious opinions" in the *Apologia pro Vita Sua* has of course had the greatest influence on his "public image" ever since, whether among admirers or detractors. Here is a profile of Newman as relentless foe of "the Liberalism of the day," a writer utterly opposed to the damage done Christianity by the liberal scorners of tradition with their march-of-mind prattling and their arrogant delusion of standing at the pinnacle of civilization.[5] This is the Newman who never ceased repeating I John 5:19: "The whole world lieth in wickedness." In the setting of the Oxford Movement he felt himself called upon always to give the benefit of the doubt to the wisdom of the ancients and to oppose innovations in church and society, fearing in his heart of hearts that the net tendency of modernity and change would be towards the uprooting of Christianity from the populations in which it had once sunk root (*Apologia*, 40).

After 1845

Critical of the modern world and its hostility to faith, Newman also become critical of the excessively regimented and overcautious ways of dealing with modern developments in the Roman Catholic church. His insertion into the Roman community led him to tack about and sail with the "liberals" among the Roman Catholics, without swerving from his lifetime course. After all, the prevailing winds tended to blow from a defferent quarter in the wake of Peter's bark. Thus, whereas in Oxford he had emphasized the pastoral dimension of the college tutor's role, as founding Rector of the Catholic University of Ireland in Dublin in the 1850s he laid stress on the basic intellectual mission of a university and its instructors. During this time he stated the case for liberal education in the unsurpassed *Idea of a University*. A similar shift can be observed in his ecclesiology: whereas in the Church of England he strove to highlight episcopal authority and responsibility, in the Church of Rome he stressed lay participation. In both cases, it was not a shift in his outlook so much as an effort to achieve a balance. As he said at a time when he still did not know the half of what had happened, he "got into hot water" (*Letters and Diaries* 19: 339) defending the interests of an educated laity with his essay in the *Rambler* of July 1859, "On Consulting the Faithful."[6]

He had a keen sense for the intellectual deficiencies of nineteenth-century Catholicism and its over-reliance on the "iron form" of received doctrine. Aware that he, as a convert, could not attempt to renew Catholic thought directly, least of all in the field of professional theology, he hoped at least that the bishops would not stand in the way of higher education for Catholics at Oxford or Cambridge. The church would need more Catholics who could take their place in the public life of the nation as did their Anglican and Protestant peers.

At the end of 1864, Newman's bishop in Birmingham, William Bernard Ullathorne, OSB, let him in on some of the backhanded scheming that took place in this matter. Apparently out of apprehension lest Ullathorne might send Newman back to Oxford (it lay in his diocese), Cardinal Wiseman and the Congregation of the Propaganda in Rome began to oppose Catholics attending the old "Protestant" universities at all. The rest of the bishops did not share the cardinal's concern, and Ullathorne wished to provide pastoral care for the Catholics in Oxford. Roman authority, however, was brought to bear to discourage any Roman Catholic presence in Oxford.

Newman observed to his bishop that there was "this secret influence" working on the cardinal and in Rome, causing trouble for Newman and for any plans connected with him. "[Ullathorne] answered that I meant Manning and Ward." Indeed he did. The way these two fellow converts had parlayed their position in the church and in the *Dublin Review* into "a dull tyranny . . . , the supremacy of Manning and Ward," was by 1863 a real grief to Newman. When the Syllabus of Errors came out in the newspapers, in January 1865, Newman acknowledged to William Monsell the same grave charge: "We are certainly under a tyranny" (*Letters and Diaries* 21:348, 84, 386; cf. 27:212). In repeated instances of this nature, however, his sense of obedience, of facing trials as a purification, and of solidarity with ordinary Catholics and their clergy in their *pietas fidei* preserved him from ever countenancing any flouting of ecclesiastical authority, no matter how mistaken its measures. The example of Newman looms in the background of the Modernists' soul-searching, every time the question of a public protest or disobedience to papal decrees comes up.[7]

The *Apologia,* Chapter V

The *Rambler* connection, undertaken by Newman only to rescue a channel of English Catholic writing and culture from extinction, brought Newman into close contact with Lord Acton, the chief proprietor of the magazine. Although the two had a great deal in common, Acton was the harsher critic of power and what he saw as the conventional mendacity practiced on its behalf, especially in the church; he regarded as necessary the accommodation of Catholicism to the new age with its freedom of speech and inquiry. Newman, in his eyes, practically condoned the abuses of power from which he too suffered, inasmuch as Newman did not look for any "great improvement of society."[8] The coming ages would languish equally as much as the past *in maligno* (in wickedness): this was the tenor of the message that Acton heard from Newman.

Just as Newman was launching into the unexpected task of writing his *Apologia,* Acton was coming to the conclusion, based on certain steps that the Vatican had taken in late 1863, that the *Rambler's* successor, the *Home and Foreign Review,* would no longer be tolerated. He informed Newman that the final issue would be that of April 1864; in the same note, he asked Newman to consider enlarging the discussion in the *Apologia* from a personal defense to deal with the whole problem of honesty and truthfulness in the church at large, including the freedom of scholars to present their findings and hypotheses to others. Newman replied on 15 April 1864 that he would "go as far as ever I can."[9]

Thus there appeared in print, in vindication of his honor and good name among Englishmen, the first of a series of discussions of the need for authority in religious beliefs, carefully balanced to exclude certain Ultramontane suppositions and thrusts. The authority that Newman extolled in the *Apologia's* final chapter was loathe to move precipitously. It would refrain from settling questions that had not yet been properly ventilated and subjected to the searching criticism of open controversy. Making good on his pledge to Acton, he added: "[T] he said authority may be accidentally supported by a violent ultra party, which exalts opinions into dogmas, and has it principally at heart to destroy every school of thought but its own" (*Apologia*, 233; *Letters and Diaries*, 20:391).

The First Vatican Council

Even though Newman explained rather bluntly to Manning and Ward what he found objectionable in their behavior, they brushed it aside as special pleading. Newman insisted that Manning and Ward should not treat their own unofficial opinions as dogma (*Letters and Diaries* 23:216-17 and 308-312). They, however, were sure that it was just a matter of time until a practically unlimited infallibility of the pope was infallibly declared. Since they knew the pope's mind on the matter, they felt it was the merest quibbling to resist and minimize at that moment, when solidarity with the pope was of the essence. Hence they strove to undermine Newman's influence of set purpose, out of a considered judgment that it was not helpful to the cause that all of them wished to serve.

It was no surprise to informed circles, but it was all the same a sensation, when a private letter of Newman's to his bishop at the council became public knowledge early in 1870. In it Newman gave voice to his dismay over the headlong rush to define papal infallibility. In his view, infallibility was a doctrine that was true enough, but hard to define accurately. The effort to push it through the council without proper deliberation was causing unnecessary scandal. In words that would become justly famous, Newman stigmatized the *Civiltà Cattolica* and other Ultramontane organs by name, and Manning, Ward, and Vaughan implicitly, as accomplices in "an aggressive insolent faction."[10]

The council went on to consider, debate, and pass a definition of papal infallibility that did not come up to the expectations of the *Civiltà* propagandists. As against Manning's stated anticipations, the council formulated the pope's infallibility not as a power given him to use separately from the rest of the church, but as an exercise in special and rare circumstances of "that infallibility with which the divine Redeemer wished to endow his Church." Furthermore, this infallibility was not extended to any and all matters of interest to the papacy, but was for the purpose of defining doctrine on faith and morals. Newman understood this reasonably enough as limiting the strictly infallible teaching to matters of revelation.

The Ultramontanes, however, proceeded to interpret the dogmatic constitution of 18 July 1870 as if the council had not bothered with any nuances. In the ensuing doctrinal confusion, Newman bided his time until an opportunity was handed him, which he seized to astonishing effect.

In the *Letter to the Duke of Norfolk* of 1875 Newman commanded perhaps the largest audience of his life—or second only to that of the *Apologia*. In a sovereign display of learning and sweet reason he defended the doctrinal import of the new dogma of papal infallibility from the exaggerations of Manning on the one side by refuting the parallel exaggerations of Gladstone on the other.[11]

It was a triumphant demonstration and won the heartfelt thanks of young thinkers and future writers such as Baron Friedrich von Hügel and, later, Wilfrid Ward. This time Newman got away with his minimizing approach to what is obligatory in Catholic thought *de fide*. Every English Catholic realized that it was essential to his devastating refutation of Gladstone's allegations. There were objections in Rome, however, and after a bit W.G. Ward returned to worrying about Newman's orthodoxy as to the decisive role he attributed to one's conscience in all matters of obedience.[12]

Leo's "Liberal" Cardinal?

At the end of all this turmoil arising from papal problems and prerogatives, or in other words from tensions with extreme Ultramontanism, Newman was able to hold his own. In the meantime, however, the situation was such as to elicit from him expressions of opinion so critical of the prevailing ecclesiastical regime that they can be surpassed by few of the subsequent Roman Catholic Modernists in the opening years of the twentieth century. Of course, the most forthright of these protests usually remained private and unknown to the younger generation until 1912 except for Newman's biographer, Wilfrid Ward (after 1905). Ward did not have access to *all* the pertinent correspondence (see *Letters and Diaries* 28:92 note 5 for Newman's list of those to whom he had "written with freedom about my dissatisfaction with the present state of Catholic affairs"), but he presented enough of a selection to allow at least his properly initiated readers to judge the depth of that dissatisfaction. One example must suffice. Lamenting the fact that, once again, an opportunity was being passed up to provide Oxford with an appropriately staffed Catholic center, Newman confided to Lord Braye (1849-1928) on 2 November 1882: "This is what I feel at the moment, but, alas, it is only one out of various manifestations of what may be called Nihilism in the Catholic Body, and in its rulers. They forbid, but they do not direct or create. I should fill many sheets of paper if I continued my exposure of this fact."[13]

Given the confusion even then surrounding the epithet, *liberal*, Newman trod a cautious line and used it primarily in its pejorative sense, focusing on its relativizing tendencies in the realm of religion. In the 1865 edition of the *Apologia* he added a "Note" on "Liberalism" to explain his usage with historical examples from the Oxford of the 1830s (*Apologia*, 254-62). Evidently people in England generally had come to associate "liberal" with democratic political reform of the type promoted by the Liberal Party, to which some of Newman's friends belonged; Catholics also knew about the Liberal Catholics who enjoyed Newman's support. Even those to whom Newman's meaning of the word was congenial tended to put it into quotation marks (*Letters and Diaries* 21:116 note 2), as if signifying that it was by now a special case departing from common usage. Newman acknowledged the same in a letter of 20 December 1868 (*Letters and Diaries* 24:191), and must have felt Monsignor George Talbot was confusing two distinct realities when he wrote to Newman on 31 May 1867 in tones of horror that a party called "liberal Catholics" took Newman for their head "in preference to the Vicar of Christ" (*Letters and Diaries* 23:242)!

To distinguish Liberalism A (subversive of Christianity) from Liberalism B (a course of action in secular politics of democratic trend), as well as, implicitly, from the late lamented Liberal Catholicism, Liberalism C (promoting freedom *and* authority in church and state, while being anti-authoritarian and anti-Erastian), Newman used the platform given him in the evening of his life on the occasion of his elevation to the cardinalate in 1879. In his address of thanks for the honor, which he took as a vindication, Newman summed up his life's work as having been a resistance to "the spirit of liberalism in religion." He then defined:

> Liberalism in religion is the doctrine that there is no positive truth in religion, but that one creed is as good as another, and this is the teaching which is gaining substance and force daily. It is inconsistent with any recognition of any religion, as *true*. It teaches that all are to be tolerated, for all are matters of opinion.[14]

The process of secularization and its negative consequences for religion are then described with great insight, but also with a keen sense of the realities of the situation, which condemnations would not alter.

One cannot resist pointing out that the occasion which brought forth a classic denunciation of liberalism in religion was the same that gave Newman's Liberal Catholic ideas a right of citizenship in the ultramontanized church. *"Il mio cardinale!"* Pope Leo later said. "It was not easy, they said he was too liberal; but I determined to honor the Church in honoring Newman."[15]

11

In the Modernist context, interest in Newman's thought focused almost exclusively on the subjects of his two major essays, *An Essay on the Development of Christian Doctrine* in the third edition of 1878 and *An Essay in Aid of a Grammar of Assent* (1870), often supplemented with the volume of Oxford *University Sermons*. The issues dealt with in these *Essays* were crucial in any attempt to update Catholic theology: how it was to cope with historical consciousness—and how it was to give an account of the certitude of religious faith in the face of a scientifically modeled ethic of knowledge.

Along with these two works, sometimes perhaps instead of them, Newman's incomparable *Apologia pro Vita Sua* had an avid readership, including many a Modernist. Here one could find succinct statements of the principle of doctrinal development as well as the role of probabilities in the certitude of faith, all in the context of Newman's own development and change of ecclesial homes.[16]

A useful reminder in taking the measure of the *Essay on Development of Christian Doctrine* is that it is a retraction of his 1837 *Prophetical Office*. There he had opted for a *via media* between Protestantism and Romanism, on patristic and seventeenth-century Anglican precedents, as he saw them. The Romish alternative was clearly impermissible, given the corrupt developments that had taken over in its doctrine and polity. Now, in the *Essay on Development*, he was challenging the presumption that developments were corruptions and suggesting that the burden of proof should lie with those who rejected the otherwise strong claims of Rome because of its corruptions of the Christian idea. In other words, the *Essay* put forward a "hypothesis to account for a difficulty."[17] Newman assumed throughout the essay that the Roman Catholic church of the nineteenth century was identical with the church of the Fathers. His aim was to account for the many historically apparent changes as not having abrogated that identity.

His starting point in chapter I of all editions is the phenomenon of 'the development of ideas." The basic analogy, then, is that of an influential "idea," one that impresses itself on many minds in a changing community over a period of generations, and by so doing makes its mark on history.[18] It should be noted that the organic development of a plant or animal from seed to maturity is not the prime analogate. Newman uses such images, even in decisive ways, but not as the leading idea. The Modernists, by viewing development of doctrine only as an evolutionary or organicist process of growth, did not do full justice here to Newman's subtlety.

The latter part of the *Essay on Development* organizes the rich matter of argument under several headings called "tests" (in the first edition) or "notes" (in the third edition) of "genuine development of an idea" as opposed to corruptive developments. It is in these chapters where the contemporary reader will most notice how timebound and obsolescent many of Newman's points were. Already by the end of the century many of Newman's examples had to updated. It was also up to Alfred Loisy's generation of scholars to push the question back historically to New Testament times, where Newman scarcely raised any critical questions. Hence one can hardly take issue with the Modernists who would modify and revise Newman's account in these ways. On the other hand, one could find fault with professed Newmanists who saw no need for such revising.

But the question that is more insistent is this: to what extent and with what right did Modernists depart from Newman's *principles* in their historical interpretations? Since Newman devoted some pages to "continuity of principles" as a mark of genuine developments in Christianity, it may be of some assistance to attend to them briefly.

"Principles" were dynamic tendencies—principles of action rather than structural features. For the 1878 edition Newman went to the trouble of formulating several principles of the sort he meant. Foremost among them, and an evident sore point in the interpretation of Newman as between Modernists and Anti-Modernists, was the *dogmatic principle*. This principle or innate Christian tendency, like the other eight that Newman enumerated, is dependent on a true doctrine expressive of a fact (the Incarnation), rather than the other way around. It is not itself a doctrine but only a characteristic way of acting. The dogmatic principle is a readiness to accept "supernatural truths irrevocably committed to human language, imperfect because it is human, but definitive and necessary because given from above."[19]

Other characteristic ways of acting, by which Catholic Christians can be differentiated from pretenders, are the principles of *faith*, of *theology,* and the *sacramental* principle.[20] Modernist thinking is not so distant from Newman in principles as it might appear, after all. Tyrrell, for example, made great use of the sacramental principle. Tyrrell's distinction between Devotion and Theology and his attacks on "Theologism" seem to lie on the very same line as Newman's distinction of the principle of *theology* (a tendency to create a "science in religion, in subservience to" faith) from the principle of *dogma*. In the dogmatic principle itself, Newman admitted the inadequacy of human language to express divine truths (see previous text). If all these points could eventually be made out of the resources of the scholastic tradition by twentieth-century Thomists, they were not at all characteristic of the theological opponents of Modernism.

13

The most basic missing element in the Anti-Modernists' mental makeup, of course, was a sense of historical change in the church. Despite the conservative use to which Newman put his theory of developments, his *Essay* made clear, however tentatively, that even the truths of faith, once delivered to the saints, have a history.[21] In the *Apologia*, he spoke of development itself as a "principle . . . giving character to the whole course of Christian thought."[22]

The second main problem area of nineteenth-century religious thought, to which Newman made a conspicuous contribution, was the ethics of belief. His concern was to justify the certitude of faith against the prevalent agnostic state of suspended affirmation or inability to get beyond the realm of probability. The *University Sermons* and particularly *An Essay in Aid of a Grammar of Assent* (1870)[23] dealt with the question: How could one responsibly give the unconditional assent of faith to propositions that were not fully comprehended and for which the evidence was not readily producible?

Unfortunately the *Grammar of Assent* begins abruptly, without any statement of the problem. As Dessain explains, however, Newman had two classes of persons particularly in mind: educated agnostics, such as his friend William Froude, whose sense of intellectual integrity forbade them to make the assent of faith (as going beyond the kind of evidence available to justify it) and the vast majority of human beings, whose right to believe had to be defended. For the broad mass of Catholics and other believers did hold "truths which they were quite incapable either of explaining satisfactorily or defending logically,"[24] and this was legitimate in principle.

In the first part of the *Grammar*, accordingly, Newman justifies the principle of dogma as corresponding to everyday patterns of ordinary, secular mental conduct. They are a function of "real assent" as opposed to "notional" assent. There are realities acknowledged by us so firmly through the power of imagination that no amount of specious reasoning could convince us that they are only probabilities. That an element of trust forms part of this knowledge does not make it any less certain (when in fact it is not mistaken). In the life of faith, similarly, the educated as well as the uneducated render a real assent through devotion to the personal and present God. It is in this connection that Newman makes his striking analysis of the role of the moral conscience in coming to an acknowledgment of the reality of God (*Grammar*, 105-121; cf. *Apologia*, 216-18). Dogma arises from and protects devotion and has to do with the same reality toward which devotion is oriented.

In Part II of *A Grammar of Assent* Newman showed how "you can believe what you cannot absolutely prove."[25] Here he establishes, again by attending to common experience, that responsible persons do in fact give unconditional assent to facts or truths or moral assessments of situations, even through apodictic evidence for their validity cannot be produced. Rationalist or "purely scientific" epistemology therefore accounts at best for a very narrow range of de facto human knowledge and that not the most important part. The name he now gave to this process of arriving at certitude in practical matters was "informal inference," an operation more basic and necessary by far than formal logic:

> . . . the processes of reasoning which legitimately lead to assent, to action, to certitude, are in fact too multiform, subtle, omnigenous, too implicit, to allow of being measured by rule . . . they are after all personal,—verbal argumentation being useful only in subordination to a higher logic.[26]

The rules for scientific investigation do not apply to "concrete matter," matter for personal decisions in conscience. It is not reasonable to put such decisions off until some sort of inappropriate "scientific" reasons could be shown to demonstrate their legitimacy. The illative sense—Newman called it a solemn word for an ordinary thing—is simply this informal or spontaneous process of reasoning in the concrete, once one has learned how to do it through practice and experience. Newman's favorite account of how it works is based on Joseph Butler's view of probability as the guide of life. The move from converging or accumulative probabilities to certitude through informal inference is not likened to a leap of faith so much as to a cable made up of many separately weak strands, or to a polygon expanding into the enclosing circle.[27]

John Coulson has noticed that his preference for complex models for the assent of faith presupposes a growth into faith quite analogous to growth in imaginative responsiveness. It goes without saying that religious language is an approximation and not an exact reproduction of the reality to which assent is given. In effect, therefore, "the most important part of what the Modernists were to ask for has . . . been conceded, viz.: the distinction between what is revealed and how it is described, defined, and spoken of."[28] That is, in spite of all the differences, there was more common ground between Newman and the Modernists than there was between Newman and their adversaries, the Anti-Modernists or integrists.

15

A scholastic critic of the *Grammar* in *The Month* had foreshadowed this nonreception, viewing it as an unnecessary and audacious departure from the conventional apologetic. A surprisingly favorable response, on the other hand, was the thesis of W.G. Ward as to the compatibility of scholastic thought and Newman's *Grammar of Assent*. Ward welcomed it without cavil, then or later. W.G. Ward commended it to Friedrich von Hügel (who swore by it) and, one may presume, to Wilfrid Ward as well.[29] It was the latter who drew attention to this side of Newman's thought in 1901 in an article entitled "Newman and Sabatier," thereby stimulating interest and the first translations of the *University Sermons* and of the *Grammar* by Henri Bremond and others.[30] Thus the stage was set for its slow recognition and reception.

In the Modernist period, Newman's contribution to the question of faith, reason, and personal conscience was that his approach constituted a serious alternative, or at least supplement, to the dominant neo-scholastic apologetic with its exclusive emphasis on intellectually probative demonstrations of the existence of God, of the credentials of Christ as his Revealer, and of the divine endowment of the Catholic church with its Petrine powers. By taking Locke seriously, Newman provided some rapprochement with the modern questions in religious epistemology as exemplified on the continent by Kant.

A Reconsideration

A special case in the republication of his works was Newman's principal anti-Romanist statement, the *Lectures on the Prophetical Office* of 1837. When he came to this task in 1877, he decided to republish it unaltered, like the rest of his Anglican writings, but with a substantial "Preface" to deal with the "main charges" he had made against Catholicism forty years before.[31] What resulted was a pearl of great price, a burnished jewel of some 15,000 exquisitely placed words, which has remained buried away in the Uniform Edition, calling no attention to itself in catalogs of Newman's works, as the "Preface" to the Third Edition of the *Prophetical Office* (i.e., vol. I of the *Via Media*). Unfortunately he gave it no other title. In fact, it would seem that only a few aficionados of Newman have enjoyed it down to the present day. Tyrrell made little or nothing of it, for example.

As John Coulson has shown, this "Preface" modifies considerably the stress laid by Newman on authority in the church,[32] carrying forward and providing a framework for the nuances and limitations we have noticed in the *Apologia* and the *Letter to the Duke of Norfolk*. The title that suggests itself for the essay is "The Three Functions of the Church," or three dimensions of its mission. These are not witness, fellowship, and service, as in the ecumenical theology of today, but a related triad: Newman calls them the Prophetical, Priestly, and Royal Offices, after the three "offices" of Christ (cf. also Vatican II, Dogmatic Constitution on the Church *Lumen Gentium*, art. 10-12). Alternatively he refers to them as teaching, worship, and rule, or as a philosophy, a religion, a society, represented respectively in the church by theology, devotion, and "the Papacy and its Curia."[33]

Students of von Hügel will immediately recognize the "three elements of religion" (the intellectual, the mystical, and the institutional) of his *Mystical Element of Religion*.[34] In fact, this is one of the few places where von Hügel explicitly acknowledges Newman's influence in his published works, along with that of William James and a certain G.T. Fechner. Curiously enough, von Hügel does not seem to have pressed this small work of Newman's on his friends, as he did with the *Essay on Development*. At the time of its publication, nevertheless, he was so struck by it that he wished it to be the first of a set of Newman's writings to be translated into German by a friend of his (*Letters and Diaries* 28:422—nothing came of this project).

Wilfrid Ward also prized the "Preface" but it did not become for him the seminal work or the norm for the reinterpretation of Newman that it became, perhaps unwittingly, for von Hügel and for some later commentators.

New Problems in a New Generation

Newman may have "blunted the edge of Ultramontanism"[35] for those concerned with the Vatican Decrees controversy. But he was by no means able to stem the tide of a Vaticanism that resulted from a continued broad construction of the council in ordinary catechetics and seminary training. Meanwhile, there was another issue on which the Vatican council had taken a new dogmatic position: the inspiration of scripture. It was in the area of biblical criticism, certainly not his special *métier*, in which Newman made a last stand for free discussion and against premature closure of open questions. It was likewise in this same crucial area where Newmanian influence would flourish briefly, now with the added aura of the cardinalatial dignity, as a sort of prelude to the full-blown Modernist controversies on history and dogma.

The tendency of Newman's 1884 articles on biblical inspiration is straightforward. His only aim was to establish that, even after Vatican I and Leo XIII's elevation of Thomistic philosophy to authoritative status in Catholic theology, theologians had no right unhistorically and a priori to settle open questions as to inspiration and inerrancy without examining them in their new context. The most likely effect, after all, would be to put the credit of the magisterium behind a position it would have to abandon again sooner or later, with results potentially as serious in its pastoral consequences as the aftermath of the Galileo affair.

After careful investigation, therefore, on what one must believe *de fide* as a Roman Catholic as to the divine inspiration of scripture, Newman published his essay "On the Inspiration of Scripture" in the *Nineteenth Century* (February 1884) and issued a reprint with additions for limited circulation in 1890.[36] The kinds of difficulties that Newman alluded to, merely as examples, were, for instance, the pseudonymous attributions of biblical books to a Moses, a David, an Isaiah, or a Paul; the several authors of a book such as Genesis or Isaiah (attributed in some cases in the Bible itself to a single historical person); the assimilation of material from ancient pagan sources or traditions; the incorporation of previous profane writings; the popular conceptions of bygone ages enshrined in the sacred text; and so forth.

Although Newman's thought on the matter only became public in 1884, he had long spotted the question of inspiration as one that was bound to give a good deal of trouble to thoughtful modern believers or would-be believers. The Vatican council had gone further than previous church pronouncements. In contrast to its definition of papal infallibility, which Newman found quite limited, at least in comparison with what was bruited about beforehand, its decree on faith, reason, and revelation (*Dei Filius* of 24 April 1870) seemed to canonize a fairly wooden concept of inspiration. Thus, for the first time in the history of the official magisterial statements, texts rather than authors seemed to be what God inspired, so that he was their author in a more direct sense than the writers were. The decree evinced no awareness of the scientific and historical anomalies that were piling up. It aggravated the situation by ruling out the more supple categories needed to come to terms with historical criticism.

Before 1870, it should be noted, even though Newman considered the problem urgent enough to work on extensive essays from 1861 through 1863, he tended to consider it an immediately practical problem more for Protestants with their *sola scriptura* than for Catholics. He argued in the *Apologia* for the living authority of the church on the grounds that scripture, though divine, "was never intended" to combat atheism and (by itself) raise up faithful populations. "It may be accidentally the means of the conversion of individuals; but a book, after all, cannot make a stand against

18

the wild living intellect of man, and in this day it begins to testify, as regards its own structure and contents, to the power of that universal solvent, which is so successfully acting upon religious establishments" (*Apologia*, 219; *Letters and Diaries* 19:487).

The council started to petrify the comparative Catholic flexibility, and other developments gave away the advantage completely. Apparently without Newman's knowledge, J.B. Franzelin, the Jesuit who had written the preliminary *schema* that became the constitution *Dei Filius* of the Vatican council, also published in 1870 his influential textbook, *De divina traditione et scriptura*,[37] closing gaps that Newman wanted left open. The upshot was that Pope Leo, when a papal pronouncement on the matter seemed called for, adopted Franzelin's line in the main. The encyclical *Providentissimus Deus* of 1893 put Catholic exegetes in a difficult position that Newman's intervention had been intended to forestall. These magisterial stands increased the tension between doctrine and history to the breaking point, at least for one like George Tyrrell. In the Irishman's eyes, the teaching of *Providentissimus Deus* called into question the infallible church authority proclaimed by Vatican I: the two inerrancies would stand or fall together.[38]

There is no denying that the problems in relation to the simultaneously divine and human character of the Bible became much more acute for Catholic scholars between the 1860s and 1884 and still more so after 1893. This is one instance where Wilfrid Ward fell decidedly behind his hero, out of a failure to grasp as well as Newman what was at stake. At least Newman had once, in the 1820s, read Genesis in the Hebrew. It became quite clear to him then "that it was the work of various authors" (*Letters and Diaries* 21:395 of 28 January 1865 to a supporter of Colenso). But he also is remarkably clear as to what he may *not* know, writing in 1877 to someone seeking his opinion on a biblical question, "I have never engaged in a critical study of the sacred text" (*Letters and Diaries* 28:240). Ward, on the other hand, had the drawbacks of a Roman Catholic education in this respect (cf. *Letters and Diaries* 30:201). Presumably, had Newman lived to see it, his reception of the encyclical *Providentissimus Deus* would have been no more positive than von Hügel's and a good deal more concerned than Wilfrid Ward's.[39]

There is one more intriguing indication of Newman's influence. Baron von Hügel wrote him from France on 1 July 1884 thanking him for the article with the printed "Postscript."[40] After giving his own positive and grateful response to the article, von Hügel went on to say that at a recent reception he had attended at the Institut Catholique of Paris, he had heard the Rector, Maurice d'Hulst, and two of the most eminent professors,

Paul de Broglie and Louis Duchesne, speak approvingly of Newman's intervention. "While discussing your papers," he wrote, they agreed "to their conclusions and maintain[ed] that their subject was the burning religious question of the hour, and that our Apologetics would cease to fail of their due effect only when the concessions you would allow can be fully applied and explicitly proclaimed."

A little further on, von Hügel mentioned his appreciation (with reservations) of the deceased William George Ward:

> [M]uch as I . . . agreed with his general philosophical principles (to which I was first won by the 'Grammar of Assent'), there was yet as complete a difference of temperament and critical questions generally as could well obtain between faithful Catholics, and at the end of nine years intercourse such subjects were all but altogether tabooed, and quite absolutely disagreed upon between us.

What I take these remarks to mean, among other things, is that the role of Newman's writings and thought in von Hügel's development was cardinal. To put it negatively, he would never have come to Duchesne and Wellhausen and Holtzmann and Loisy with the same openness, had it not been for the large doses of Newman he took in at critical junctures along the way.[41] One wonders: without that exposure, would he ever have paid any special attention to Charles de Smedt's little book on historical method?

Newman's "Liberal" Legacy

History and Dogma was not only the name of an important work by Maurice Blondel published at one highpoint of the Modernist crisis in 1904; it was also a fundamental problem for all of nineteenth-century theology and, in his particular circumstances, for Newman. Even though a Manning might say that, for faithful Catholics, "Dogma has conquered history," it could not remain that way. The Thomistic renaissance in Catholic thought was unable to cope with this challenge except by transforming itself, a process that did not get well under way until after the defeat of Modernism. Newman's fostering of the idea of developments in doctrine, of a dynamic rather than a static tradition, was, therefore, the foremost instance of his influence on a younger generation of open-minded Catholic intellectuals.

His *Grammar of Assent* also had to do with dogma: its importance and fittingness to the religious mind, in the first place, but also its dependence on conscience and the religious imagination, that is, on religious experience. Here again, the conventional theology favored by Rome had developed a horror of the appeal to experience in theology, and here again Newmanian thought was in a position to offer a healthy alternative to scholasticism.

Finally, Newman was known to have taken a moderate stand, one that minimized dogmatic claims, on the perennial issue of freedom of scholarship in the Roman Catholic church. For this reason his name was suspect in Ultramontane circles from 1860 on and he was reputed to be a "Liberal Catholic." For the same reason, the scattered adherents of Liberal Catholicism were attracted to his writings and took heart when he was made a cardinal in 1879. A man, in that year, who could say ("emphatically") that theology "makes progress by being always alive to its fundamental uncertainties" (*Letters and Diaries* 29:118; Ward 2:591), was in touch with the intellectual temper of his times. Such attitudes would make him the most revered thinker of the age for those younger Catholics who keenly felt the shortcomings of scholastic theology at the end of the nineteenth century.

NOTES

1. Wilfrid Ward, *Life of John Henry Cardinal Newman*, 2 vols. (London: Longmans, Green and Co., 1912), 2:460; and Charles Stephen Dessain, *John Henry Newman* (London: A. and C. Black, 1966), 165. Citations from *The Letters and Diaries of John Henry Newman*, ed. Charles Stephen Dessain et al. (31 vols., London: Nelson, 1961-72; Oxford: Clarendon Press, 1973—) will be indicated by the abbreviated form *Letters and Diaries* with volume and page numbers.

2. I adopt the remarks in the next five paragraphs from a paper prepared for an American Academy of Religion meeting with the author's permission: Charles Davis, " 'Fluent Benthamites and Muddled Coleridgians'—The Liberal and Conservative Traditions of Discourse," *Papers of the Nineteenth Century Theology Working Group*, ed. Garrett Green and Marilyn C. Massey, 8:45-53 (Berkeley, CA, at the Graduate Theological Union, 1982).

3. J. Derek Holmes, "Liberal Catholicism and Newman's Letter to the Duke of Norfolk," *Clergy Review* 60 (1975):510. See also the same author's *More Roman than Rome. English Catholicism in the Nineteenth Century* (London: Burns & Oates; Shepherdstown, WV: Patmos, 1978) for further background.

4. Jacques Gadille, *Les catholiques libéraux au XIXe siècle* (Grenoble: Presses Universitaires, 1974), 16.

5. *Apologia pro Vita Sua*, ed. Martin J. Svaglic (Oxford: Clarendon Press, 1967), 26; cf. *Fifteen Sermons Preached before the University of Oxford* (London: Longmans, Green, and Co., 1896 [1871]; henceforth *University Sermons*), 102-103.

6. Dessain, *John Henry Newman*, 106-118; *On Consulting the Faithful in Matters of Doctrine*, ed. John Coulson (New York: Sheed and Ward, 1962).

7. Paul Misner, *Papacy and Development: Newman and the Primacy of the Pope* (Leiden: E.J. Brill, 1976), 145-46; Lawrence F. Barmann, *Baron Friedrich von Hügel and the Modernist Crisis in England* (Cambridge University Press, 1972), 214.

8. Hugh A. MacDougall, *The Acton-Newman Relations. The Dilemma of Christian Liberalism* (New York: Fordham University Press, 1962), 172. On "conventional mendacity," see John E.E.D. Acton, "Notes on Archival Researches 1864-1868," in *Lord Acton: The Decisive Decade 1864-1874. Essays and Documents* by Damian McElrath in collaboration with James Holland et al. (Louvain: Publications Universitaires, 1970), 140; cf. 10-11.

9. *Letters and Diaries* 21:94; cf. MacDougall, *The Acton-Newman Relations*, 92-95.

10. *Letters and Diaries* 25:19 and Ward, *Life* 2:288; cf. Dessain, *Newman*, 137-9.

11. Holmes, "Liberal Catholicism and Newman's Letter to the Duke of Norfolk;" MacDougall, *The Acton-Newman Relations*, 132-33; and Misner, *Papacy and Development*, 150-53. *A Letter Addressed to His Grace the Duke of Norfolk on Occasion of Mr. Gladstone's Recent Expostulation*, by Newman, may be found in his *Certain Difficulties Felt by Anglicans in Catholic Teaching* (2 vol.; London: Longmans, Green, 1896), 2:171-378.

22

12. *Letters and Diaries* 27:189-92 and 30:382-84; 31:152; 27:402-411 and 28:24. Cf. Dessain, *Newman,* 142-46 and see below, note 39.

13. *Letters and Diaries* 30:143 and Ward, *Life* 2:486.

14. Ward, *Life* 2:460-62, here 460.

15. *Letters and Diaries* 24:426 and Dessain, *Newman,* 165.

16. *Apologia,* 178-81 with 22, 30-32 and the annotations by Svaglic.

17. Newman, *Essay on the Development of Christian Doctrine,* 3rd ed. (London: Longmans, Green, 1878), 30.

18. Nicholas Lash, *Newman on Development: The Search for an Explanation in History* (London: Sheed and Ward; Shepherdstown, WV: Patmos, 1975), 46-54; Misner, *Papacy and Development,* 63.

19. Newman, *Essay on Development,* 323-26, here 325.

20. For the dogmatic and sacramental principles, see also *Apologia,* 54-55.

21. Lash, *Newman on Development,* 15 and 72.

22. *Apologia,* 179, cited in the third edition of *Development,* 326.

23. *An Essay in Aid of a Grammar of Assent* will be cited according to the pagination in the Uniform Edition of Newman's works (London: Longmans, Green, 1870).

24. Dessain, *Newman,* 148-59, here 152.

25. Ibid., 148, 151.

26. Ibid., 156, citing *Grammar of Assent,* 303.

27. Cf. *Apologia,* ed. Svaglic, Index, s.v. Butler; Ward, *Life* 2:43; *Grammar of Assent,* 320.

28. John Coulson, *Religion and Imagination: 'In Aid of a Grammar of Assent'* (Oxford: Clarendon Press, 1981), 73.

29. *Letters and Diaries* 27:189 and 30:383; Wilfrid Ward, *Last Lectures* (London: Longmans, Green, 1918), 72-100.

30. B.D. Dupuy, "Newman's Influence in France," in *Rediscovery of Newman. An Oxford Symposium,* ed. John Coulson and A.M. Allchin (London: Sheed and Ward, 1967), 153-167.

31. *The Via Media of the Anglican Church* (2 vols.; London: Longmans, Green, 1899), 1:xv.

32. Coulson, "Newman on the Church—His Final View, its Origins and Influence," in *The Rediscovery of Newman* (cited earlier, note 30), 123-43.

33. Preface to the *Via Media,* 1:xl.

34. Friedrich von Hügel, *The Mystical Element of Religion as Studied in Saint Catherine of Genoa and Her Friends* (2 vols.; London: J.M. Dent, 1908, 2d ed. 1923), 1:50-52, esp. 53 and xxxi; cf. Coulson, *Newman and the Common Tradition* (Oxford: Clarendon Press, 1970), 175-77.

35. Acton's words in Owen Chadwick, *From Bossuet to Newman. The Idea of Doctrinal Development* (Cambridge University Press, 1957), 194.

36. Newman, *On the Inspiration of Scripture* [1884], ed. J.D. Holmes and Robert Murray (Washington: Corpus Books, 1967); see also the 1861-63 *Theological Papers of John Henry Newman on Biblical Inspiration and on Infallibility*, ed. J. Derek Holmes (Oxford: Clarendon Press, 1979).

37. T. Howland Sanks, *Authority in the Church: A Study of Changing Paradigms* (Missoula, MT: Scholars Press, 1974), 42-61.

38. David Schultenover, *George Tyrrell: In Search of Catholicism* (Shepherdstown, WV: The Patmos Press, 1981), 252, 289.

39. Barmann, *Baron Fredrich von Hügel*, 41-49. The reasons for this presumption lie partly in Newman's correspondence with Prof. St. George Jackson Mivart (on whom see *Letters and Diaries* 25:488 and Holmes, "Newman and Mivart," *Clergy Review* 50 [1965] : 852-67). Because Mivart died under ecclesiastical censure in 1900, Newman's encouragement of his efforts in the 1870s went unmentioned in Ward's *Life* of 1912. The elder Ward (William George) pursued both Newman and Mivart in 1876 in separate pieces in the *Dublin Review* for their refusal to countenance violations of conscience, even on behalf of Christianity (*Letters and Diaries* 28:24 and 71). This would be a "*Dottrina men favorevole a dottrine e principi strettamente cattolici*" (*Letters and Diaries* 27:407: "a view unsupportive of strictly Catholic doctrines and principles"), as Cardinal Franchi had written to Bishop Ullathorne à propos of the *Letter to the Duke of Norfolk*. Mivart picked up the same theme in *Contemporary Evolution, An Essay on Some Recent Social Changes*, 1876. Newman could guess about the background with a sure instinct. He wrote to Mivart (*Letters and Diaries* 28:71-72):

> You must not be surprised at finding yourself the object of criticism in consequence of passages of your book. No one but will incur the jealous narrowness of those, who think no latitude of opinion, reasoning or thought is allowable on theological questions.
> Those who would not allow Galileo to reason 300 years ago, will not allow any one else now. The past is no lesson for them for the present and the future: and their notion of stability in faith is ever to be repeating errors and then repeating retractations of them.

Mivart defended himself in the pages of the *Dublin Review*, to which W.G. Ward replied in a long article in the January 1877 issue, with an Appendix in April. Newman wrote again (*Letters and Diaries* 28:195):

> My dear Professor Mivart,
> I have seen with great concern the way in which Dr Ward has treated you. Controversy is his meat and drink—and he seems to consider it his mission to pick as many holes in others as he can, and to destroy to the uttermost the adhesive qualities of Catholic brotherhood.
> I have suffered from him quite as much as you. He has before now written to Rome against me— but I have never answered him, and doubt whether it is worth while for any one to do so. A Review goes on for ever—and thus he is sure of having the last word.

Newman's correspondence with Mivart is especially pertinent inasmuch as Mivart was in many respects a sort of Modernist before the name.

40. *Letters and Diaries* 30:382-84; cf. Holmes, "Newman's Attitude Towards Historical Criticism and Biblical Inspiration," *Downside Review* 89 (1971):22-37.

41. Holmes, "Newman's Attitude," 34-36; Barmann, *Baron Friedrich von Hügel*, 9-11.

Part Two

ENGLISH MODERNISTS

AND

NEWMAN INTERPRETERS

2

Wilfrid Ward's Interpretation and Application of Newman

Mary Jo Weaver

Whatever else history makes of him, Wilfrid Ward (1856-1916) will endure as a master of biographical skill. The biographer, Ward insisted, paints a faithful portrait: "what the writer must attempt to do is to make the subject of his biography known to his readers as he would have been known to those who came across him in real life. He cannot do much more. He will have achieved signal success if he does as much."[1] Ward achieved that success four times, each time adapting his skills to his subject and each time following his own dictum that "[n]o one should write the life of a man who does not admire him."[2] His first three biographies—of William George Ward, Nicholas Wiseman, and Aubrey de Vere—were, by all accounts, triumphs of a consummate talent; the Wiseman biography especially was hailed as a masterpiece.[3] In some sense, however, these first three lives, now nearly forgotten as their subjects have drifted into obscurity, were but the practical prolegomena for his major work, the biography of John Henry Newman (1801-1890).

The Life of John Henry Cardinal Newman (1912) both suffers and profits from Ward's close identification with his subject. However closely Ward followed his own biographical principles[4]—intimate knowledge of the subject, total mastery of all available material, scrupulous accuracy and objectivity, unmistakably lifelike characterizations—he nevertheless shaped his material according to his own predilections. Sheridan Gilley has shown that Ward's self-understanding closely paralleled that of Newman, an identification that was crucially important in writing the biography.[5] Because Ward not only wrote the life of Newman, but in some ways *lived* it,[6] our understanding of his use of Newman rests on an understanding of his own life.

The outlines of Ward's life are clear: son of a famous and controversial father, he was an apologist for Roman Catholicism,[7] a biographer, an essayist, an editor of the *Dublin Review* (1906-1916), a founding father of the Synthetic Society, a political conservative, and an intellectual and social elitist. He was drawn to those who worked on the edges of a new religious vision, but not ultimately comfortable with them; his religious dream was the triumphant and traditional authority of medieval Catholicism. Perceiving Newman to be an intellectual oligarch and determined to follow in his footsteps, he spent his life as he believed Newman had spent *his* life, in "the preservation of religion against the incoming tide of rationalism and infidelity."[8] His friendships with some of the more controversial religious figures of the time—Friedrich von Hügel, George Tyrrell, Henri Bremond— changed in character or ceased completely during the early years of the twentieth century. His differences with them were complex, but more often than not, they hinged upon the departure from Newman's principles as Ward understood them.[9]

Ward agreed with many of the progressive thinkers of the time that the Roman Catholic church ought to be brought into fruitful dialogue with the modern world. With them he recognized the inadequacy of scholastic philosophy and the attractiveness of Newman's thought. So long as those thinkers stayed within the limits of Newman's principles—provisional freedom of discussion for experts within the boundaries of an institution with a divinely established teaching authority[10]—Ward understood them and made common cause with them. Once they departed from any of those principles—by insisting on total freedom of discussion, by making an untrained foray into a theological discussion, or by questioning ecclesiastical authority—Ward was quick to sense their deviation and often hastened to point it out in print.[11]

If we must know Ward before we can appreciate his Newman, how can we interpret Ward? Maisie Ward's description of him in the aftermath of *Pascendi* helps to set the problem: he was, she says, "under the three-way pull of Modernists accusing him of cowardice, orthodox Catholics accusing him of Modernism, and puzzled Catholics appealing to him for help in the distress of their minds."[12] Ward cannot be classified as a Modernist or even as much of a progressive thinker, yet neither was he welcomed by ecclesiastical officials as champion of orthodoxy. His early support of Alfred Loisy[13] and others made him suspect to conservative Catholics, yet he parted company with nearly all his progressive friends. In his attempt to interpret modern thought for ecclesiastical officials and explain official documents to incredulous progressives, he misrepresented both; yet his dogged attempts to find a positive reading in almost anything written either by experts or ecclesiastical officials gave him a wide audience and a strong sense of responsibility for the "simple faith of devout minds." A posthumous interpreter tried to picture Ward as a moderate, loyal to the church, alive to change, and careful of popular piety.[14]

The picture of Ward occupying a middle ground surrounded by extremists of various kinds may have been the most satisfying way out of the interpretive problem fifty years ago when Maisie Ward wrote the life of her parents. "If you can keep your head when all about you are losing theirs and blaming it on you," Kipling said,[15] you were manly; Maisie Ward's picture of her father is heroic in that sense.[16] I would be inclined to agree with those who finish Kipling's remark by saying, "then you do not have a firm grasp of the situation." Ward may have understood Newman better than anyone else in the nineteenth century, but he did not have an adequate grasp of his own times. His comparisons between thirteenth- and nineteenth-century Catholicism do not allow for real historical change, his failure to address the questions raised by biblical criticism kept him from the center of important controversies, and his almost complete deference to ecclesiastical authority made it impossible for him to understand some of the most important questions raised by Modernists and progressives. His interpretation of Newman *qua* Newman (in the biography and in *Last Lectures*) is superb;[17] his application of Newman's style and thought to his own times was myopic.

Ward's understanding of Newman was, by almost all accounts, remarkable. His gifts as a biographer had been proven and extolled in earlier work, and eager anticipation surrounded his *Newman.* Critical acclaim showed that Ward had met these high expectations; critics were nearly unanimous in praising it "as a great book, and even as a great event."[18] Negative reviews in *The Tablet* and the *Edinburgh Review* were directed against Newman, not against Ward's work; both drew responses from Ward arguing a point that he would take up later in his Lowell Lectures at Harvard, that one cannot criticize someone without knowing the person's career as a whole.[19]

The biography of Newman was written under extremely stressful conditions. On a purely technical level Ward had to contend with serious threats to access and approval by Newman's literary executors.[20] On a strategic level he had to vindicate Newman from any suspicion of Modernism at a time when some church officials, Newman scholars, and Modernists themselves were saying that *Pascendi* condemned Newman along with Modernism.[21] On a professional level, he wanted to produce the most accurate account of Newman's thought so as to discredit what he considered to be travesties of Newman, especially the interpretation of Henri Bremond.[22]

The Modernist controversy and *Pascendi* gave Ward a nightmarish atmosphere in which to write his biography of Newman. That situation would have been bad enough had Ward himself not believed Newman to have been condemned by the encyclical. Those who "really know" Newman, Ward told his wife's uncle, the Duke of Norfolk, see that he has been condemned.[23]

When Tyrrell and Williams published their beliefs about Newman's condemnation in *The Times*[24] Ward was frantic not because he disagreed with them but because he thought that at all costs connections between Newman and Modernism had to be ignored or minimized.[25] In an earlier conflict with ecclesiastical authority—the controversy over the Joint Pastoral Letter in 1901—Ward attempted to relieve an awkward situation by explaining it away.[26] Even Ward, however, could not ignore *Pascendi*, or its condemnation of Newman:

> I don't believe the Pope *meant* to condemn Newman. But he has done so beyond all doubts so far as the words of the Encyclical go—not only on development but so much else. Here is the nemesis Newman foresaw arising from Popes trying to give the Church *intellectual* instructions by Encyclicals—which has never been done before Pius IX's time. It is a piece of "modernism," . . . .
> Its theology is drawn up not by a keen mind alive to the religious controversies of the age (or even to the *established facts* of history), but by a scholastic theologian who may either be an anti-Newmanist, as they often are, or does not know Newman's work and condemned the modernists on certain points in terms which beyond question equally condemn Newman's theories. The situation is, I cannot but think most serious.[27]

Ward was determined to deny connections between Modernism and Newman. From the day he first read the encyclical he began to formulate a strategy to keep Newman's name out of any discussion about *Pascendi*. He thought it useless to try to extricate the pope from the position or to try to prove that his words did not condemn Newman: the best tactic, he thought, was to argue that the doctrines specified in the encyclical were condemned only in the sense in which they were to be found in the writings of the Modernists. In an editorial in the *Dublin Review*,[28] Ward combined deference to authority with a defense of Newman. He claimed to be surprised that "the name of Cardinal Newman should have been, even tentatively, associated by anyone with a system based on the idea which he has dismissed with more absolute scorn than any other."[29] The encyclical was explained as a "solemn warning" against "irresponsible speculation" and no more condemnatory of Newman than of Aquinas. In his defense of Newman he exploited the connection between Jansenius and Augustine, an analogy he apparently intended to use in the biography. After agreeing not to write a paragraph about it,[30] he prepared a long footnote on the similarities between the Modernists and the Jansenists and sent it to von Hügel for comment; but when the baron asked him to omit it, he did. The biography contains no explicit connection between Newman and the Modernists.[31]

Ward was fifty-six when the biography was published (1912), suddenly feeling very much an "old man."[32] His wife attributed that feeling to the Newman biography:

> the Cardinal's Life was a big enough job to break a stronger man's health than Wilfrid's. The mental strain, and I may say it, his absolute conscientiousness has made that worse, is really too much for him . . . Wilfrid has been allowed to overwork himself at a tension of which they [Newman's literary executors] have no notion. They have no consideration for his health and they will break his nerve effectually without knowing what they are doing, or perhaps caring![33]

The strain began with Newman's death (1890) and persisted until Ward actually got access to the papers in 1905; it was intensified by the Modernist controversy and Newman's condemnation in *Pascendi*. I wonder what kind of biography we would have, had William Neville not withheld the papers from Ward for nearly fifteen years. Would a biography written in the 1890s have been more optimistic, but perhaps less deeply felt? Or did Ward's own experience in the first decade of the twentieth century allow him to identify with Newman emotionally as well as intellectually? Whatever its source, the identification Ward felt with Newman's life and work supported him and, in the end, helped him produce a classic.[34]

The Life of Newman—more than 1,200 pages in two volumes—contains hundreds of letters from Newman to various people and very many others *to* him. It is a masterpiece of research and arrangement, thoroughly judicious and focused on Newman *after* his conversion to Roman Catholicism.[35] For the most part, Ward let the documents tell the story, intruding only occasionally to underscore Newman's obedience to ecclesiastical authority or his intellectual oligarchy. While one could argue that Ward did insinuate himself into the biography by virtue of his selection of documents, the sheer volume of sources he published suggests that he made an essentially fair interpretation. In any case, his selection remains to be challenged. The biography was the capstone of a life devoted to Newman's thought and gave Ward the confidence to develop into the fine Newman scholar we find in "The Genius of Cardinal Newman."[36]

The Lowell Lectures enabled Ward to clear up popular misconceptions about Newman and so were useful to him as a way to answer his critics. They also show a mature understanding of Newman and gave Ward more freedom than he had in the biography to comment and explain. Ward covered six topics in these Harvard lectures: Newman's critics, the unity of his work, the sources of his style, his philosophy, his personality, and his psychological insight. His Newman was "a genius, spiritual and intellectual, marked by rare concentration and unity of purpose, and rare variety of gifts and perceptions."[37] He was constrained to show that while people agree that Newman was a genius, they do not agree as to why. Newman did not win an intellectual reputation, Ward says, because he did not seek one, yet he anticipated some major intellectual trends—found later in Auguste Sabatier, Adolf von Harnack, and William James—in his work. He was not "objective;" isolated quotations can make him appear narrow-minded. Yet, Ward insists, he was an artist, not a dilettante, and his "overmastering desire was to secure the influence of Christian faith in an age in which Christianity appeared to him threatened with complete overthrow . . . this is the key to his greatness."[38]

Ward's lecture on the unity of Newman's thought is masterful. Newman, he says, saw clearly the demise of belief in the supernatural and set out to strengthen contemporary Christianity. Having understood agnosticism and seen the value of the imagination, he was able to conclude that "the great antidote to this agnostic atmosphere was . . . the atmosphere created by the teaching and ordinances of the visible Christian Church."[39] His work in different fields, therefore, is held together by a unified vision: the seeds for a philosophy of faith in the Oxford *Sermons,* the historical justification for Christianity in his work on the Arians, and his theological theory of development put forth in the *Essay* all support his aim of strengthening Christianity from "an unprecedented outburst of infidelity."[40]

Ward argues for Newman's artistry, for his genius in anticipating such "modern" trends as the subconscious, pragmatism, and a theory of development,[41] and for his psychological acuity. Newman, Ward says, knew what others felt, was "alive to the trying thoughts which often subconsciously haunt" us.[42] His belief that the human mind contains more than it can master and that we know the truth only in glimpses made him less ready to argue and more willing to spend his energies strengthening existing systems.[43] Perhaps it is best to let Ward himself summarize Newman:

> He was steeped in Christianity. And he endeavoured to impart
> to others the visions and the feelings as well as the arguments

32

which inspired his own faith . . . . He brought to the aid of the Christian Church in winning and keeping human sympathies all the force of his great individuality . . . . he realized his own chosen motto, *Cor ad cor loquitur* . . . . He was by nature and culture alike a true artist, and he communicated to his disciples by means of his art his own self with its many-sided living and intensely Christian way of looking at the world. This really sums up all I have said of his philosophy, his history, his apologetic and his style. When he argued he communicated not dry, formal, theoretical arguments, but the living process of mind through which he had himself passed. So, too, in history . . . . All his views were presented through the pictorial medium of his own mind . . . . In this sense the German insistence on Newman's subjectivity is just. It lies at the root of his strength and of his limitations alike. His most objective study was the genius of the Church as manifest in succeeding civilizations . . . . Still, from first to last the method is the same. It is that of an artist who is likewise poet, historian, thinker and theologian, painting, with a minuteness which only great literary endowment can achieve, the living process of his own mind—his philosophical thought, his historical studies, his imagination, his emotion—presenting to others the picture of Christianity which this process first paints for himself, depicting also the depth of his own conviction as a testimony to the force of the considerations which have convinced him. Occasionally rhetoric and irony are invoked . . . . But the main outcome of the writings is that they convey his own vision of Christianity to the intellect and imagination of his readers, and his own resultant passionate conviction; his principal aim being to form in them the Christian mind and Christian character . . . to draw them within the ark of the Christian church while the deluge of unbelief is being poured throughout the world at large.[44]

Ward's *interpretation* of Newman, distilled from massive documentary evidence, reflects some of Ward's own views and was surely tempered by the limitations Newman's literary executors placed upon him. It was clearly colored by the fact that it was written in the aftermath of *Pascendi*.[45] Still, it is a magnificent piece of work and, insofar as such a thing is possible, one does have a sense of Newman as others knew him. Particularly impressive, I think, is the fact that Ward did not shrink from presenting the tragic elements of Newman's life.

When one turns from interpretation of Newman to Ward's *application* of him to his own times, however, one finds a different story. I once compared Newman to Jean-Antoine Houdon's statue of Voltaire with its witty, intelligent face and impish smile. "Newman smiles, to my mind, because he knows he cannot be pinned down. One cannot devise an interpretive framework and then fit Newman into it; one cannot clarify a definition and then test Newman against it. He slips away from the designs of one school and turns up in those of another. The range of people who have claimed him as a doctrinal or spiritual godfather is large and varied, but he remains elusive."[46] It seems bizarre, perhaps, that Newman could elude his best interpreter; but I think he did. For all the insight Ward brought to Newman *qua* Newman, his attempt to apply Newman's style and principles to developments in the late nineteenth and early twentieth centuries was sadly shortsighted.

Having grown up under the heavy-handed tutelage of William George Ward, Wilfrid Ward was an eager disciple of John Henry Newman. In Newman he saw someone who consistently practiced a species of civility which is especially attractive, yet someone who was tough-minded about essentials—*suaviter in modo, fortiter in re.* His attraction to the charm blinded him to Newman's limitations, and his idealization of Newman's principles did not equip him to deal forthrightly with the problems of his own times. Reading Ward's essays or letters from his friends, one gets the sense that he did not really understand what was going on around him, or that he was hopelessly sanguine. He was not ignorant about the problems of the late nineteenth century: the epilogue to his father's biography—whether he owes its insights mainly to von Hügel or not[47]—at least shows that he could identify the problems. The current assault on Christian faith, he said, draws its strength from three sources: historical criticism, biblical criticism, and agnostic metaphysics in various forms. The "[n]umber is daily growing in England as elsewhere of those who feel the necessity that Christian thinkers should deal not only reverently and cautiously, but also frankly and fully with each of these branches of study."[48]

Perhaps it was his hope for a "Catholic revival" that led him to see more hope in those issues than grief. Looking around at the end of the century he saw a new budding of Christian life and urged those "who see in the Catholic Church the great instrument for the preservation of the belief in the supernatural which is now on the decline all around us"[49] to take note of these signs. For him, the very issues which were threatening theism carried in them a great opportunity for the Catholic church: if the Roman church raises no barrier to those who feel that they must confront the problems of the time, he said, the great fight now engaging all Christian thinkers will become, "to some degree a Catholic Movement."[50] And, if it becomes a Catholic movement—we can almost feel his excitement here—then the Roman Catholic church can finally move beyond its post-Reformation "siege mentality" to take its place as the religious leader of the Christian world.

I think it was this great hope of Ward's which led to his touchingly naive essays of the 1890s. Unfortunately, that hope was not grounded on reality: the Christian world was not ready to make common cause with Catholicism, especially the kind of Catholicism Ward espoused. The epilogue to the Wiseman biography, meant to awaken Catholics to the legitimate claims of modern thought, was a plea for the renewal of medieval Catholicism under the rubric of doctrinal development.[51] Articles like "New Wine in Old Bottles"[52] and "The Rigidity of Rome"[53] were "an appeal to the thinking world outside the Church, to recognize the reasonableness of Rome or at least to consider the Catholic point of view fairly and without prejudice."[54] Ward's activity in the Synthetic Society and his friendly overtures to people like Arthur Balfour were attempts to gather a wide variety of Christian thinkers into his dream.[55] His more daring essays[56] and his early support of the work of Alfred Loisy and George Tyrrell were reflections of his eagerness to associate with the great Catholic thinkers of his time.

All of his work was grounded on his interpretation of Newman. His application of Newman's principles in the 1890s was hopeful and, within the limits of Newman's thought, it welcomed dialogue with the modern world. Those very principles—provisional freedom of discussion for experts within the boundaries of a divinely established teaching authority—were severely tested at the turn of the century and judged inadequate by progressive or Modernist thinkers. Ward had always warned against total freedom of discussion. Newman had insisted on "provisional freedom,"[57] and Ward made it a leitmotiv of his own work. Furthermore, Newman was an intellectual oligarch, extending that freedom only to "experts" guided by the teaching authority of the church. When "nonexperts" like William Gibson or Robert Dell proffered *their* theological opinions in print—opinions highly critical of ecclesiastical authority—Ward was quick to denounce them.[58] In doing so, he set down a rigid standard of orthodoxy which began to alienate him from his "expert" friends like von Hügel and Tyrrell.[59]

One might think that as Ward distanced himself from the progressives, he secured for himself a warm reception by ecclesiastical officials. Not so. By the early part of the twentieth century Ward found himself increasingly isolated. Curial officials committed to scholasticism were suspicious of

Newman and progressive thinkers committed to scholarly autonomy and "real" development of dogma did not find in Newman the freedom they needed to move ahead. Ward, as Newman's foremost interpreter, found himself without friends in either camp. Yet he continued his campaign, insisting at the end of his life that it "is hardly too much to say that the encyclical *Pascendi* would not have been written had Newman's ideal been realized."[60]

At almost every point, Ward simply misread the issues. His historical interpretations were amazingly naive. Charlotte Blennerhasset criticized his assessment of the present situation,[61] and Edmund Bishop thought him "too ignorant of recent history to undertake [the] role . . . as 'liaison officer' between Catholicism and modern thought."[62] His historical analogies—between Newman and Aquinas, or between the Modernists and the Jansenists—offended conservatives and progressives alike since they tended either to use orthodox scholasticism to justify the novelties of Newman or odious comparisons to denigrate the Modernists. Ward's analogies did not account for real historical differences—they implied that all questions would be or should be resolved in the same way forever. One can only guess what Williams thought when Ward, trying to counsel obedience to *Pascendi,* asked if it were any worse than the rack used by the Inquisition.[63]

Ward adopted Newman's intellectual oligarchy easily; it suited his temperament and his purpose to limit free discussion to experts and to consider himself as one of those experts. Elitism had always infected Ward's vision, though it did not show up with hostility until the end of the century. Having explained Newman and the genius of Catholicism throughout the 1890s, Ward anticipated the new century with much optimism. His "Time Spirit of the Nineteenth Century"[64] is the clearest statement of his hopes for the twentieth century, a celebration of the "essentially optimistic" character of evolution. At the close of the nineteenth century, however, he began to see his hopes threatened by "agitators" and "comparative tyros,"[65] and he answered them with a contempt rooted in his own understanding of orthodoxy and expertise. If theology were to grow, he said, it would be due to the serious work of "a few wise men," the experts and specialists working in conjunction with the teaching authority of the church. Who were the experts? Himself, the Newman scholar, and others "who have inherited Newman's spirit."[66] Once he identified himself as an expert, able to speak on religious issues, he held to it. When the Joint Pastoral letter (1901) did to him what he had done to Gibson and Dell—dismissed him from the conversation by arguing that he had no right to speak at all—he stubbornly refused to believe it.[67] His defense of the pastoral and his strategy of explaining it away precipitated his break with Tyrrell[68] as his "Liberalism and Intransigence" article changed his relations with von Hügel.[69] His articles in the first two or three years of the new century were more defensive than hopeful, much stronger articulations of the essentially conservative nature of Newman's principles.

As the century wore on, Ward's distance from progressive or Modernist thinkers grew, especially as he began to emphasize Newman's obedience to authority and the church's obligation to guard the devotional life of the faithful from dangerous theological speculation. His former friends might have been able to overlook his ignorance of historical and biblical questions, agree with the substance of his elitism, and accept his optimism as an eccentric character trait, but they could not live with his almost total deference to authority. Ward believed that Newman "did carry non-resistance or non-protest one step too far,"[70] and he did, with some courage, refuse to publish an article by the bishop of Limerick which was uncritical in its acceptance of *Pascendi*,[71] but in the last analysis he upheld the principle of authority to the letter. During the *Pascendi* crisis Ward continually quoted a letter in which Newman said, "Theirs is the responsibility, I have only to obey and help them with my prayers."[72] His articles immediately before and after *Pascendi*—especially "Cardinal Newman and Creative Theology"[73]—insisted on the necessity of discipline and purification of the intellect by ecclesiastical authority. His interests had shifted from scholars to "the faithful" and he underscored Newman's views of the church as the protector of devotional life: "[t]hus authority may rightly check the intellect not merely for falling into excesses which are untrue or misleading, but for pressing on the community speculations which upset the faith and devotional life of the masses."[74]

The wrenching irony of the situation lies in the fact that in distancing himself from progressive thinkers and extolling the wisdom and value of ecclesiastical authority, he came no closer to acceptance by the official church. The condemnation of Newman's thought by *Pascendi*, and the implicit condemnation of his own work, stunned him and changed his life. No longer was he the optimistic herald of the new theology; from 1907 until his death in 1916 Ward worked to vindicate Newman from any suspicion of Modernism. Newman was called a "liberal Catholic" by many, Ward said, but "he most strongly repudiated that eptithet . . . Later came a phenomenon yet more surprising—such advocates of Modernism as Loisy and LeRoy claimed Newman's philosophical thought as being in line with their own speculations . . . . Newman was never a Modernist."[75]

Ward understood Newman's life and his principles, and was surely not alone in thinking that Newman's thought was the key to a new and splendidly creative period of theological speculation. In placing all his hopes in Newman, he idolized him and failed to see his limitations as a guide through the thicket of new theological questions raised at the end of the century. Newman had virtually no acquaintance with biblical criticism; and Ward, hampered by the liabilities of his hero, had none either. He was content to leave the question to experts like von Hügel and Loisy, but did not understand that their expertise would take them into questions Newman never dreamed of.[76] As he did not understand the autonomy questions which went hand in glove with critical questions, his continual application of Newman's provisional freedom was inadequate for scholars and too daring for ecclesiastical officials. His upholding of the "principle of authority" and citation of Newman's ever and ready obedience begged the very questions the Modernists asked.[77] Yet, since his obedience was rooted in Newman's principles, Ward never endeared himself to church officials. At the time of *Pascendi* he was, as Maisie Ward said, caught in the middle of a three-way pull. I do not think, however, that he was therefore a "moderate" or a man of the middle. He was, as Father Cuthbert noted, "an open-minded conservative."[78]

Heroic action in a crisis is rare, which is why we notice and reward it. Ward was no hero: he was too blind to Newman's limitations and too bound up in his own conservative inclinations to be fully committed either to the pursuits of the Modernists or to the excesses of Roman authority. When forced to choose between them, he chose the church knowing that "things are terribly bad in Rome," hoping that "at any moment the 'regime' may change," and insisting that "direct resistance is in every way unwise."[79] No one will remember Ward for his *application* of Newman's principles to the problems of the late nineteenth century; he joins a significant company of religious thinkers who misread the signs of the times in one direction or another. He will be remembered, however, for his *interpretation* of Newman in the biography and the Lowell Lectures. In spite of his overeager and myopic responses to his own situation, Ward was a brilliant biographer: the Newman we get from him is a genius, full of subtlety and passion, whose life was, in many ways, tragic. I think the identification Ward felt with him as he saw his own hopes collapse during the Modernist controversy deepened his understanding of Newman and helped Ward produce an enduring and faithful portrait.

NOTES

1. Wilfrid Ward, *Last Lectures* (London: Longmans, 1918), 151.

2. Ibid., 169. Apropos of his desire to be in sympathy with his subject was Ward's refusal to write the biography of Lord Acton. Letters from Acton's children can be found in the Wilfrid Ward Papers at the University Library, St. Andrews, Scotland. Ward's letter of refusal was published in Maisie Ward, *The Wilfrid Wards and the Transition* (London: Sheed and Ward, 1934), 245f.

3. Wilfrid Ward, *Last Lectures*, 255; Maisie Ward says, "competent critics have told me that they place it highest among my father's works,—even above the *Life of Cardinal Newman* usually held to be his magnum opus."

4. Ward spelled out his biographical principles in a series of lectures delivered at the Royal Institution in London, 1914-1915. See Wilfrid Ward, *Last Lectures*, 150-221; the principles I have summarized appear on pp. 170-73.

5. "Wilfrid Ward and his *Life of Newman*." *Journal of Ecclesiastical History* 29 (April 1978): 177-93. Gilley contrasts Ward's interpretation of Newman with that of Bremond and concludes that the Ward biography "stands as a massive refutation of the psychological simplicities of Bremond, by showing that to understand a Newman one must see the vision which held him through his life, and judge of his achievement by his vision" (193).

6. His wife remembered later that "Wilfrid lived in the person whose life he was writing—and so much was this the case that I, too, lived successively in the company of his father, whom I had never known, of Cardinal Wiseman and of Aubrey de Vere. All our life together was lived under the shadow of Cardinal Newman" (Maisie Ward, *The Wilfrid Wards and the Transition*, 239).

7. Ward was ever an apologist, attempting to explain Roman Catholic traditions, beliefs, and personalities to a non-Roman Catholic audience. His *Life of Wiseman* is a case in point: "Wilfrid Ward had accomplished the two things that meant most to him. He had done his duty as a biographer of Wiseman. What in the long run mattered more, he had helped his readers to a better understanding of the Church" (Ibid., 256).

8. Wilfrid Ward, *Last Lectures*, 7.

9. Ward's arguments with George Tyrrell are a case in point. See my *Letters from a "Modernist": The Letters of George Tyrrell to Wilfrid Ward 1893-1908* (Shepherdstown, WV: Patmos Press, 1981).

10. These three principles—provisional freedom, expertise, and ecclesiastical authority—form the main themes of Ward's interpretation of Newman as a guide to contemporary scholars. One can find them reiterated in almost all of Ward's apologetic works and many of his reviews and essays. In the biography of Newman he outlines them this way: "Yet, together with his protests against intellectual narrowness . . . we have indications of two lines of thought tending in the opposite direction . . . . One was that, although reason rightly exercised would in the long run justify belief in Theism and Catholic Christianity . . . still in man . . . a force is needed to keep alive and vivid those first principles on which religious belief depends. And that force is supplied by the living Catholic Church. Secondly, while free discussion is essential . . . the intellect

of man has . . . a constant tendency to exceed its lawful limits and arrive at unbelief . . . .
Here again the antidote was the controlling action of the Catholic Church in arresting
speculation when it ran to excess" (*The Life of John Henry Cardinal Newman*
[London: Longmans, 1912], 413).

11. This tendency in Ward, especially evident in such essays as "Liberalism and
Intransigence" *Nineteenth Century* 47 (June 1900): 960-73, or "Catholic Apologetics: A
Reply," *Nineteenth Century* 45 (June 1899): 955-61, led von Hügel to write to Ward
saying, "I have to admit that I am generally a little fearful of finding that you have
treated the questions *under the aspect of orthodoxy, and the limits of the latter.* Now
whilst quite prepared to think or declare such and such a view or such and such a man
inadequate, impoverishing or even downrightly untrue, I find I should be acting quite
against my whole interior movement and spontaneous conscience if I allowed myself to
shift it on to the ground of orthodoxy, and drawing the list as to who or what is
within, who or what is without the pale. I should wish to work all those questions well
into a very devoted spiritual life, and, as to the results, leave the question of their
orthodoxy to God and the Church authorities" (Wilfrid Ward Papers, 18 June 1900).

12. *Insurrection versus Resurrection* (London: Sheed and Ward, 1937), 272.

13. Even in 1907, Ward was not totally negative about Loisy. Writing a brief review
of William's *Newman, Loisy, Pascal and the Catholic Church,* Ward said that though
he regretted that Abbé Loisy's name was included in William's title, "We are quite
in accord with Mr. Williams' view as to the place which Abbé Loisy's ostensible
aim—namely a careful analysis of the results of modern criticism—would occupy
in the carrying out of theological development along the lines of Newman's *Essay.*"
At the same time, he said, "his actual writing has aroused a degree of criticism,
even apart from its official censure by the Holy office, which makes [William's]
brief treatment of [Loisy's] position unsatisfactory." See *Dublin Review* 140 (January
1907): 183.

14. Father Cuthbert, "Apologist of the Catholic Church," *Dublin Review* 159
(1916): 1-22. Cuthbert addresses the problem directly: "Amongst his fellow-Catholics
this sincerity of mind gave him a secure place in their esteem: it carried him safely
through the period of acute feeling aroused by the condemnation of modernism,
when one party regarded him as a drag on the wheel whilst their extreme opponents
wondered whether modernism itself was more dangerous to the Church or the 'liberalism'
of Wilfrid Ward. To those who knew him at all intimately the charge of 'liberalism'
was too ludicrous to be taken seriously, though it caused himself much pain at the
time. He could hardly have been a liberal in thought even had he tried" (p. 1). I find
Cuthbert's phrasing provocative, especially that anyone could wonder if Ward's so-called
"liberalism" was "more dangerous to the Church" than Modernism itself. I take it that
Cuthbert could only come up with such a remark in light of "extreme opponents"
(of the Modernists). For an example of the kind of criticism Ward did receive from
right-wing Catholics see the letter from a Monsignor Croke-Robinson (1907) which
claims to delate Ward for suspicion of intellectual pride. The letter was reprinted in its
dismal fullness in Maisie Ward, *Insurrection verus Resurrection,* 227-9.

15. Rudyard Kipling, "IF."

16. Maisie Ward's work on her father is excellent for its use of materials and its ability
to explain her father's life and work to a world ready to forget him. Her characterization
of her father as the "philosopher of the Church's constitution" and as a moderate is an
insightful accounting of the facts. Whether such an interpretation continues to be useful
today, however, is arguable. Unless one is willing to argue (by way of Aristotle, perhaps)
that there is something intrinsically good about being "in the middle," a rehearsal of
Maisie Ward's view adds nothing to our understanding. William J. Schoenl's "English
Liberal Catholicism in the Early 1980's," *Clergy Review* 62 (1977): 92-105, would have
profited from an argument for the goodness or rightness of a middle-ground position.

17. These works on Newman are still cited and consulted by Newman scholars, and lately by students of Victorian culture. See A.O.J. Cockshut, *Truth to Life: The Art of Biography in the Nineteenth Century* (New York: Harcourt Brace Jovanovich, 1974): Ward's Newman is one of five "classics" of nineteenth-century biography used here to prove that critical studies of biography can illuminate the culture in which they were written.

18. Maisie Ward, *Insurrection versus Resurrection*. For an account of the writing and reception of the biography see the chapter in this book, "The Newman Biography," pp. 332-57. Letters to Ward (Wilfrid Ward Papers) are overwhelmingly favorable, though von Hügel scarcely says more than "thank you."

19. See his letter to *The Tablet* 119 (3 February 1912): 183 and his long article, "The Edinburgh Review on Cardinal Newman," in *Nineteenth Century* 72 (July 1912): 69-87. The article in the *Nineteenth Century* contains some of the strongest words Ward ever published: he says the review feeds those who hate Newman; does no service; is unjust, absurd, and intellectually contemptible. His main point, that too many critics fail to take Newman's career as a whole and so do not understand him, became the basis for his Lowell Lectures. See Wilfrid Ward, *Last Lectures*, 1-150.

20. For a recounting of how and why Newman's first literary executor, William Neville, withheld papers from Ward, see Maisie Ward, *Insurrection versus Resurrection*, 332-57. The correspondance in the Wilfrid Ward Papers between Ward and Longmans gives some indication of the horrendous problems Ward had dealing with Newman's literary executors: he was promised a "free hand" but submitted copy to them nevertheless and was constantly being asked to change words delete phrases, and recast chapters. They forbade Ward to publish a third, supplementary volume of letters and so dashed his hopes for completeness. The most sympathetic and insightful account of these aspects of the Newman biography is Sheridan Gilley's "Wilfrid Ward and his *Life of Newman*," cited, n. 5. He notes, rightly, that in recounting the story earlier Maisie Ward says too little about the ways in which Modernism exacerbated Ward's already delicate relationship with Newman's literary executors.

21. For an overview of this episode see Edward Kelly, "Newman, Wilfrid Ward and the Modernist Crisis" in *Thought* 48(1973): 509-18.

22. *The Mystery of Newman* (London: Williams and Novak, 1907). Ward had nothing but contempt for Bremond's reading of Newman. See Weaver, *Letters from a "Modernist,"* 109f, or Ward's review, "Newman Through French Spectacles," in *The Tablet* 108 (1906): 86-89, where he says that the French mind is not suited to understand Newman and that Bremond apparently cannot handle the English language.

23. On 2 November 1907 Williams wrote to *The Times* to say that Newman had surely been condemned by *Pascendi*. That day, Ward wrote to Norfolk:

> Williams is a friend of mine . . . he is, I suppose, except myself, the Catholic who knows Newman's writing the best. [His] letter is likely to bring to a head what I still think is a most grave crisis. Please look at my letter to you of October 10th and you will see this is no new impression, and please observe what I there said as to the disingenuous quibbling likely to come in the attempt to prove that the Encyclical did not hit Newman. I believe such an attempt may be made seriously by some, *because they do not really know Newman's writings and thought* thoroughly and believe on the face of it that Rome cannot have condemned him (Letter in Wilfrid Ward Papers [emphasis mine]).

24. Weaver, *Letters from a "Modernist,"* xxv-xxix.

41

25. Ward believed minimizing was the best strategy for interpreting *Pascendi*. Two letters in the Wilfrid Ward Papers to Williams (14 and 24 December 1907) articulate his position quite clearly. "I think the logical minimism a necessity. Yet it is now getting to a point when it runs very close to sheer equivocation owing to the high hand of Roman authorities. I am tempted to apply a saying of my father's in 1863, in the days before the ballot: 'The British constitution is a democracy tempered by bribery and intimidation—one bad thing largely neutralized by another.' So, 'our present system is papal absolutism tempered by theological equivocation.' But I repeat that I believe even excessive minimism to be justifiable *under* this system while it lasts, as the only way out of greater evils. Yet one should not in any way approve of the system, as involving such excesses through some minimism is even necessary on account of human imperfection" (14 December 1907).

26. See my "George Tyrrell and the Joint Pastoral Letter," *Downside Review* 99 (1981): 18-39.

27. To Norfolk 10 October 1907. In Wilfrid Ward Papers.

28. "The Encyclical *Pascendi*," *Dublin Review* 142 (January 1908): 1-10. Ward's strategy about the editorial began to take shape as early as October when he wrote to Norfolk saying "The only simple way out, preliminary to a more accurate statement for which they [Roman authorities] *must* employ competent people and not exclusively mere scholastics, is to say that the doctrines specified in the Encyclical are only condemned in the sense in which they are found in the pages of the Modernist writers alluded to and based on their principles" (10 October 1907). He was more specific as to his editorial strategy in a letter to Williams (24 December 1907). In that letter he outlined his principles of "the golden bridge" saying "it is the theological interpretation which enables the authorities to retreat from an untenable point without explicitly admitting a mistake." He assures Williams that he deplores the encyclical, that the true course is to make authority realize that "a great deal which it includes in modernism is true and indispensable" and that the "Vatican confirmed [this] view so far as the Newman passages were concerned." At the same time, he tells Williams, the archbishop has told him that his Dublin editorial must "accept" the encyclical and that he has done so, "Plainly showing, however, that while I obey I do not approve, though obedience ties my tongue." He urges Williams to take a historical view and asks him if Popes have never been wrong before. "Is Pascendi," he asks, "worse than the rack?" He quotes Newman, but says, "I clearly intimate in my article that I sacrifice none of my convictions and that intellectually it is only the most minimistic sense that I accept the document" (Wilfrid Ward Papers).

29. Ibid., p. 1.

30. In a letter to Archbishop Bourne (16 August 1911) he says, "As to the Modernism paragraph, I have cut it out of the text, and have put instead a brief footnote on the subject near the end" (Wilfrid Ward Papers).

31. Ward felt caught between demands from Newman's literary executors (to villify the Modernists and exonerate Newman from any connections with them) and von Hügel's request that he omit his remarks from the biography. See a series of letters between Ward and von Hügel (in Wilfrid Ward Papers and von Hügel Papers at St. Andrews).
A. Ward to von Hügel (20 September 1911)

> . . . my life of Newman . . . is an absolutely frank book and I have stood to my guns as to publishing all documents . . . [Newman] carries the doctrine of obedience in my opinion too far.

B. von Hügel to Ward (2 October 1911)

> I cannot but feel, more strongly than formerly, and doubtless quite finally, one, to my mind now grave, peculiarity and defect of the Cardinal's

temper of mind and position. His, apparently absolute, determination never to allow—at least *to allow others*—*any* public protestation, any act or declaration contrary to current central Roman policy, cannot, surely, be pressed, or imposed as normative upon us all. For, taken thus, it would stamp *our Lord* Himself as a deplorable rebel . . . . Such like considerations and the sense as to all Fr. Tyrrell had to suffer and of all he did—in spite of faults and failings,—for the heroic, . . . fruitfully true conception of Catholicism,—make the note on p. 26 impossible for me.

C. Ward to von Hügel (3 October 1911)

I think JHN did carry non-resistance or non-protest one step too far, thus you and I should quite agree . . . as to my note, it is disliked by the ultra-montanists as not strong enough . . . the comparison to Jansenius just hits the nail—for Loisy was inspired by JHN, yet clearly he would not have embraced Losiy's conclusions.

Ward had not given up his determination to say what Newman would have made of Loisy even though von Hügel had written to him (20 January 1906) to comment on Ward's "Function of Prejudice" article. "I am sorry to note," von Hügel wrote, "the attempt to guess what Newman would personally have held about Loisy, were he now alive."

D. Ward to von Hügel (20 November 1911)

I am omitting the note on "modernism" partly *in consequence* of your criticism, but not from agreement with it. I do think that the explanation I have been at infinite pains to elicit from theologians shows that what will ultimately be ruled as being condemned by the Holy See is the . . . exaggeration by Loisy of all JHN has said, just as Jansenius was condemned for a[n] . . . exaggeration of St. Augustine.

E. von Hügel to Ward (23 November 1911)

Thank you for your card, and now for your letter, concerning that St. Augustine-Jansenius, Newman-Tyrrell note in your "Life of Cardinal Newman." I cannot help being sincerely pleased that you have now omitted that note, and am taking serious note of your reasons for doing so, as thus given me by yourself.

32. Ward wrote to George Wyndham in 1911 to say, "I wonder if you will feel, at 55, as I do, that quite suddenly old age has begun. There has hardly been any preparation. I did not feel it when I turned 54. It has all come quite suddenly in a few months" (Quoted in Maisie Ward, *Insurrection versus Resurrection*, 347).

33. Quoted in Maisie Ward, *Insurrection versus Resurrection*, 348.

34. Whether Ward's identification with Newman was helpful or not can be argued; empathy with a subject often allows a biographer to understand things deeply, though it may also blind one to the subject's faults. Gilley (see note 5) believes that it was precisely this identification that gave Ward the "vision" to write the biography, and I am inclined to agree with him. Louis Wetmore, however, said, "the life of Newman has never impressed me as a vital piece of work. There is too much of the element of the magnum opus and the official biography about it; again, too, much of the suggestion of the disciple and the master." (Wilfrid Philip Ward: Victorian" in *America* 15 [1916]: p. 36). Whatever the merits of the identification, critical appraisal of the biography was excellent and continues to be good. Nicholas Lash has high praise for Ward's work: "I would wish to argue," he said, "that Ward's value as an intelligent and not uncritical interpreter of Newman has been seriously [in modern times] underestimated." (*Newman on Development* [Shepherdstown, WV: Patmos Press, 1975], p. 151).

35. Ward treated the first thirty-five years of Newman's life in about fifty pages; his virtual neglect of Newman's youth led Maisie Ward to write *Young Mr. Newman* (London: Sheed and Ward, 1948).

36. Title of his Lowell Lectures, delivered at Harvard in 1914. See Wilfrid Ward, *Last Lectures*, 1-150.

37. Ibid., 145.

38. Ibid., 10.

39. Ibid., 43.

40. Ibid., 24, quoting a letter written about Newman by Aubrey de Vere.

41. Ibid., 74.

42. Ibid., 135.

43. Ibid., 104-8.

44. Ibid., 122f.

45. I do not think Stephen Dessain is quite fair when he says, "Wilfrid Ward claimed to know Newman's teaching through and through, but a real disciple ought to have been less perturbed [about Newman's connections with Modernism]." *The Letters and Diaries of John Henry Newman*, vol. II (London/New York: T. Nelson, 1961), xix.

46. In review of Lee H. Yearly, *The Ideas of Newman: Christianity and Human Religiosity* (1978) in *Victorian Studies* 23 (1980): 525.

47. Ward did claim that he owed the Epilogue to von Hügel—see *William George Ward and the Catholic Revival* (London: Longmans, 1893), xii—but that hardly justifies citing it as one of von Hügel's own works as does Thomas Michael Loome, *Liberal Catholicism, Reform Catholicism, Modernism* (Mainz: Matthias-Grünewald, 1979), 209.

48. *William George Ward and Catholic Revival*, 431.

49. Ibid.

50. Ibid., 432.

51. *The Life and Times of Cardinal Wiseman*, 2 volumes (London: Longmans, 1897), volume 2, 533-83. The epilogue had nothing to do with Wiseman (see a letter from Ward to his son Leo, 1916, Wilfrid Ward Papers), but provided a medium for Ward's application of Newman's ideas. It was predicated on the belief that the Roman church is the appointed guardian of revelation and must be, accordingly, exclusive and judging. At the same time, he argued, that same church's genius is its ability to assimilate "all that is worthy, in the civilizations in which, from time to time, it finds itself" (p. 534). The epilogue is replete with slogans and warnings about hasty conclusions, all of which, Ward says, are suggested by Newman: intellectual life and freedom must be balanced by alert and ready obedience. Finally, Ward's vision is of a wise and holy pope ruling a gratefully obedient people (p. 583). In light of the essentially conservative nature of the epilogue, it is fascinating that, in 1911, he was asked by Rome to delete it from further editions; see Maisie Ward, *Insurrection versus Resurrection*, 318-28.

52. *Nineteenth Century* 27 (June 1890): 942-56. Here he presents Newman as a mediating position between Lord Acton's "liberalism" and William George Ward's conservatism, but his real apologia is for Roman Catholicism. Ward believed that the combination of

44

real scientific study and a strong, eternal deposit of faith would lead to properly sober conclusions and that the Catholic church could march triumphantly into the modern world neither wrecked by hasty conclusions nor hopelessly mired in anti-progressive patterns of thought. "Holding fast to the substance of tradition yet alive to the new outlook," Maisie Ward interpreted; see Maisie Ward, *Wilfrid Wards and the Transition*, 184.

53. *Nineteenth Century* 38 (December 1895): 786-804.

54. Father Cuthbert, "Apologist of the Catholic Church," *Dublin Review* 159 (1916): 14.

55. Ward admired Balfour and pubished highly favorable reviews of his work; see my "A Bibliography of the Published Works of Wilfrid Ward" in the *Heythrop Journal* 20 (1979):399-420, numbers 49, 115, 157, 184, and 245. Louis Wetmore (see note 34) in a critical assessment of Ward said, "The influence that Ward has on the philosophical development of Arthur Balfour is one of those curious intellectual adventures that delight the soul of man in his ironic moods . . . [it] remained for Balfour cordially to hate the Church . . . . Yet His anti-Catholic prejudices were held in check by the powerful influence that Ward exerted on his mind. Ward's admiration for Balfour was intense" (36).

56. "The Ethics of Religious Conformity," *Quarterly Review* 189 (January 1899): 103-36 is one example. In a letter to Ward (7 March 1899, Wilfrid Ward Papers) Balfour said, "I think that at the appropriate time and place [in the past] you would have been burnt for writing it." Ward compared the work of Sabatier, Henry Sidgwick, and Newman and concluded that those who hold a theory of the evolution of dogma can conform to a religious creed *while separating themselves from orthodox positions*, while those who do not (namely, Sidgwick) do not have tenable positions (136, emphasis mine).

57. Wilfrid Ward, *Life of Newman* 1: 400

58. See "Catholic Apologetics: A Reply," *Nineteenth Century* 45 (June 1899): 955-61, and "Liberalism and Intransigence," *Nineteenth Century* 47 (June 1900): 960-73.

59. See Weaver, *Letters from a "Modernist."*

60. See the Introduction to John Henry Newman, *On the Scope and Nature of University Education* (London and New York: Everyman's Library Edition, 1915), xv.

61. See Maisie Ward, 192, *Insurrection versus Resurrection*, where Maisie Ward repeats Blennerhasset's criticism but does not give its source.

62. See Nigel Abercrombie, *The Life and Work of Edmund Bishop* (London: Longmans, 1959), 198.

63. Ward to Williams, 24 December 1907 (Wilfrid Ward Papers).

64. *Edinburgh Review* 194 (July 1901): 92-131.

65. "Liberalism and Intransigence" (cited note 11), 961.

66. Ibid., 972.

67. See "Doctores Ecclesiae" *Pilot* 2 (22 June 1901): 774-76. Also see my "George Tyrrell and the Joint Pastoral Letter." He argued from what he considered to be the nature of pastoral letters and said that those who wished for intellectual support in the thirteenth century did not go to a pope or a bishop but to Aquinas and that those who want similar help in "our own day are more likely to go to the pages of Cardinal Newman than to those of a pastoral."

68. See Weaver, *Letters from a "Modernist"*, and "George Tyrrell and the Joint Pastoral Letter."

69. See letter from von Hügel to Ward, June through October 1900, in Wilfrid Ward Papers.

70. In a letter from Ward to von Hügel (3 October 1911) MS 3153 in the von Hügel Papers at St. Andrews.

71. See Maisie Ward, *Insurrection versus Resurrection*, 254-95. Ward wrote to Williams (14 December 1907) saying that he accepted the encyclical but did not like it. "Moreover, I made certain conditions in my own mind as to what was necessary for a candid and truthful article on that subject from anyone and have declined the Bishop of Limerick's paper because they were not observed in it. I gave him warning first. He threatens to denounce me publically, but I think he will have the worst of it. Yet I should be sorry if it leads to my resignation as this storm must pass and I do not want my 'Dublin' work terminated forever" (Wilfrid Ward Papers).

72. Quoted in a letter to Williams (24 December 1907), Wilfrid Ward Papers.

73. *Dublin Review* 138 (April 1906): 233-70.

74. Ibid., 263.

75. See Ward's Introduction to *On the Scope and Nature of University Education*, cited, vii.

76. As early as 1894 von Hügel wrote to Ward to say, "The real question in my mind is whether there is or is not such a thing as the Science of the Bible (as distinguished from its dogmatic and devotional use) and whether it is to be allowed to pursue its own methods (as distinct from proclaiming any and every conclusion) and whether suppression of labour or even publication (as distinct from broadcast dissemination) is not a danger as great as any that is attempted to be met" (Wilfrid Ward Papers).

77. Von Hügel wrote to him (5, 7, July 1900) saying that critics can often care more for *religion* than church officials; did Ward, von Hügel asked, wish to leave all criticism to Protestants? Wilfrid Ward Papers. In his Introduction to *The Scope and Nature of University Education*, written in 1915, we can see that he still, even then, did not understand the nuances of the Modernist issue. "The history of Modernism would have been widely different," he argued, "had Newman's ideal been fully realized. Highly sensitive and easily overwrought intellectual natures may be driven to extremes by a lack of understanding in authoritative quarters of the problems which exercise them intensely" (xiii).

78. "Apologist of the Catholic Church," see note 14.

79. In his letter to Williams (24 December 1907), Wilfrid Ward Papers.

Ward's Newman: The Struggle to be Fair and Faithful

Nadia M. Lahutsky

A successful biography requires mastering several factors. The first is a rather basic one of securing access to the evidences still available. The difficulty of this task will vary according to the time elapsed and the specific circumstances surrounding the materials. The second necessary factor is the development of a general framework into which the evidences are to be placed. Without this element of interpretation, the assorted vignettes of a life do not become a biography. John Henry Newman's life provided an abundance of available materials and a fascinating human story begging for an interpretation. Wilfrid Ward's writing a life of Newman ought to have been a biographer's dream; in fact, it was more like a nightmare.

The nightmare quality of Ward's work came from an external source, the Birmingham Oratorians' general distrust of him, and an internal source, his own tendency at rare but noticeable points to confuse a biographical interpretation with his own contemporary use of Newman. This paper will explore aspects of Ward's *Life of Newman* with attention both to the details of his obtaining the material and to the way his use of Newman influenced his implementation of the evidences at hand. Ward's *Life of Newman* is a good biography, attentive to the sources and alive to contextual issues. The three episodes chosen for scrutiny here—1846 plans for a theology school, the *Rambler* incident, and Newman's relations with J. J. Ignaz von Döllinger—represent areas where Ward may have been especially tempted to bend the narrative to coincide with his own understanding of what should be known of Newman, an understanding that was in conflict with both those of the Oratory and of other—more daring—interpreters of Newman.

Ward vs. the Oratory

Getting the Assignment

William Neville served as literary executor by dragging his feet for fifteen years after Newman's death, never assigning the Newman biography to Wilfrid Ward, the only obvious candidate for the job. Several reasons explain this delay. First was Newman's own reticence regarding a biography. Actually, "reticence" is not strong enough to describe what seems to have been a holy horror of biographers. This horror became an effort by Newman to preempt the biographical task.[1] Had he not done an autobiography, the *Apologia pro Vita Sua* in 1864, which covered all the important stages of his religious development up to that time? Surely little remained to be said once he had escaped "the city of confusion and the house of bondage."[2] Newman's own careful efforts to organize his correspondence would have given to his life the shape he intended. Whatever his fears of a future biographer, they were transmitted to his fellow Oratorians who worked with fervor to protect the memory of their founder.

Secondly, there was the Oratorians' reasonable fear that the son of Newman's old bête noire could not possibly do a fair and sympathetic treatment of the cardinal. W. G. Ward, with H. E. Manning, had often made Newman's life difficult by opposing his plans and person. The Oratorians ought to have looked more closely. Indeed, in Ward's biography of his father we encounter a strange threesome—W. G. Ward, once the most fervent follower of Newman but eventually his severest foe; Newman, at one time a leader of opinion, now reduced to leading a small group of Oratorians and schoolboys; and Wilfrid Ward, biologically son of the first, intellectually son of the second. The elder Ward is the principal character in the biography, but lurking throughout every chapter is Newman, either as Ward's acknowledged leader in the Oxford Movement or as a force in the Catholic Revival.

A third reason for the delay lay with the Oratorians' inability to perceive a pressing need for a biography. Newman may have had some public moments in his triumph of 1872 with the *Letter to the Duke of Norfolk* and he was warmly acclaimed by all England on receiving the cardinal's hat in 1878. But in all important matters, he was, by the time of his death in 1890, primarily one of them. He belonged not to the English public, but to the smaller world of the Oratorian communities. They saw no great need for a "Life and Times" of the man they all knew so well. Thus, they would not initiate steps toward a biography.[3]

There were discussions in 1890 about a biography and even some letters congratulating Ward on his "assignment." However, those plans called not for a genuine biography, but rather for "something of a biography," namely, the publication of Newman's letters with a sparse narrative to link them.[4] Neville no doubt assumed that such a design would eliminate the dangers any biographer might bring to the task, reducing the biographer to little more than a secretary. In retrospect Ward must have been glad that the ersatz biography project died, else he would not have had the later opportunity to embark on what was to become his finest, most mature work. We, too, should be grateful, for the project proposed in 1890 would have been a pale imitation of a genuine biography. It would have contained little of Newman's correspondence, much of which was collected during the 1890s when Neville put out his call for letters and was nearly buried in the response. Furthermore, some of what is now available to Newman scholars in the *Letters and Diaries* may well have been omitted then in the interests of prudence and the cardinal's good name.

In sum, it is a good thing that the project did not materialize. At the time, however, Ward was less than pleased. He wrote complaining letters to the Duke of Norfolk (uncle of his wife, Josephine Hope) about Neville's inconstancy. He resented the cat and mouse game that Neville played with him, inviting him to the Oratory to give him some papers and then taking the material back before Wilfrid could leave.[5] To do the life of Newman was the project for which Ward was best prepared and which he wanted most passionately. Ward must have realized, however, that this mouse was not likely to be nabbed soon. For in 1894, he agreed to write the life of Wiseman.[6] Ward's acceptance of the Wiseman project suggests that he did not believe a Newman project was forthcoming.

When the Wiseman project was completed in 1898, Neville wrote to Ward that it caused him anxiety. "I find what are to me as phantasies of events in wh. I cannot recognise J.H.N's real self, and I can only put down the book wondering with distress as to what is to become of him in the future."[7] Reading the *Life of Wiseman* today, we can only wonder what so distressed Neville that he could not clearly express those concerns. H. I. D. Ryder, fellow Oratorian, gave some advice to Ward regarding Neville. "You must treat him as an old aunt from whom you have expectations."[8]

Ward's turn to worry came when he saw an announcement for a life of Newman by Edmund Purcell. He had critiqued Purcell's *Life of Manning* as a mere caricature and not a biography. What would happen to Newman if Purcell should have the biography was more than Ward could fathom. To Norfolk Ward wrote, "If Neville has supplied him with material it is quite upardonable. I thought it a bad sign that he evidently rejoiced in Purcell's Manning because of the glorification of Newman and disparagement of Manning. And he was very dissatisfied with my treatment of Newman in the Life of Wiseman. He judges everything simply by the amount of butter which Newman personally receives and the total absence of any shade of criticism of him."[9]

Ryder's advice to Ward was perceptive. A trip to Birmingham shortly after the Purcell scare seems to have improved Ward's position with Neville. He reported to the Duke, "I think I have made some impression on him as to the misfortune of delaying to begin the biography until many people are dead whose information would be most valuable . . . . He said, 'The fact is that I have not been wisely treated. Lord Emly tried to use violence with me and to give you the letters to write a book in six weeks. And now they don't make enough of me. I ought to be fussed over and petted, then perhaps I should do something.' "[10]

If Ward's financial future had depended on his ability to fuss over and pet an elderly relative, the family may well have ended up in the Poorhouse. He did not do well at the task with Neville and the hoped-for Newman papers. He did receive a quantity of manuscript material in 1902, but only because Neville thought Ward needed to clarify his misunderstanding of Newman. "I cannot describe the distress my further perusal of your two Dr. Ward vols., and your life of Dr. Wiseman has given me."[11] Neville was, at least, consistent. Perhaps he simply could not bring himself to trust Newman's memory to *anyone*. Ryder suggested that Newman had named Neville as literary executor, knowing that he would stall endlessly. Elsewhere Neville has been described as "always a hesitant, undecided person."[12]

George Tyrrell wondered at Neville's ability to put off the inevitable and asked of Ward: "What is going to be done for the Newman centenary? I should suggest the assassination of F. Neville and the appropriation of his goods by Wilfrid Ward. There is no one who could do the work as you could and it would be for you *monumentum aere perennius.*"[13] No one assassinated Neville, but he did die in 1905, leaving behind the unresolved problem of Newman's papers and Ward's desire for them. Neville's will named as executors Edward and Henry Bellasis; their brother Richard acted informally as an executor. In 1906 they asked John Norris, superior of the Birmingham Oratory, to work with them. Since Henry was in Rome, he was not closely involved with the project, and Richard tended to defer to Edward's judgment. Norris, who was a supporter of Ward's work, was not so strong or long-lived as Edward. Disputes with the Bellasis brothers over the extent of Edward's literary responsibilities took some time to resolve. Nevertheless, by the summer of 1905 Ward was ready to begin work in earnest on the long-desired biography project.

Keeping the Assignment and Completing It.

If Neville had not been such a hesitant, undecided person or if he had died in 1900, Ward would have begun work on the Newman biography five years earlier. Working at roughly the same pace, he would have completed the task by 1907. Undoubtedly, it would have been a rather different book, for all parties involved would have worked out their positions on it apart from the crisis occasioned by *Pascendi*. Nothing—not even Neville's eccentricities, inherited by Edward Bellasis—so colored the shape and content of the biography and determined the nature of the difficulties Ward would face in its writing as did the developments of 1907. When the encyclical was issued on 8 September 1907, reaction from Catholics was mixed. Ward's own response to it cannot be quickly characterized. Its vehement tone and ugly language bothered him; its lack of clarity on the matter of condemned issues was troubling; but what most disturbed Ward was his conviction that no matter what their intention, Roman theologians speaking through the pope had condemned Newman's thought.

Maisie Ward describes her father as "distracted" during the months following *Pascendi*, "under the three-way pull of Modernists accusing him of cowardice, orthodox Catholics accusing him of Modernism, and puzzled Catholics appealing to him for help in the distress of their minds." While some of this may be overstated, it does seem that many people were clamoring in Ward's direction to hear the right thing from him. Ward was, apparently, unable not to say what was on his mind. "He wrote rashly and he talked rashly—and the talk lost nothing in repetition." Without consideration of consequences due to the peculiar situations of his listeners, he told them what he was thinking.[14] Most disastrous of all the rash comments were those that were sent or found their way to the Birmingham Oratory.

From the first, Ward was distressed that the text of the encyclical, as it stood and as it would be read by many, seemed to condemn various items important in Newman's thought. He did not scruple to present this difficulty to John Norris, writing him on 2 November to lay out the problem and preclude any wrong moves; "as I told Norfolk three weeks ago it not only hits him but the analysis of modernism includes all on which his heart was set for 40 years and brands it as false and absurd . . . he would have been horrified at the system as a whole—a God immanent and not transcendental, religion as emotion, dogma as merely analysing emotional experiences, Christ's divinity explained away. I could write—and must in the Life— showing conclusively that JHN was poles apart from the extreme conclusions of the Modernists. Nevertheless we cannot defend him successfully without going in the teeth of the Encyclical, which brands also positions essential to his views . . . . I think the situation simply tragic." The very next day, Ward sent a clarification. "I did not mean in my last that Newman is condemned, but that his chief positions are included in the exposition of Modernism which is condemned."[15]

That was the problem—that Newman's main lines of thought showed up in the encyclical as condemned propositions. The great fear Ward had during October and November as explained in the same letter was "anxiety lest anyone should rush in indignantly and say 'Newman's positions are not included.' " The public effect of such a disingenuous claim would be disastrous, thought Ward, for there were a considerable number of ordinary, educated people in England who could read Newman all over the encyclical. They would be scandalized by a simple claim that Newman is untouched without any explanation of how.

Ward did not want someone from the Oratory making any such claim. Someone needed to state squarely that Newman's ideas were included in *Pascendi* and then indicate how Newman himself and his thought were not condemned. Anything less would be dismissed as dishonest. To this end, Ward attempted to elicit such an article for his *Dublin Review* from Edward O'Dwyer, Bishop of Limerick. He did everything short of writing the article for O'Dwyer: "I do want a very candid recognition of what is quite clear to me the more I read the Encyclical—that there are parts of the system described as 'modernism' which to the ordinary educated reader seems to be precisely J.H.N.'s philosophical system . . . . I am anxious for two things—(1) that you should expressly recognize what is a fact that while the system as a whole as described in the Encyclical is simply poles asunder from JHN, there are parts which *apart from the context* he held, and which he was prepared to defend from identification with or even suspicion of fideism . . . (2) that the Encyclical only censures the system it describes *as a whole* and the parts only *as component parts*."[16] A number of letters passed between Ward and O'Dwyer over a month, as Ward's initial hope of getting what he needed faded. When the article did come from O'Dwyer, Ward wrote back that he could only publish it minus the first eight pages because the *Dublin Review* was limited in space and because O'Dwyer had failed to give what Ward needed, a recognition that on the surface the encyclical did seem to touch Newman. Without that important admission, Ward could not publish the article. O'Dwyer was outraged and withdrew the entire piece.[17]

During his correspondence with O'Dwyer late in 1907 Ward had also to contend with the response of the Oratory to his letter of 2 November. If Ward assumed that everyone interpreted the encyclical in relation to Newman as he did or that everyone would appreciate frankness in dealing with this difficulty, he soon discovered how wrong he had been. Norris was appalled by the entire episode. "That you should take it for granted that the Cardinal was implicated by the Encyclical and are ready to agree with Williams that the Cardinal's characteristic propositions were condemned and proposed to draw up a list of such propositions is to me a proof that you are looking at the Cardinal's teaching from a wrong point of view and with a preconceived notion in your mind as to what his teaching was."[18] Ward's letter caused Norris "a great shock" and "renewed feelings of distrust" and created a "present feeling . . . that the *Life* may never appear." Subsequent efforts to clarify his meaning and to convince the Oratorians of his position only weakened their estimation of Ward. Richard Bellasis too declared his wish that the biography "never see the light of day."[19] Even more strongly a few days later, Bellasis claimed that "the question is whether your action, objectively considered, does not rather savour of treachery" to the cardinal's memory, since it is wrong to disparage a papal encyclical. Richard Bellasis further hoped that Ward would, on more mature reflection, modify his views. He must have been distressed to receive Ward's letter dated 12 November: "Therefore I am confident that if you give things a little time you will come to realize that I am only recognizing difficulties which are recognized; and that it is fortunate that a friend of the Cardinal should see them at once and guard against consequent dangers."[20] The other dangers were that Tyrrell or Williams would make further capital out of inane disclaimers made by persons who were not students of Newman.

The Oratory never did accept any part of Ward's argument. Neither Norris nor the Bellasis brothers ever were convinced that any of Newman's thinking appeared in *Pascendi.* Thus, they could not see that Ward was aiding Newman's reputation by working out a way of minimizing the effects of the encyclical. The bothersome letters continued for several months; the matter reached a stand-off of sorts.

The crisis was calmed by both the passage of time and the intervention of Edmund Talbot, younger brother of Norfolk. In his role as mediator, Talbot urged the recognition of Ward's good intentions and the need for a truthful *Life*; he warned Ward against sending off half-finished drafts and thereby arousing "alarm and suspicion in what is and must be the most susceptible and sensitive spot on earth regarding Newman." He urged Ward to realize that the Oratorians feared he would so emphasize the intellectual aspect of Newman as to overshadow the spiritual.[21]

Time calmed some fears, and by November, Norris's distrust and fears had changed into mild pleasure at the part of the manuscript he had seen. He wrote to Ward, "I have read it through several times and say very heartily that I like it very much and have found it very interesting." Norris closed the letter with a few minor criticisms and then playfully added, "apart from them I have nothing to say but express my great pleasure and perfect contentment, and like Oliver I ask for more."[22]

Talbot's analysis was accurate, for the root of Ward's problem with the Oratory grew out of the varying estimations of the importance of Newman's life and witness. For the Oratory, Newman was a great spiritual guide. This is clear from Norris's letter of conciliation of 25 September 1908 in which he assures Ward "that all I want is that Newman should be put before the public in his true light . . . the true key to Newman's life" being the recognition of him as the man of God he was.[23] To be a disciple of Newman was to protect this reputation and keep it alive in the Oratory he founded.

One cannot imagine Ward disputing that Newman was a man of God. But spiritually minded individuals were not rare in nineteenth-century Catholicism; thinkers of Newman's quality and style were. It was Newman's intellectual legacy which Ward prized most highly. As he told O'Dwyer in November 1907, "Newman to the end, stood by the philosophy of the University Sermons. That philosophy saved my faith."[24] Extrapolating from his own situation, Ward assumed that other minds also needed the witness of Newman's thought to guide them to the right balance of faith and intellect. In continually pressing this matter onto Norris and the Bellasis group, Ward was engaging in a futile exercise. Norris might eventually say to Ward, "I quite agree that everything must be told" and "that I do not wish to keep anything (i.e., any papers) back from you."[25] But he could not share Ward's enthusiasm for displaying Newman's intellectual work so publicly. Ward and the Oratory were the heirs of Newman's bequest to the twentieth century, and like siblings quarreling over a family estate, they could reach no agreement on which portion of it was most valuable.

Ward's strongest support at the Oratory was John Norris, who from 1908 was reading proofs. Norris had sufficient confidence in Ward that he could both send criticism and express pleasure over what he had read. Unfortunately for Ward and for the progress of the *Life*, by March 1911 Norris was too ill to take any further active role. One of his last official acts was a letter of 14 March to the publisher Longman denying Ward's request that a third volume of letters be published six months after the first two volumes of the narrative and directing further correspondence to Frs. Richard Bellasis and Joseph Bacchus of the Oratory.[26] Norris's death in a few months left responsibility for the guardianship of Newman's memory with a group of men wholly opposed to Ward's representation of Newman and unable or unwilling to compromise on it.

The last year of work on the *Life* was a difficult time. Because of the criticisms of Joseph Bacchus (backed by Richard Bellasis) and John McIntyre, Ward was kept busy adjusting his text where possible or persuading his critics why a change was not advantageous. Bacchus was particularly concerned over Ward's treatment of the theory of development. "People will be up in arms at once if they think that a private interpretation of Newman is introduced into a life having a more or less official character." Ward needed to be more careful, for "matters where people are on the look out for affinities between Newman and the Modernists (e.g. the significance of dogmatic formulae) should be passed over."[27] Ward's response to Richard Bellasis reflects the difficulty of his position. He tried to be conciliatory: "So far as merely prudential considerations are urged you will find me very ready to meet you." But, he had to express his irritations: "I may say to you in confidence that Fr. Bacchus' paper, short as it is, shows that he is quite unfamiliar with Newman's writings on the philosophy of dogma."[28] Ward could not risk appearing ignorant of Newman's thought, as would surely occur were he to adopt Bacchus's suggestions. He acknowledged that Newman did use language different from Roman theologians, but since it had to do with philosophy of dogma and not theology, there could be no danger in using that language today, and no suggestion of unorthodox theology.

Bacchus was irritating, but hardly less so to Ward than the surprise of discovering that Oscott theologian John McIntyre had been given proofs to read, or rather, to censor. McIntyre urged that Ward substitute for Newman's term *idea* the clearer word *picture* to speak of Christian realities. He believed this was important because those Modernists, "the sons of rebellion have been working might and main, both here and abroad, to steal Newman's (chiefly Anglican) language, to fill that language with their own thought, and then to claim Newman as a kindred spirit."[29] In another letter McIntyre tried again to persuade Ward that "Newman's position was that the objects of faith were not mere notions, but concrete realities."[30] Newman's own masterful exposition of the "Christian idea" notwithstanding, McIntyre feared that such language was not specific enough in the post-*Pascendi* era and insisted that since the impressions on the mind were of real things for Newman, they should be termed pictures. Ward successfully resisted this use of language that was not Newman's.

Throughout 1911 Ward fielded numerous criticisms from the Oratory and McIntyre, as both sides prepared to bring the work to a close. The criticisms were legion. "Ward is interpreting too much and not allowing Newman's own words to tell the story." "Ward is using Newman's own language when perhaps other terms would be more discreet." "The text gives positions and ideas from the Anglican period without sufficient reminder that it is not Catholic thought." They objected to including Newman's own claim that he was saved from skepticism by religious experiences. They wanted Ward to omit Ambrose St. John's proposal for circumventing the rule for flogging during Lent. "Do not use the comparison of Newman and the Birmingham Oratory as identified with the moderate group and Faber and the London Oratory with the extreme one—analogous to Montalembert and Veuillot in France." "Soften some phrases from Newman's diary testifying to his personal sadness." "Do not include so many letters from other persons; they detract from Newman's central role in the biography." Ward must have been exasperated at having so many assistants stirring the stew he thought was his own. To many of the points he said simply "Criticism adopted." To others he responded, "I can't see any reason for its omission. But I do not mind omitting it." Often he went into lengthy detail on the facts as they stood against the claims of his critics. Occasional insuppressible tirades appear against their carelessness in reading his text. There is even appeal to literary privilec "You will recall the agreement whereby I am responsible for what I write."[31]

A further problem arose as Ward attempted to settle problems raised by the Modernism controversy. He had, it will be recalled, seen Newman's thought "all over" the encyclical. What to do about this in the *Life*? Ward's solution was to employ the analogy he had used from the start. That is, just as Jansen took the orthodox language and ideas of Augustine and distorted them out of proportion, so did Loisy, Tyrrell, and others do the same with Newman's thought. A version of this analogy appeared in an early manuscript of the introductory chapter, but its inclusion brought Ward trouble from two sides. The Oratory and the Archbishop wanted stronger words. But von Hügel protested that the argument was "impossible" for him, due to the suffering of Tyrrell at the hands of Roman policy for the sake of a "fruitfully true conception of Catholicism." Unable to please, Ward told von Hügel, "I go back to what I think proper."[32] Silence was, in this case, golden, and Ward omitted all reference to Modernism and his own often-used analogy.

Again, the intervention of Talbot may have ensured the biography's completion. The acrimony between Ward and the Oratory over a third volume of letters had reached outrageous proportions. When Ward wrote to Richard Bellasis that correspondence with Norris discussing the proposed volume should serve as evidence of Norris's approval of the plan, Bellasis virtually accused Ward of having forged the letter.[33] Talbot cautioned civility and calmness to Ward, but generally seemed to think he could help convince the Oratorians that Ward's claim was just. He advised Ward all through 1911 not to appear angry. "Also for heaven's sake, be careful to avoid talking of the difficulty that has arisen." He censored Ward's letters to the Oratory to ensure that he did not needlessly alienate anyone there. Talbot's optimism that the Oratorians would approve the third volume turned out to be unfounded. Permission was never granted for Ward to bring out a collection of *pièces justificatives* to supplement the *Life*. Two reasons were given to Ward. "It is entirely opposed to the well-known and clearly expressed wishes of the Cardinal." The second reason ran counter to the first. In 1912, Bellasis argued that a volume of letters would hurt their own recently formulated plans to publish letters from Newman.[34]

To Talbot, however, the Oratorians offered another reason for refusing permission—their desire to avoid any further expression of confidence in Ward as an exponent of Newman. "A most serious obstacle arises from the association of Ward's name with the Modernist controversy of recent times, and the duty the executors feel they owe to the Cardinal's name that it should be in future as little as possible connected with it . . . . It is often necessary in private conversation to point out that Ward was given the *Life* before Modernism was ever heard of." It did no good to point out that the *Life* was a monumental vindication of Newman against any charges or fears that he was less than orthodox. "It is not Modernism in the Life which is in question, but the general estimation in which Ward's views and writings are held by theologians and others both at home and abroad."[35] Talbot, who called the Oratory's position "wickedly unjust," was convinced that they "feel they are not on very solid grounds as gentlemen, and in groping about for another excuse have persuaded themselves that this modernist question supplies the deficiency."[36]

The troubled relations between Ward and the Oratory were never healed. In August 1912 Talbot tried to persuade Richard Bellasis and the Oratory to express thanks and appreciation to Ward, for it "rankles in Wilfrid's mind that amidst all he has had to endure he has never had a word of what might be called official gratitude and thanks from the Oratory."[37]

Ward felt keenly his sense of isolation; three years later he said of a plan to remove him from the *Dublin Review* what he no doubt had felt earlier in his difficulties with the Oratory. "I comfort myself by thinking that the disciple is not better than the Master" recognizing "that Newman's biographer should receive at the hands of a Catholic Organization just the kind of treatment which he received, and just the same signs of total want of appreciation of his work."[38]

Plans for a Theology School

This second section of the paper will look at three specific areas in Newman's life to see how they appear in Ward's *Life of Newman.* Of particular interest is the way Ward shaped his presentation of Newman to avoid what he considered to be two extremes of interpretation—that offered by the Oratory and that of the so-called Modernist interpreters of Newman.

The first point considers whether Newman entered the Catholic church with his own plans for revitalizing the church in England or whether he had only the desire to be obedient to the wishes of legitimately authorized ecclesiastical authority. There permeated the Birmingham Oratory a "myth of the passive Newman," a Newman whose life as a Catholic was played as a passive pawn to the schemes of Wiseman and Manning. While we can not know the ultimate source of this myth, we can examine one place where it seemed to be operating.

In 1846, after his conversion, Newman and a group of fellow Oxford converts were at Maryvale, Old Oscott, considering their futures. What would Newman's service to the Catholic church be? Would he determine on his own an arena for his work or would he await some direction from Wiseman and/or Rome? As early as 6 July 1846 Newman was writing to J. D. Dalgairns, "Now first see what St. John and I would do, if we were advisers of the Midland District . . . . *We* should make Oscott a boy's School and no more, and should send the Divines down to Maryvale." Later in the same letter, returning to the subject, "I see nothing except that the notion of a theological school is a great idea" and a natural response both to the needs of England and the gifts of his little group (*Letters and Diaries* 11:196). The plan for a theology school was Newman's.

A later generation of Oratorians objected to letting others know that Newman had been so bold as to come up with such a plan. Ward, in his 1911 response to criticisms of the proofs, wrote, "The facts are as I have given them, and not as many critics give them. The scheme of teaching theology was Newman's own and not Wiseman's."[39] Apparently, a reader had argued that Newman considered the theology-school plan because it had been proposed by Wiseman, or even worse, that Ward should say this, even if it were not true. A look at the published version of the *Life* indicates the compromise Ward made on this matter. He does quote from Newman's letter of 6 July and rather fully narrates the ideas Newman was developing about putting Maryvale and the converts to best use (Wilfrid

Ward, *Life of Newman* 1:128-29). At a later point, however, Ward seems to have capitulated to complaints from Bellasis. In discussing details of Newman's stay in Rome and the dismal reception of his *Development,* Ward returned to the idea of the theology school, but with a surprise. Ward wrote, "The task of teaching divinity to theological students would be exactly the opportunity he wanted to bring out clearly and persuasively his philosophy of faith and to instill it into the rising generation—a far more effective mode of influence than mere controversy, with its attendant misunderstandings." The converts "were absolutely trusted by one man of genius among their English co-religionists—Bishop Wiseman. And the scheme, both in itself and in its ultimate object of stemming the tide of modern infidelity, had been Wiseman's own" (Wilfrid Ward, *Life of Newman* 1:159). What happened? Ward blatantly contradicted himself. Did he give in to Oratory criticisms that he was making Newman appear "too scheming"? Did he think he could fool them with this rather hazy description of the matter here but put the more accurate details seven pages later? Whatever he thought he was doing, it worked. The proofs were approved. But it does startle one to read Ward's later description. "He had written definitely to Wiseman within a few weeks of his arrival, proposing to found a theological seminary at Maryvale; and Wiseman had accepted the suggestion" (Wilfrid Ward, *Life of Newman* 1:166). It seems that Wiseman welcomed either a school or an Oratory. "Your proposals on the subject, therefore, (supposing the Oratory given up as I did) naturally met my most cordial wishes: but there was no disappointment at all at finding this plan abandoned for a return to our first one."[40]

From our perspective, it seems strange that the Oratorians should be concerned about such a small matter. Ward responded to their criticism, "I entirely agree that the key to Newman's action was the indication of Providence given him by the voice of authority, and have said so. But he had to frame schemes, and his letters show him at this time engaged entirely in framing alternative schemes. I cannot make Newman's schemes Wiseman's schemes, or contradict the whole tenor of the letters which show both the desire to please authority and the active initiation of schemes."[41] If there was a "myth of the passive Newman" and if the myth had begun with Newman himself, then it should not be surprising that the second generation would cling to it most tenaciously, even in the face of a witness to the contrary. In this case, the evidences were forced to give way in part to an "official" interpretation.

A second event in Newman's life where the evidences may have been forced to create the desired image is his connection with the *Rambler* and its associates Richard Simpson and John Acton. W. G. Ward had found the principles of the *Rambler* to be "thoroughly detestable" (*Letters and Diaries* 19:76). Since those who gathered around the *Rambler* proudly wore the label "Liberal Catholic," it is reasonable to expect that some individuals in the post-*Pascendi* era would take care to protect Newman's memory from too close a connection with such a group. Would Ward try to protect Newman from the *Rambler*? Would he disavow Simpson in Newman's name?

In spite of his own distaste for the title and style of "Liberal Catholicism," Ward attempted to give a fair treatment of the incident in Newman's life. A comparison of the several chapters in the *Life* with the relevant materials in the *Letters and Diaries* reveals that Ward did not distort Newman's association with Acton and Simpson, nor did he try to prejudice the reader into adopting the simple interpretation that Simpson was always wrong. Thus, Ward's narrative of the events surrounding the *Rambler* is good, but not without fault.

In their early 1911 response to proofs the Oratorians had a considerable number of criticisms of the chapters that cover the period of the *Rambler/Home and Foreign Review*. Ward began his typed response to these criticisms: "As to the general account, I have exactly followed Newman's lead in the papers on the subject he has put together. He began with more sympathy with Acton and Simpson than he ended. To put the final attitude as though it were the initial would be historically false."[42] To the fathers at the Oratory, apparently, it was a grievous liability to demonstrate to the world any of Newman's sympathy with the "Liberal Catholics." Ward, nevertheless, used Newman's letters to indicate the nature of his sympathies with Acton and Simpson. He included a paragraph out of Newman's 13 January 1859 letter to Acton with its comments on Simpson, "I have a great opinion of his powers, and a great respect for his character, and a great personal liking for him."[43] Ward thus conveyed well Newman's convictions at this time. Although he omitted reference to Newman's letter to Ullathorne on 19 February conveying Simpson's grievances and a mild suggestion of his own support of them, Ward also did not include in his account a number of criticisms from Newman of Simpson.[44]

In two ways, however, Ward bent the *Rambler* incident to fit his own image of what should be seen of Newman. The first was the omission of some material and the second was the addition of some words of his own.

It seems that Ward did not distort any of Newman's own language about Simpson; he faithfully used the materials given him. But he did not fully use them. An examination of volume nineteen of *Letters and Diaries* indicates significant collaboration between Newman and Simpson on the May issue of the *Rambler,* the first under Newman's editorship. In fact, on 7 April Newman wrote to Simpson, "I think you are making a capital number. I say you because the articles you have written or are preparing are so good" (103). In his brief account of the production of that issue, Ward gave nothing about Simpson's involvement, so the reader assumes that there was little or none. His silence implies a state of affairs which was not so, and thus is distorting.

In the second place, the biographer's narrative was constructed to color the reader's impressions of the individuals involved. Ward did of Simpson what Newman would not—he spoke ill of him. Various phrases throughout the account betray Ward's attitude. "Simpson and Acton both professed to fall in with the idea of henceforth excluding theology from the *Rambler,* and Newman rejoiced" (Wilfrid Ward, *Life of Newman* 1:485). The choice of language suggests they did not really mean what they said. Ward described Simpson as "now eager for the fray" (488) and of Acton and Simpson, "the flings at the Bishops were such a favourite indulgence that self-denial on this point seemed unattainable by them" (495). These are small items in a fine piece of work written under considerable duress. In truth, they tell us more about Ward, who had once spoken of Acton as "a monomaniac" with whom he had little sympathy, than they tell us about Newman.[45]

Newman's Relationship with Döllinger

A third area of interest and potential for distortion in Ward's presentation of Newman is the treatment of his relations with J. J. Ignaz von Döllinger. Several complicating factors should be kept in mind as we read Ward's account. One problem is Döllinger's excommunication in 1871 and his relationship to the Old Catholic church. That he did not accept the definitions of the Vatican council would explain the unwillingness of some Catholics to admit any association with his name. The problem is compounded by the similarity of Döllinger's claim of independence for scholarly pursuits in the church with that of Modernists. One wonders: would Ward deemphasize or even hide the friendship between Newman and Döllinger, thus covering up an embarrassing matter?

Ward's portrayal of Newman's attitude toward Döllinger may be the weakest portion of the biography. There are at least three points at which

Ward has obscured details sufficiently to allow his readers to assume something which was not so. Ward devoted two substantially detailed chapters to the plans for and progress of the Catholic University of Ireland, not concealing Newman's disappointments about the difficulties he encountered there. Newman invited Döllinger to "undertake the office of 'Lecturer extraordinary' for the year running from Autumn 1854 to Autumn 1855." Döllinger's inability to add additional responsibilities to his schedule meant "a great disappointment" to Newman.[46] Ward, however, omitted any reference to Döllinger and to Newman's conviction that the university needed the prestige of his name. Ward gave a list of those old Oxford contacts who disappointed Newman by refusing his request to join him (Manning, W. G. Ward, and Henry Wilberforce), but made no mention of Döllinger. Newman's letters on the matter suggest that it was important to him; why did Ward omit this serious matter? No doubt, he wished to avoid such a significant link between Newman and Döllinger.

A similar omission occurs in Ward's account of the 1864 Munich Brief. Newman did not attend the Munich Congress of September 1863 and did not seem greatly affected by its proceedings. When Acton's enthusiastic article appeared in the *Home and Foreign Review*, Newman was already plunged into his response to Kingsley's outrage and was too preoccupied to give serious attention to other things. However, in a letter of 12 February to T. W. Allies, in a passage marked "Most Private," Newman replied to Allies's request that he write against a recent display of anti-Catholic prejudice by noting how difficult *his* kind of writing was in the church then, due to the strength of the dominant party. He—Newman—could not write without demonstrating that his sympathies were so counter to those of the powerful party and such would not be wise. A brief intriguing comment preceded this assessment. Newman wrote, "The more I know of Döllinger's views (I mean in his German works) the more I find I agree with him" (*Letters and Diaries* 21:48). In less than a month the archbishop of Munich would publish the letter from Pius IX condemning the views proposed at the congress. Newman's earlier qualified endorsement of Döllinger was not mentioned by Ward. He did include the substance of Newman's analysis of the Munich Brief and a draft of his response to Acton's news that he was suspending the *Home and Foreign Review*. But he made no mention of the comment on Döllinger. Assuming that the executors had the letter to Allies at the time of writing and that it was among the materials given to Ward, his reason for its omission must have been a concern to protect Newman. He had given Newman's nuanced response to the brief—an acceptance of the points contained in it coupled with a fear of how they would be applied to specific persons and situations in the present ecclesiastical climate. Ward (or perhaps the executors) did not wish to risk including too much.

A final area concerning Döllinger and his relationship with Newman falls in the post-Vatican council era. Ward gave a number of examples of Newman's written discussions against the manner and speed of proceeding on the question of infallibility. He stressed Newman's pleasure at the moderation he noted in the text finally adopted and his utter lack of difficulty in accepting the new dogma. And he included a number of letters from Newman attempting to help other Catholics appreciate the decrees.

But Ward did not give his readers a full sense of Newman's reactions to the events of and following the council. Ward was extraordinarily captivated by Newman's letters and said of them that they demonstrated the reserved nature of Newman's self-disclosure, and that "they express the character as a whole rather than mirror completely the thoughts and feelings" (Wilfrid Ward, *Life of Newman* 2:316). Given this understanding of Newman's wide-ranging letters, it can be expected that Ward would use those letters which demonstrate something of the man Newman and which convey the complexity of his feelings and concerns. In regard to Newman's thoughts on Döllinger's inability to accept the Vatican definition of infallibility, Ward carefully omitted various sentiments. Newman wrote a long letter on 11 November 1871 to Malcolm MacColl. It included this strong comment: "I think, certainly, Dr. Döllinger has been treated very cruelly." Ward printed the remainder of the paragraph without indication of any omission and gave no notice that Döllinger was directly the topic of the letter.[47] Ward included in the text of the biography several passages from Newman letters predicting that no good would come from Döllinger's stand or from the Old Catholic movement (Wilfrid Ward, *Life of Newman* 2:380, 556-57), but he chose not to include strong statements of sympathy for Döllinger and enduring respect for his historical work. Most notable here is Newman's address to Döllinger himself on 9 April 1871, a letter which opens, "I hope I am not wrong to intrude upon you just now, when you have so overpowering an anxiety upon you. At least, in doing so, I am able to assure you that you are continually in my thoughts and prayers. I am sure you must have many hearts, feeling and praying for you, and astonished that so true a servant and son of the Catholic Church should be so tried" (*Letters and Diaries* 25:311).

By omitting this valuable material, Ward prevented the reader from being able to make fully informed judgments about not only Newman's positions on important matters but also his personality. No doubt Ward feared for the memory of his beloved Cardinal Newman, should it be widely known that he held such sentiments unpopular in the church which produced *Pascendi*. Ward wanted Catholics in his day to read Newman's works and to embrace his spirit of both openness to inquiry and commitment to Catholicism. The value of Newman's thought for the church as it moved into the twentieth century would decline as lay people, church leaders, and professional theologians ceased to read Newman; and no one would read the works of one who had "fallen into ill odour." It was a cautious approach which contained minimal expectations for the future.

Ward's task was a difficult one. In trying to preserve Newman's good name for the future service of Catholics, he erred on the side of caution. He fought this battle in the same way he imagined that Newman had fought his own battles, and although he eventually admitted to von Hügel that even Newman had carried the principle of obedience a bit too far,[48] criticism remained a paper theory for Ward and not a principle of action. Ward was, it seems, doomed to repeat Newman's own life story; the highly acclaimed *Life of Newman* was, like Newman's red hat, a moment of glory destined not to bear fruit in its own season.

NOTES

1. See *The Letters and Diaries of John Henry Newman,* edited by C. S. Dessain, et al. (London: Thomas Nelson & Sons and Oxford: Oxford University Press, 1961—), 27:92. where Newman's instructions regarding his biography appear. He did not want a Catholic writer to treat his Anglican years, any "sickening panegyric," or that H. I. D. Ryder have a part in any biography or defense of him against unjust attacks.

2. As quoted in Wilfrid Ward, *The Life of John Henry Cardinal Newman,* 2 vols. (London: Longmans, Green, and Co., 1912), 1:581. Newman sent this to the *Globe* in 1862 in response to the rumor that he would soon return to the Church of England.

3. Robert Whitty, S.J., to Wilfrid Ward, 25 April 1895, Wilfrid Ward Papers VII/315 (3). Whitty wrote, "There is no chance of anything being done towards Newman's life until both Wiseman's and Manning's lives have appeared. There is then a chance that the Birmingham Oratory may be *forced* to move." Wilfrid Ward Papers, at St. Andrews University Library.

4. Maisie Ward, *The Wilfrid Wards and the Transition,* vol. 2, *Insurrection versus Resurrection* (New York: Sheed & Ward, 1937), 333.

5. Ibid., 334.

6. Von Hügel advised Ward to consider if he would soon be offered a Newman project before taking on the Wiseman life. Von Hügel to Ward, 5 December 1893, Wilfrid Ward Papers, II/6(68).

7. William Neville to Ward, 8 May 1898, Wilfrid Ward Papers VII/219(10).

8. Maisie Ward, *Insurrection versus Resurrection,* 334.

9. Ibid.

10. Ibid., 335.

11. Neville to Ward, 5 January 1902, Wilfrid Ward Papers VII/219(13).

12. As mentioned in Sheridan Gilley, "Wilfrid Ward and His Life of Newman," *Journal of Ecclesiastical History* 29 (April 1978):177-93, comment on p. 184. The comment about Neville is from *Letters and Diaries* 31:557.

13. Tyrrell to Ward, 16 February 1901, printed in *Letters from a "Modernist": The Letters of George Tyrrell to Wilfrid Ward, 1893-1908,* introduced and annotated by Mary Jo Weaver (Shepherdstown, WV: Patmos Press, 1981), 64.

14. Maisie Ward, *Insurrection versus Resurrection,* 2:272, 279.

15. Ward to Norris, 2 and 3 November 1907, Wilfrid Ward Papers IV/L(6i, 6ii).

16. Ward to O'Dwyer, 12 November 1907, Wilfrid Ward Papers VI/25c(5).

17. The remainder of the Ward and O'Dwyer correspondence tells of the ensuing conflicts brought on by this misunderstanding. See Wilfrid Ward Papers VI/25c(3-13) for

the Ward to O'Dwyer letters. Wilfrid Ward Papers VII/226a(52-62) give O'Dwyer's side of the story. Maisie narrates the dispute and blames part of it on Ward's fear of crossing the Irish Channel in December. Maisie Ward, *Insurrection versus Resurrection*, 82-89.

18. John Norris to Ward, 6 November 1907, Wilfrid Ward Papers VII/223a(5).

19. Richard Bellasis to Ward, 10 November 1907, Wilfrid Ward Papers VII/25a(1).

20. Ward to Richard Bellasis, 12 November 1907, Wilfrid Ward Papers VI/4.

21. Edmund Talbot to Ward, 7 and 12 August 1908, Wilfrid Ward Papers VII 281a(14, 15).

22. Norris to Ward, 5 November 1908, Wilfrid Ward Papers VII/223a(11).

23. Norris to Ward, 25 September 1908, Wilfrid Ward Papers VII/233a(10).

24. Ward to O'Dwyer, 12 November 1907, Wilfrid Ward Papers VI/25c(5).

25. Norris to Ward, 29 June 1909, Wilfrid Ward Papers VII 233a(14).

26. Norris to C. J. Longman, 14 March 1911, Wilfrid Ward Papers VII/223d.

27. Fr. Bacchus's criticisms to Ward, from March 1911, Wilfrid Ward Papers VII/11a.

28. Ward to R. Bellasis, from a draft, n.d., but sometime in March 1911, in response to criticisms from Bacchus, Wilfrid Ward Papers IV/L/1(4).

29. John McIntyre to Ward, typed copy, n.d., Wilfrid Ward Papers VII/202(1).

30. McIntyre to Ward, n.d., Wilfrid Ward Papers VII/202(2).

31. Ward's Response to Criticisms (perhaps those of R. Bellasis), an eight-page draft, n.d., Wilfrid Ward Papers IV/L/11. Last quotation from Ward to R. Bellasis, 22 March 1911, Wilfrid Ward Papers IV/L(2).

32. For von Hügel's response, see von Hügel to Ward, 2 October 1911, Wilfrid Ward Papers II/6(183). Ward's comment is in Ward to von Hügel, 20 November 1911, von Hügel Collection, St. Andrews, MS 3154.

33. Ward to R. Bellasis, dated "June," Wilfrid Ward Papers IV/L/1(14), and "Statement" from R. Bellasis to Ward, Wilfrid Ward Papers VII/25d, in which Bellasis pointed out that *they* could not find *the* letter among Norris's correspondence, nor any reference to it. Ward took this as an accusation of dishonesty.

34. First reason given in R. Bellasis to Ward, 17 May 1911, Wilfrid Ward Papers VII/25a(13). Second in R. Bellasis's "Statement," Wilfrid Ward Papers VII/25d.

35. R. Bellasis to Talbot, 1 July 1912, Wilfrid Ward Papers VII/25g. This letter was marked "Private and Confidential." Talbot did not share its contents with Ward. The second comment is from R. Bellasis to Norfolk, 15 August 1912, Wilfrid Ward Papers VII/25h.

36. Talbot to Norfolk, 18 August 1912, Wilfrid Ward Papers VII/281d(2).

37. Talbot to Norfolk, 25 August 1912, Wilfrid Ward Papers VII/281d(3).

38. Ward to Lord Halifax, 13 April 1915, Wilfrid Ward Papers VI/13/1(124i).

39. Ward's Response to Criticisms, n.d., Wilfrid Ward Papers IV/L/11.

40. Wiseman to Newman, 27 February 1847, as quoted by Ward in Wilfrid Ward Papers IV/L/11. The emphasis is, I think, Ward's.

41. Ibid. Some interpret the theology-school incident more strongly. Gregory Goodwin, "Newman and the Matter of Reputation: The Contribution of the Letters and Diaries, 1845-1853," Ph.D. diss., Vanderbilt University, 1981, proposes that Newman was so mortified by his rejection in Rome that he turned to the unassuming Oratorian model as penance for the sin of ambition. He argues that Newman is himself responsible for the "myth of the passive Newman."

42. Ward's Reponse to Criticisms, n.d., Wilfrid Ward Papers IV/L/11.

43. Wilfrid Ward, Life of Newman 1:485. Also appears in Letters and Diaries 19:13-14.

44. Ward has omitted reference to several critical comments from Newman on Simpson, judgments which might have aided his (Ward's) own case. See, Letters and Diaries, 19:167, Newman to Acton, 5 July 1859, urging Acton to see that it was a bad idea to have Simpson as sub-editor. The very next day, Newman said the same thing to Simpson himself. "I don't think you should be sub-editor for the Success of the R" (170).

45. Ward to Norfolk, n.d., Wilfrid Ward Papers VI/24(32), on whether he should take the offer to write Acton's life, sometime in 1902.

46. Newman to Döllinger, 15 December 1853, in Letters and Diaries 15:506. Newman expressed his disappointment at Döllinger's negative response in a letter 18 August 1854, Letters and Diaries 16:225. Newman did not give up and urged him to remain open to offering occasional special lectures.

47. Wilfrid Ward, Life of Newman 2:332. The full letter appears in Letters and Diaries 25:430.

48. Ward to von Hügel, 20 September 1911, von Hügel Collection, MS 3151. Of his forthcoming work Ward said, "It is an absolutely frank book and I have stood to my guns as to publishing all documents, though I have been ready to modify the rhetoric of my own words. I do not think you will expect, as Tyrrell did, that the documents would show any inculcation of the duty of public protest against a policy among the authorities, which he deplored. On the contrary he carries the doctrine of obedience in my opinion too far." It is an amazing thing to hear from Ward!

67

4

William J. Williams, Newman, and Modernism

John D. Root

In most accounts, William John Williams (1868?-1930) is the hopelessly absent-minded "little Willie" as immortalized by Tyrrell: "Willie W. is here in my armchair, smoking and swooning. He does not know where he is; or who I am; or what century he is living in."[1] It is perhaps because of such patronizing descriptions that WIlliams awaits recognition as a significant intellectual figure. After failing to designate Williams even as a significant "lesser light" in his *Varieties of Catholic Modernism* (1971), Alec Vidler has taken the first step toward establishing Williams's historical reputation.[2]

Very little is known of Williams's early years, not even the exact date of his birth. Anglican by birth, he lived most of his life with his mother, brother, and sister Dora at Meadhurst, Eastbourne, on a small, unearned income. Williams's close friend, the novelist and critic John Cowper Powys, described him as, though diminutive in stature, a "noble figure" with "soft black-brown hair . . . his nobly rounded forehead, . . . his deep hazel eyes, eyes that had the peculiarity of turning black, yes: of shooting forth *black fire* when he got excited."[3] Williams matriculated at Corpus College, Cambridge, but after converting to Roman Catholicism in 1890, fled to Queen's College, Oxford, for his B.A.[4] His introduction to English Catholic intellectual life began with frequent visits to the Wilfrid Wards, who had moved to Eastbourne in 1891. Soon afterward, Ward introduced Williams to Friedrich von Hügel, who, by September 1895, would characterize him as "more than ever, rarely thoughtful, and sensitively perceptive and distinguished in mind and feeling," telling Ward that he was "glad indeed that we have him."[5] Williams briefly became a seminarian at Oscott and at St. Edmund's, Ware, in 1893 and 1894. It was while at St. Edmund's that Williams first demonstrated his intellectual liberalism. Letters to Ward reveal that he closely followed the reception of the encyclical *Providentissimus Deus,* concluding that recent criticism "must surely show most people that the game of Biblical conservatism is up."[6] It is not clear why Williams was not ordained, though Maisie Ward recalls that "we as children credited the story that he had failed in his Seminary course from inability to put his boots on in the morning, when absorbed in thought."[7]

Cardinal Vaughan, at the request of Wilfrid Ward, took a personal interest in Williams's case, but was not encouraging:

> I do not see what I can do for Williams. I do not feel justified in spending Diocesan money upon him, . . . If you can get some friends to keep him until he is further proved as fit for the Priesthood, I shd be willing to do what I can. . . . Bernard [Ward] & his staff have no great opinion of his vocation &c.[8]

Williams returned to Eastbourne, but at least through 1895 von Hügel continued to refer to him as the "reverend" W. J. Williams and, in letters to Ward, implied that he was still looking for a Bishop to ordain him.[9]

We may only speculate what course Williams's intellectual life might have taken had he become a priest, though it is unlikely that he would have, in 1896, become one of the original members of an extraordinary philosophical and religious discussion society known as the Synthetic Society, the membership of which represented in microcosm the best of religious and philosophical thought in late Victorian and Edwardian England. The Synthetic Society met regularly from 1896 to 1910, and its membership was broad enough to include scientists and philosophers, priests and bishops, Roman Catholics and Anglicans, politicians and poets—all united by the common goal of finding a "working philosophy of religious belief." For the most part, the membership of the Synthetic were believing Christians united in an attempt "to defend the theistic postulate against the negative presumptions of the critical and scientific spirit."[10] Wilfrid Ward was the real founder of the Synthetic, while Arthur Balfour used his considerable prestige to recruit many in the initial membership.[11] Ward drafted the program and a set of rules, and recruited the Roman Catholic contingent which would include Friedrich von Hügel, Canon William Barry, Fr. Robert F. Clarke, Fr. George Tyrrell, and Williams.[12] Von Hügel happily accepted Ward's nomination: "What capital people you are getting together! . . . Williams is really an exquisite thinker—I am glad you are proposing him. And, I suppose it can hardly damage his chances of getting a Bishop to ordain him."[13] During the first eight years of the society's existence, Williams was among the most active participants at the monthly (January to June) dinner meetings.[14]

In March 1898, Williams presented his first formal paper. A month earlier, Henry Sidgwick had presented a brilliant and wide-ranging critique of all previous discussion at the society, entitled "On the Nature and Evidence for Theism." While he thought it unlikely that a complete philosophical proof of Theism was possible, Sidgwick argued that it was "especially impossible, in attempting the construction of a Theistic Philosophy, to leave Ethics on one side," and that therefore "arguments drawn from the indications of ethical experience" should not be discarded from the Synthetic's discussions.[15] In his follow-up paper, Williams agreed that "the fundamental assumption of ethics—the only motive of altruism and the law of sacrifice—is not justifiable and cogent without a theistic hypothesis" and that this consideration provides a motive for seeking to prove Theism. However, Williams did not think that the argument from Ethics could be "made into the basis of a working philosophy of religious belief," nor could mere speculative proofs "lead to the full conception of a God which we require." He suggested that "we are looking for something more, and that something more—the living Reality with which religion desires to deal—cannot be found . . . in statical arguments, it can only be observed in the dynamic changes of human life, . . . in that living organism [the church].[16] Ward termed this meeting "almost the best we have had. . . . There was more life in the discussion than we have yet had."[17]

Williams's next Synthetic paper, in April 1899 was so controversial that eventually it was excluded from the printed record of the society's proceedings. Responding to F.W.H. Myers's March paper, entitled "Provisional Sketch of a Religious Synthesis," Williams asserted that "there can be no doubt that the Catholic idea in religion provides a basis for such a synthesis." A few days before the meeting, Balfour expressed his feeling of dismay to Ward: "I do not see how it is possible to discuss Mr. Williams' Paper without plunging into doctrinal controversy. The theory therein expounded may be, and I doubt not is, a very proper one for a Roman Catholic to hold, though some of the statements rather surprise me even from this point of view."[18] According to Clement Webb, Williams gave "his often-expressed view of the Catholic Church as a growing society capable of assimilating everything, whose dogmas only as it were 'report progress' on the religious development of humanity. . . . The paper benched too nearly on theological controversy. . . . An interesting evening."[19] Tyrrell agreed that "some expressions in Williams's paper were unfortunate as having at least the appearance of theological colour," but was upset by the rudeness of some of the respondents.[20] Williams presented no further papers at the Synthetic, though he remained one of the most active members.[21]

Williams's participation in the debates of the Synthetic Society exemplified his broadening contacts in Edwardian religious and philosophical circles and his growing intimacy with the Roman Catholic liberal party. Early in 1897, von Hügel provided him with introductions to Loisy and Blondel; later that year, scarcely a week after their own first meeting, von Hügel invited Tyrrell to meet Williams, whom he described as "so shy and sensitive, thoughtful and original."[22] It was a momentous meeting. Meetings with Tyrrell and von Hügel became more frequent,[23] and when the first rumblings of the crisis in English Liberal Catholicism were heard in the spring of 1899, Williams began his own foray into ecclesiastical politics by reacting strongly to Pope Leo XIII's condemnation of "Americanism." "The matter about Hecker *in America*," he told Ward, "is so serious as absolutely to require the protest of English representative laymen."[24] Williams impatiently waited for someone to follow William Gibson's journalistic lead in challenging the recent activity of the Roman congregations. "I think he feels vexed," wrote von Hügel, "that the fact of the unsatisfactoriness of the situation should not irritate, and should not arouse any ready sympathy."[25] Concerned lest Williams drift into the more radical camp of Gibson, von Hügel implored Tyrrell to counsel him: "As you know, I think him very interesting and thoughtful, but with one whole side of his nature curiously paralyzed. I am very sure that you wd be a person who could help him much."[26] Later in the year, Tyrrell vowed to get to know Williams better, "though I do not want to get into the Gibson-gang which I know is playing into the hands of the Philistines & bringing discredit on the broad & intelligent party."[27] Williams never disavowed his association with "the Gibson-gang," and Tyrrell himself grew closer to them in the coming years.

Williams continued to expand his participation in English Catholic intellectual circles, notably with his membership in the Rota, a dining and discussion club begun by Edmund Bishop and Robert Dell late in 1900. In Februrary 1901, he presented a paper attacking the scholastic method of intellectual inquiry, entitled "Differences between Private Judgment and the Freedom of the Scientific Spirit."[28] Williams's life became that of a peripatetic scholar, moving frequently between his family home in Eastbourne, the Wards' new home in Dorking, Powys's and Gibson's in Sussex, von Hügel's in Kensington, and Tyrrell's outpost in Richmond. Maisie Ward recalls humorously that sometimes "the hostesses arranged between themselves when he would be moved. He could begin a conversation at 'Lotus' [Wards'] and finish it at 'Moorhurst' [Gibson's] , quite unconscious that this transfer had been effected, or that he had left a puzzled family in ignorance of his whereabouts."[29] But no matter where he moved, Williams now carried Newman with him. Late in 1899, he had begun a series of articles on Newman destined for the *New Era.*[30] When that publication died in January 1900, a victim of the Mivart Affair, Tyrrell hoped that they might appear in the *Weekly Register,* "the only blow-hole left for those who like a little fresh air."[31] Von Hügel also looked forward to seeing them in print. The projected series never appeared, but Williams thus had begun to bring together the notes which would culminate with the publication of *Newman, Pascal, Loisy and the Catholic Church* nearly seven years later.

There is no evidence that Williams appeared in print, on Newman or any other subject, until he engaged in a journalistic controversy with another lay Catholic, J. Herbert Williams (no relation), in the pages of the *Weekly Register* in 1901. The controversy was fired by the appearance of an article by Wilfrid Ward on the occasion of the centenary of Newman's birth. Ward emphasized a familiar theme:

> If St. Thomas was the first Doctor of the Church under the new intellectual *regime* of the thirteenth century—the *regime* which combined the wisdom of the Fathers with the Aristotelian culture—Newman may prove to be the first of the new series which is to combine the essential teaching of Catholic tradition with the scientific and historical culture of the nineteenth and twentieth centuries.[32]

J. Herbert Williams would have none of Ward's "liberal" Newman, and objected strenuously to the claim that Newman would prove to have combined traditional Catholic doctrine with modern culture.[33] When Ward chose not to respond, W. J. Williams stepped into the breach.[34] He argued that Newman's *Essay on Development* was a clear proof of his willingness to adopt or to recognize modern methods of scientific criticism: "the book is a wholesale adoption of modern methods of historical inquiry," precisely "what we must all do if we are to be understood by the present age."[35] J. Herbert Williams dismissed this rebuttal, demanding clear proof that Newman believed in "progress" and emphasizing that the *Essay* was "a Protestant work, without authority for Catholics."[36] The two Williamses now were engaged in a battle of quotations from which no victor would emerge, but after two more exchanges W.J. Williams had the last word.[37]

Williams began drafting a larger essay on Newman's thought in relation to the modern world. Though the paper was apparently not published, Ward described it as "a very subtle bit of writing on the English intellect in general."[38] Tyrrell later saw the manuscript and reported to Ward:

> Williams sent me a badly constructed but most interesting study of J.H.N.'s philosophy a short time ago; I hope you have seen it. I wish you would show how and why it is possible

for both Williamses (W. J. and J. Herbert) to claim him as their prophet. I should say it is because . . . he was a liberal in intellect and conservative in sentiment. . . . Our Eastbourne Williams has the spirit of J.H.N. on his side; while Herbert Williams has the letter.[39]

A few months later, Tyrrell told von Hügel that Williams's manuscript on Newman presented "a far deeper apprehension, I think, than Wilfrid Ward's. The latter never thinks freely, but according to some system of mental politics by which his conclusions are first elected—the premises selected accordingly."[40] Williams's work on Newman was interrupted for most of 1902, however, when some sort of illness left him in a severe depression.[41] Von Hügel, Maude Petre, and Tyrrell all assisted in his rehabilitation.[42]

During the next two years, Williams resumed work on his Newman manuscript and renewed his activity in the Rota and Synthetic Societies. When von Hügel and others created the London Society for the Study of Religion in 1904, Williams became one of six Catholic members and presented an occasional paper. He also participated, despite von Hügel's reservations, in the planning of the "New Tracts for New Times" scheme. While von Hügel thought Williams "a rarely appropriate man for the work," he also feared that Williams's indiscretion might compromise Tyrrell's position with his Jesuit superiors.[43] Strange paranoia on the part of von Hügel; Tyrrell himself earlier had discussed the plan extensively with Williams and had reported as much to Lilley.[44] Fears of Williams's "unreticence" did not, however, prevent von Hügel from suggesting Williams as one of four possible English correspondents for the forthcoming progressive Catholic review *Demain*. Tyrrell candidly told von Hügel that Williams "would be at best dilatory," but that he "certainly could do excellent work—far better than I, because he has keen political as well as ecclesiastical interests & discernments."[45] When the first issue of *Demain* appeared in October 1905, the honor of the lead article went to Williams, with his *"L'Affaire Loisy et la situation religieuse en Angleterre."* Williams was surprisingly blunt in his estimation of the church's treatment of Loisy: *"L'Eglise romaine a prouvé ainsi son entière impuissance et qu'elle a détruit pour toujours son prestige et son autorité dans la personne de ses represéntants officiels."*[46] The following month, a second communication by Williams appeared which invoked the name of Newman against the church's excessive demands of intellectual discipline.[47] Tyrrell humorously advised Dora Williams that "your Willie is going to wreck the *Demain* and get himself excommunicated. . . . I have now to sit down and define W. J. Williams. There's a nice job!"[48]

Williams did not experience ecclesiastical censure, and none more than Tyrrell took all of Williams's idiosyncracies in stride. In fact, as Tyrrell's estrangement from the Society of Jesus grew, he seriously considered going to live with the Williamses.[49] At the time of his dismissal from the society in January 1906, after sojourns at Tintagel and Clapham, Tyrrell then went to the Williamses, "there to await what I do hope will be a final word from Rome."[50] Tyrrell remained in Eastbourne for two weeks, and it was there that he said his last Mass and preached his last sermon on 14 February 1906.[51] He visited two more times that year, and continued to speak of there being "a slight chance that I might live with the Williamses."[52]

The same year saw the publication of Williams's long-promised book on Newman. It appears that the work was complete, although in need of extensive revision, by the middle of 1904. Tyrrell reported to Lilley that Williams's manuscript "is really *quite* excellent & he is perfectly willing to be excommunicated for it. . . . It is a stand for a sane Catholic Christianity such as we all want. If all fails, we must chop it into articles."[53] In the same month, Tyrrell told Bremond that "Williams' book is *very* good; but a wilderness; I am hoping to get him to tidy it up."[54] It took nearly two years to amend the manuscript and to find a publisher, Francis Griffiths, and the book finally appeared in 1906.

Newman, Pascal, Loisy and the Catholic Church is much more than a commentary on Newman; it is a work of apologetics which incorporates the religious philosophy of Newman and Pascal, and a defense of intellectual freedom within the church. The book consists of a "General Introduction" and two parts. The four sections of Part One deal almost exclusively with an exposition of Newman's thought. Also in four sections, Part Two deals with the actuality, ideal, and mission of the church.

In the Introduction, Williams lays down some epistemological guidelines, interpreting Newman as saying that

> . . . revelation was not made simply from outside, but grew up also from within. The truth which makes us free and which causes a religion to prevail is not a something without ourselves alone, but is only to be recognized as something objective because it is immanent in the human race as a whole, and is inherent in all things from the first. . . . If it lives, it grows; and growth is the test of its life.[55]

The question before us is, as Newman might put it, "Can we not express in terms of the thought of our day what the schoolmen considered it their duty to express in terms of the thought of theirs" (p. 19). Now, as then, men are in search "not of some abstractly perfect proof, not some mathematical or scholastic demonstration, . . . not some fixed idea; but life—life of a kind so central to the nature of man as to give life to all the spheres of his thought and action. If he has found this life for himself, he has found God and the absolute" (pp. 21-22). Furthermore, Newman found in the Catholic Church a religion able "to assimilate all the moral and spiritual truths that are found in other religions." Indeed, he "found in the Church's capacity for assimilation a proof for the very kind of Catholicity we now require" (p. 23).

While authority is essential to the survival and development of religion, it does not put an end to speculative intelligence: "It does not forbid analysis, explanation or the philosophic account of the history of religion. . . . It does not remove the right of scientific doubt. It does but involve the demand that this religious tradition shall be dealt with as a fact" (pp. 30-31). The first essential of relgous authority is that "it should be able to answer with religious infallibility the question: What is essential to religion?" (pp. 35-36). This external and rationalistic argument for the Catholic religion, writes Williams, is implicit in the works of Newman, but in modified form.

Williams decries the misrepresentation of Newman's philosophical opinions. Though he was not a systematic philosopher, he has been categorized as a sceptic, an empiricist, an intuitionist, an idealist, a traditionalist, and a mystic. In fact, Newman conceived of philosophy as "on a journey," always in a state of transition, and late in his life "he cast aside . . . the whole set of statical arguments in which he had been brought up and fought his way to that dynamic conception of truth which has caused so much terror to the orthodox, not only in religion, but in every department of thought" (p. 44). Newman's method resulted in a "cautious, tentative movement in the direction of a synthesis which he never completed, and [a] bold analysis . . . of arguments for religion which he believed to be incomplete or sophistical or false or unreal" (p. 46). Accused of denigrating reason while exalting the authority of conscience, Newman in fact condemns all attempts to separate the reason from the religious or moral element in man. Yet he insists that the religious element is the primary element in the history of man, that man is permanently and progressively a religious animal.

The great test of religious truth, as elaborated in Newman's theory of development, is "the vitality consequent on its answering in every generation to the necessities of man. . . . And of this vitality and its real value the only test is its steady growth or development; . . . *its power to assimilate from what is without; in short all the tests of growth which can be applied to an organism*" (pp. 61-62). The Catholic church claims to be "the natural medium—the only possible protectress and guardian" of this religious element. The essential ambiguity in Newman's thought is that he seems to write in favor of scepticism, decrying, for example, the pretensions of natural theology. Yet he insists that by "a process of reason and an act of judgment we shall confer a sort of infallible authority upon conscience" (p. 83).

The question which lies at the bottom of the *Essay on Development* is how to ascertain the true object of the religious element in man. When criticized for not first having set out to find "the germ idea of Christianity," Newman correctly pointed out that we cannot, "in spiritual things, discover a germ except from the nature of its growth," and the main idea of Christianity is still "in the process of expressing itself and cannot be known in its completeness till Christianity itself has run out its course" (p. 99). It is not through theology but through history that religion can be regarded dynamically as a living growth. The *Essay* is, therefore, "a criticism of theology and not, in the first place, a theological work" (pp. 110-11).

For Newman the abuse of reason consists in its being disconnected "in such a manner as to make it indifferent to the conscience and to other faculties" (p. 125). How does Newman determine the right use of reason?

> It is by the use of what Newman called the 'illative sense'—which brings 'the whole man' to the task of making truth; it is by the perception that action as well as thought takes part in the pursuit of truth; it is by the perception that it is only in the complete realization of type both in the individual and in the mass—in variety and in unity—that any proposition becomes realized so as to be 'true' for the whole man or for the whole race (p. 149).

The religious sense is the elementary capacity for the recognition of law in the nature of man, and man's aspiration for the ideal begins, not with the question of whether God is knowable, "but with the question whether there is a religion for man" (p. 152).

Williams devotes several pages to the fundamental relationship between the thought of Pascal and Newman, especially as regards "the interior argument." Both Pascal and Newman sense an "immanental conception of the Divine in the original constitution of man which alone can account at once for his greatness and his misery; for the steady and unchanging consistency and growth of his religious hopes. . . . Man is great because he

77

seeks for God, and miserable because he cannot find Him" (pp. 154-56). Both conceive of a tradition in religion that is "based on the internal revelation made to man by the exigencies of his nature in his battle with circumstance" (p. 157). Newman and Pascal do not disavow theory or speculation, but insist that "what the philosopher may discover by the immediate action of his intellect, the human race discovers by experiment, by action, by the slow processes of experience" (pp 163-64). Both agree that scepticism has a place in the history of religion, but to make God incomprehensible is not to make him unknowable. The Pascalian vision of the *fait intérieur* is present in Newman's "interior argument." For Newman, the moral certitudes slowly gained by the conscience of man parallel the religious certitudes slowly developed by the church, admit of the same test, and are liable to the same corruption. The church, "thus regarded, began with the beginning of conscience; has devleoped in accordance with the same law and claims the allegiance of man on the same title."[56] Williams brings Part One of his book to a close with a pointed reminder "that the great religious vision which the Church represents to mankind owes its immediate validity to the free testimony and active experience of the individuals who have freely accepted it as in accordance with the exigencies of their nature." This same freedom must in time be granted "to criticism and history as well" (pp.183-84).

The last chapters of the book contain a vigorous apology for the church, which he regards "as having found the only possible way in which to make a great religious experiment, to organize and objectify the religious idea" (p. 197). In a remarkably Darwinian reading of Newman's theory of development, Williams argues that the church "has been in religion the natural ground for *that struggle for existence between ideas,* that struggle between the past and present, and that struggle between authority and the individual in which alone a survival of the fittest becomes possible, and order and continuity are united with progress, advance and development" (p. 198). Only those ideas which can prove their consistency with the continued vitality of the organism (the church) ultimately can survive. Williams then proposes that in a church ruled in accordance with the genius of the Saints, intellect ought to be more completely liberated than outside it. His not so subtle intention is to convince the reader that the authoritative church should not fear that "the Bible will suffer any real disadvantage from a criticism of its mere historicity, or the Church, from a criticism of the immaturity of its methods of action or of the crudity of its forms of expression." Thus great Catholic luminaries such as Erasmus and More, Simon and Pascal, and Newman and Loisy "have been able to let their thoughts play freely round subjects with which the Church and the Bible are concerned."[57]

Williams argues that conservative theologians err in thinking the development of dogma as final and absolute, and citing Newman, he regards the medieval scholastic formulations only as a "channel for a true philosophical development" (p. 252). The church compels us to accept a particular dogma, but not its philosophical expression. For centuries the avenues to religious development have been blocked; the church has "ceased to be the ground and centre in which philosophical and ethical development are made and reconciled." Those who could have modified the church from within were content merely to repel hostile attacks. In the present age "the responsibility . . . and the necessity for making these changes from within is far greater," and it is precisely this task that "the Abbé Loisy, with the aid of Newman's theory of Development, has had the boldness and the patience to undertake."[58]

It is only now, in the last fifty pages of the book, that Williams draws a series of connections between Newman and Loisy while appealing for the broadest intellectual freedom within the church. Though perhaps necessary to her preservation at one time, some pronouncements of church representatives have produced "untold mischief." In her general acquiescence to the philosophy of Aquinas, the church "committed herself to exaggeration as great as her former condemnation." Today the church's interpretations of the scripture will not hold, though formerly "her infallibility in the expression of the life of religious and Christian thought was perfectly consistent with false interpretation of texts" (pp. 288-89).

Williams's views on the nature of the church's infallibility and the relationship of the "*ecclesia docens*" to the "*ecclesia discens*" are nearly identical with those we associate with George Tyrrell. He insists that no one went farther than Newman "in showing how the '*ecclesia docens*,' if left to itself, on more than one occasion, would have destroyed the faith which the laity preserved," and that "the '*ecclesia docens*' only speaks infallibly so long as the whole body is faithfully represented" (p. 290). Needless to say, the hierarchy of the day did not share Williams's assertion that

> . . . there has never been a definition made or a dogma enunciated
> which did not owe its origin to traditions held among all Catholic
> peoples and taught with the consent of the laity; . . . The basis
> of infallibility ever remains in the mass of catholic peoples and
> ultimately depends on their consent (p. 294).

The notion of infallibility of the church is not clearly revealed in the New Testament, but something "historically built up" (p. 296).

Turning again to Loisy, Williams is most outspoken:

> The Abbé Loisy's treatment of the Gospels may be regarded as an application of the best thought of Newman and especially of his theory of development to the whole history of religion in the light and by the aid of modern criticism and the modern spirit. His thought is not, indeed, in any sense borrowed from Newman. . . . But Newman's theory of development came to him as a confirmation and an independent witness to a fact (p. 302).

Newman's doctrine of Development commends itself to modern writers such as Loisy in that "it is felt to apply and to be as necessary to belief in the authority of the Bible as to belief in the authority of the Church. . . . On no other basis than that of some development of ideas . . . [do we find] in the Bible the authentic revelation of the Divine" (p. 303). So also do we understand the meaning of the church's infallibility.

Williams concludes that, because both see a development of Christian ideas, Newman and Loisy regard the later ages of the church to be the best. Both consider it a fatal defect in Protestantism that it claims to have discovered the "essence" of Christianity and thereby denounces all the past history of development in the church as so much corruption. A final apology. The church has made many mistakes, and Protestantism arose, in a sense, from necessity as a protest to the crudities which then prevailed in the Catholic world, but "it substituted something so vague and so entirely individualistic that the whole social basis of religion was destroyed" (p. 313). The Catholic church alone holds the hope of "a base for authority and an orientation in inquiry. . . . She has given to man the possibility of union and progress in the religious sphere" (pp. 314-315).

George Tyrrell's first reaction to Williams's book was qualified: it was "the best plea for the 'liberal' reading of Newman, about which I grow more and more sceptical."[59] After reading the book several times, Wilfrid Ward told his wife, "It is like champagne, *very* strong champagne."[60] Ward's first notice of the book appeared in the January 1907 issue of the *Dublin Review:*

> Mr. W.J. Williams has given us a most remarkable work, a veritable treasure-trove of deep thought on the foundations of religious belief, and a book which is, for those who rightly understand it, a very powerful Apologia for the Catholic Church. . . . The thought is absolutely genuine, honest and impartial, even when it passes into regions beyond bounds encouraged by the Church.[61]

Ward especially praised Williams's analysis of Newman's "deeper thought on Faith and Reason . . . [which] contains the most important contributions towards the elucidation of the problems under discussion which we know." He regretted, however, that the name of Loisy appeared in the title, because "to many people the prominent association of the Abbé Loisy's name with Mr. Williams's theory may make them, however unjustly, approach his book with less symapthy than they otherwise would do" (pp. 182-83).

There were few other prominent reviews of the book. A strong review from the pen of Maude Petre appeared both in the liberal *New York Review* and in *Il Rinnovamento*. In "A New Catholic Apology," Petre emphasized Williams's argument for "the collective aspect of religion, the Church's 'Catholicity' and a democratic sense of ecclesial authority."[62] One of the most sympathetic reviews was that of a non-Catholic writer, the Rev. F.W. Orde Ward, who declared that "Newman is fortunate in finding such an acute and able champion."[63] Orde Ward also noted that "It will be a matter for surprise, if this powerful and opportune book does not flutter the dovecotes of the Vatican and add another Jewel to that great treasure, the *Index Expurgatorius*" (p. 464.).

In the July *Dublin Review*, Wilfrid Ward noted the appearance in English of Bremond's *The Mystery of Newman* by derisively contrasting his views with those of Williams: "the whole of Newman's speculative intellect . . . is almost a sealed book to M. Bremond; . . . . It is not a psychological study, it is a novel suggested to a very imaginative writer."[64] To underscore the grievous faults found in Bremond's work, Ward praises Williams's book far beyond the tentative approval shown in his earlier review: "Mr. Williams' book is so completely on the track of Newman's reasoning that there is hardly any thought in it which one cannot fancy passing through Newman's mind" (p. 14). Ward bemoans Williams's "entire absence of intellectual self-restraint," but recognizes that in order to help "those who need help in justifying philosophically their faith," it is sometimes necessary to "startle those to whom these fundamental questions do not in the ordinary course present themselves" (p. 15).

For Tyrrell, whose split with Ward was complete by this time, the kind words for Williams were overshadowed by the "spiteful and silly attack" on Bremond. "There is meanness in every line of it: and nobody will fail to see it," he told Bremond.[65] Tyrrell then dashed off a letter to *Demain*, noting the implications of Ward's apparent preference for Williams's view of Newman as the true father of modern liberal Catholicism, and reminding his readers to take note of the full title of Williams's book with Newman, Pascal, and Loisy lumped together "as three persons in one Nature."[66]

Williams himself, despite his own friendship with Bremond, wrote a brief critical review of *The Mystery of Newman,* sadly noting that Bremond seemed to enjoy a "mischievous delight in collecting evidences of Newman's defects."[67]

In the wake of the publication of *Newman, Pascal, and Loisy,* Williams's relationship to the progressive party in the church became more intense; especially did his intimacy with Tyrrell grow. Early in 1907, Williams and Tyrrell spent two weeks together at the home of William Gibson (later Lord Ashbourne). Tyrrell cryptically wrote to Bremond: "Spent a fortnight with Gibson, Fawkes, Williams & made a new Religion—'Pre-Gallicanism.' "[68] In April 1907, Tyrrell settled in with the Williamses in Essex for five weeks. And in May, Tyrrell and Williams again spent several days together at Gibson's, a visit which Tyrrell thought "would be a good occasion to elect an anti-pope and depose Pius X."[69] During the summer of 1907 Williams also published "The Divinity of Christ and Modern Criticism," an essay, he told Ward, which "completes much that wanted completing in my book."[70] Williams denied that New Testament criticism threatened the doctrine of the Divinity of Christ. To the contrary, he declared that "modern criticism does not destroy but construct, and does but teach us to find a deeper and more Universal Christianity in the Gospel of Christ."[71]

In September 1907 appeared the encyclical *Pascendi dominici gregis,* and the crisis was at hand. Williams would be nearly alone among lay Catholics who publicly protested the wholesale condemnation of philosophical and theological ideas offically designated as "modernism." He was, however, slow to react. "Williams will not admit that anything has happened," Tyrrell wrote to Kitty Clutton, "for earthly events do not trouble his platonic world of subsistent ideas."[72] Two things aroused Williams from his stupor: his growing perception that *Pascendi* condemned a multitude of ideas central to Newman's thought and the excommunication of his closest clerical friend, George Tyrrell, at the end of October 1907. Tyrrell was the first English Catholic to throw down the gauntlet, and his two-part article in *The Times,* "The Pope and Modernism," was the immediate cause of his excommunication.[73] In the second of these articles, Tyrrell raised the question of the implicit condemnation of Newman. Though Wilfrid Ward did not publish his own views during the last months of 1907, he privately admitted, in a long and important letter to the Duke of Norfolk, that it was "beyond question . . . that *the whole of Newman's life* is an account of his work for ideas apparently condemned in the Encyclical . . . [and] to maintain that the Encyclical does not *say* what it does will make things worse."[74] Meanwhile, Cardinal Merry del Val wrote to Archbishop Bourne of Tyrrell's "scandalous rebellion," stressing that "though there are not many English Modernists, there is quite a sufficient number of them, of *different* grades, . . . who are in position to discuss matters, half-tinkered converts, etc."[75] At the petition of Bishop Amigo of Southwark, Tyrrell was excommunicated before the month was out. Williams, one of the "half-tinkered converts" described by Merry del Val, now resolved to act.

Williams's first letter to *The Times* hit like a bombshell:

> I have been asked to make the following statement on behalf, not only of those who call themselves Liberal Catholics, but also of many who have hitherto taken no part in the conflict between modernist and Pope. . . . They regard it as an unprecedented evil that, while one Pope has implied a direct approval of the writings of an English Catholic by making him a Cardinal, his successor should reverse the decision by condemning every characteristic proposition for which that writer made himself responsible. . . . They would urge that arguments which led them to become Catholics if they are converts, or enable them to defend Catholicism if they are Catholics by birth, cannot be . . . flung aside afterwards.[76]

Ward told Norfolk that Williams's statements about Newman were "precisely true," that "not one or two but all the characteristics and fundamental positions of Newman are included in close detail in what the Encyclical describes as Modernism."[77] Ward told Fr. John Norris of the Birmingham Oratory much the same thing.[78] For his part, Norris told *The Times* that he was able "to state on information received today from the highest authority that 'the genuine doctrine and spirit of Newman's Catholic teaching are not hit by the Encyclical.' "[79] In *The Times* of the following day, Dom Aidan Gasquet repeated Norris's disclaimer and openly attacked the assumptions and the tone of Williams's letter.[80] Neither Norris nor Gasquet identified the "highest authority,"[81] but the *Osservatore Romano* also printed what it said was an authoritative response to Williams's "tendentious assertion," proclaiming that, if he lived today, Newman would "stigmatize with fiery words . . . these self-styled Newmanists." The article contained, however, the important qualification that this does not mean that Newman's works may not contain some opinions or theories which would not be approved.[82]

Williams's final public statement in the controversy was a second letter to *The Times* in response to Norris and Gasquet. The mere act of their having to cite "the highest authority . . . seems to show that the Encyclical was, to say the least, sufficiently ambiguous on this point to cause some perplexity even among the Oratorians themselves."[83] Both Gasquet and Norris responded the following day, the former expressing his amazement that Williams had not "withdrawn so erroneous a view," the latter to say that the only reason he had applied to Rome for an authoritative declaration was the publicity given the question in Williams's first letter to *The Times*.[84] Tyrrell saw clearly that Gasquet's "preposterous letter" had not met Williams's challenge and vowed to Ward that if the pope would say "openly that 'no theory, no idea, no opinion' contained in 'The Essay on Development' or in 'The Grammar of Assent' is condemned by the Encyclical, ... I for one will withdraw all I have written against the Encyclical, and confess my utter inability to comprehend its meaning."[85] When no other Catholic stepped forward, Tyrrell wrote what he termed an "inspired" and "decisive" article for the *Guardian* to sum up the controversy.[86] The scholastic authors of the encyclical surely must be totally ignorant of Newman's work, wrote Tyrrell, for "in the expert judgment, not only of Mr. Williams, but of all who have studied Newman, . . . his condemnation is written all over the face of the Encyclical." Fr. Norris's assurances from "the highest authority" are worthless without a more comprehensive statement from Rome.[87]

As the leading lay Catholic writer in England and the official biographer of Newman, Wilfrid Ward was in the strongest possible position to make a public pronouncement, but he published nothing on the question until January 1908. Ward's perplexity is seen in the intense correspondence he carried on into the winter. Fr. Norris did not appreciate the subtlety of Ward's position and was shocked at finding him so "ready to agree with Williams."[88] Ward once again reminded him that it simply was not a matter for debate, that the "notorious characteristic lines" of Newman's thought "are at least apparently included in the [encyclical's] account of 'Modernism.' "[89] While Norfolk encouraged Ward to write something, especially after Tyrrell's article in the *Guardian,* Norris was convinced that "Newman's biographer should keep out of the matter altogether."[90] Ward's other approach was to try to obtain a stronger, unequivocal pronouncement from Rome. Mgr. Vaughan wrote to say that he had spoken privately with Pius X, who had expressed his admiration for Newman, but advised Ward that the Roman authorities "will read what you write with a judicial not to say critical spirit."[91] Vaughan later told Ward that "It seems 'Williams' has done you harm. They [Roman authorities] seem to connect you two together; . . . my impression is that they think you are inclined to sail too near the wind."[92]

Ward clearly felt that any response to *Pascendi,* any resolution of the Newman-Modernist question, meant coming to terms with Williams, and this he tried in vain to do. From the start Williams urged Ward "to join him in public criticism of the Encyclical," even to the extent of resigning his editorship of the *Dublin Review.* Defending his letter to *The Times,* Williams wrote that to exempt Newman from the strictures of *Pascendi* "would be to destroy him forever."[93] Ward agreed that "the facts of the situation must be faced, and the authorities made to face them," but did not feel he could "move one finger to diminish the effect of Norris's authoritative disclaimer without the greatest disloyalty to J.H.N." Hence he could not "in any way, however indirect, participate in your action or your policy. . . . I am almost as isolated as J.H.N. was in 1862."[94] Williams sympathized with Ward's "terribly difficult situation," but denied he was imprudent in pressing the issue of Newman's implicit condemnation: "Is not insubordination the only thing which the authorities pay any attention to?"[95] In another letter, Williams argued that if Norris's disclaimer really came from the pope, which he doubted, then "a certain amount of reparation is absolutely due us & Cardinal Newman. . . . I really do not see how it is possible for us, with any intellectual self-respect, to ask for anything less." If Newman is not touched by the encyclical, then neither are the Modernists, for they "have never gone further than Newman's doctrine."[96]

During this period, Maude Petre recorded that "W.J. Williams is frantic with W. W. for his shiftiness on the Newman question—and no wonder!"[97] Von Hügel also had concluded that there was no way to get Ward to stand up publicly.[98] Ward, however, protested to Alfred Fawkes that he had "spoken most strongly to everyone of [*Pascendi's*] most unfortunate character. I have done this privately but without reserve." Ward hoped thus to help the authorities to construct "a golden bridge of retreat."[99] Fawkes answered that he would be disappointed if Ward were to "defend what is indefensible. . . . I frankly can't go with you as to a 'public attitude of obedience to the Encyclical.' "[100] In early December, Ward told Williams he had come to a conclusion concerning Newman and *Pascendi*: "The very narrowness of the document justifies the view of theologians that *technically* speaking the only *censure* is on the *whole* system—which includes sheer subjectivism and a God immanent and not transcendent. . . . Thus I feel justified in the 'Dublin' in making the most of the official declaration that J.H.N. is not censured—his God was entirely transcendent, he is no mere subjectivist."[101] Williams responded with a plea for stronger resistance, for "it is of no use to put on the brakes now, as the brake no longer touches the wheel."[102] Ward still felt compelled to convince Williams of the judiciousness of his formulating a "theological interpretation which enables the authorities to retreat from an untenable point without explicitly admitting a mistake. . . . This 'golden bridge' is the only way out of the position except revolution."[103]

Williams's response shows that the specific question of Newman's condemnation no longer was in the forefront of his mind, no doubt reflecting the influence of Tyrrell who was with him most of the month of December 1907. "I start from a different point of view & with a different object from you," Williams told Ward:

> My hope has always been that Catholics would take the first opportunity of showing that . . . the Pope's power is not absolute against an actual majority of educated Catholics. I am always looking out for an opportunity of establishing a clear precedent for what you call rebellion, but what I call lawful & constitutional resistance. Such an occasion has now arisen.[104]

Williams reminded Ward that Newman had discussed several occasions, for example in matters of conscience and science, when the pope is not to be obeyed. This correspondence now came to an end. Ward's letters to Williams, according to Tyrrell, had become "more deplorable every day," and there no longer were grounds for compromise.[105]

Following this inital period of controversy over the meaning and import of *Pascendi*, Williams seemed to retreat into himself. After spending the Christmas holidays with Williams at Eastbourne, Tyrrell reported: "I found Willie W. rather lethargic; and as I saw he was going to do no serious work, I ran away."[106] Both Tyrrell and von Hügel continued to encourage Williams to write, Tyrrell because he regarded him "as out and out the best interpreter of Newman's subconscious philosophy," von Hügel because he saw a desperate need for more non-Italian correspondents for *Il Rinnovamento.*[107] The only known publication of Williams in 1908 was, however, an uncontroversial article in the *Hibbert Journal* entitled "The Burden of Language in Religion, and Authority as the Means of Release: A Catholic Study," a version of an earlier London Society for the Study of Religion paper.[108]

During the spring of the tragic year 1909, Williams spent much of his time near Tyrrell in Storrington and once again took up his pen. Maude Petre recorded that he was "much occupied with his new work, which is to represent the views of an old-fashioned Catholic on the Encyclical," and be entitled "The Diversity of Christianity."[109] In June, Williams accompanied Tyrrell to Exeter College, Oxford, to hear Tyrrell's last public address.

Inexplicably, however, there is no evidence that Williams was among those called to Tyrrell's deathbed in July, though he and his sister Dora were among the handful of Catholic friends who attended the funeral. In a note to G. W. Young, "the modernists' unofficial liaison officer in Oxford," Williams comments lightheartedly on Tyrrell's passing:

> I am glad to say the sense of a dead man's being really alive was never stronger in my mind than after his burial. . . . Indeed, the monstrous behaviour of the authorities (which would have made F. Tyrrell himself laugh till he screamed) made it impossible to feel the dismal sensations of ordinary funerals. What a humour he had! . . . We could not think of him without remembering the delicate shafts of wit he would have discharged had he known that the authorities continued to demand recantation after he was speechless and even after he had died![110]

Williams had lost his closest and greatest friend, and now he nearly would disappear from the center of progressive English Catholic activities. Williams's last defense of Tyrrell was on the occasion of the publication in the *Guardian* and *The Tablet* of a letter from Tyrrell to Dr. Herzog of the Old Catholics. He defended Tyrrell's denial of the intellectual legitimacy of many Papal claims, saying that in this matter Tyrrell was at one with Newman.[111]

We know little of Williams's life and activities after 1909, except that at least until the eve of World War I he had not wavered in his Modernist sympathies. Von Hügel continued to think of him so highly that he named him and Edmund Bishop to be second, after Edmund Gardner, as his literary executor.[112] It also is a little-known fact that Williams was the only lay English Catholic besides Maude Petre to announce publicly, after the infamous *Motu Proprio* of November 1910, that he never would sign his adherence to *Pascendi*. Williams remained convinced that

> It is a really doubtful matter whether the Encyclical *Pascendi* is valid. It is also a doubtful matter whether it is not, in certain particulars, even heretical. . . . If this should turn out to be the case, the present Pope has already, *ipso facto*, ceased to be Pope, and everything that he does, except in cases of ordinary discipline, is invalid.[113]

There is no evidence that Williams was asked to sign.

Williams's last known publication was a review of Ward's biography of Newman which he chose to praise rather than criticize, concluding that "the book merits itself a place among those things that are true and just and lovely and of good report, for it is a book which will do good to all to read."[114] The most significant references to Williams in the post-Modernist years are provided by John Cowper Powys, who spent much time with Williams and his sister, delighting in their "delicious diffusive spirituality."[115] Powys later dedicated his book, *Religion of a Sceptic* (1925), to Williams.[116] Though he apparently maintained contact with Maude Petre, von Hügel, and Gibson into the 1920s, we know nothing further of his activities. Williams died in obscurity in France in 1930.[117] His death went unnoticed in the English press, not uncommon for one of the "lesser lights" of Modernism.

NOTES

1. Tyrrell to Mrs. William Gibson, 17 June [1907], in the Wilfrid Ward Papers, St. Andrews University Library, VII/294H(li). Research for this essay was supported by a Fellowship from the National Endowment for the Humanities.

2. Alec R. Vidler, "An Abortive Renaissance: Catholic Modernists in Sussex," in *Studies in Church History* 14 ("Renaissance and Renewal in Christian History"), ed. by Derek Baker (Oxford: Basil Blackwell, 1977), 386-88.

3. John Cowper Powys, *Autobiography,* new ed. (London: Macdonald, 1967), 325; Vidler, "An Abortive Renaissance," 286.

4. Powys, *Autobiography,* 337. See also *The Catholic Who's Who & Year Book* (London: Burns & Oates, 1912), 413.

5. Von Hügel to Ward, 19 September 1895, Wilfrid Ward Papers. In another letter, dated 26 December 1895, von Hügel describes Williams as "really an exquisite thinker."

6. Williams to Ward, [April] 1894 and an undated letter, Wilfrid Ward Papers.

7. Maisie Ward, *The Wilfrid Wards and the Transition,* (London: Sheed & Ward, 1934), 360.

8. Vaughan to Ward, 23 September [1894], Wilfrid Ward Papers VII/297c(44).

9. Von Hügel to Ward, 26 December 1895, Wilfrid Ward Papers. Powys describes Williams as "half a priest," adding that it was "an instinct with him to wear dark clothes." (*Autobiography,* 381, 416).

10. Alan Willard Brown, *The Metaphysical Society: Victorian Minds in Crisis, 1869-1880* (New York: Columbia University Press, 1947), 303.

11. See John D. Root, "The Philosophical and Religious Thought of Arthur James Balfour," *Journal of British Studies* 19 (Spring 1980): 121-41.

12. "The Rules of the Society" may be found in Arthur Balfour, comp., *Papers Presented Before the Synthetic Society, 1896-1908* (London: Printed for Private Circulation by Spottiswoode and Co., 1909), vii. See Appendixes to Maisie Ward, *The Wilfrid Wards and the Transition.*

13. Von Hügel to Ward, 26 December 1895, Wilfrid Ward Papers.

14. Ward describes Williams in a letter to Lord Halifax as "a very popular member of the Synthetic" (21 April 1901, copy, Wilfrid Ward Papers VI/13/1(7ii).

15. *Papers Presented Before Synthetic Society,* 175.

16. Untitled paper for 25 March 1896, *Papers Presented Before Synthetic Society,* 182-86.

17. Ward to Oliver Lodge, 9 April 1898, Lodge Papers, University of Birmingham Library, 1/420/10.

18. A copy of Williams's paper is among recently discovered papers of Charles Gore in the House of the Resurrection, Mirfield, W. Yorkshire. Balfour to Ward, 26 April 1899, Wilfrid Ward Papers.

19. Clement Webb's Journal, 28 April 1899, Bodleian Library, MS.Res.e.125.

20. Tyrrell to Ward, 2 May 1899, Wilfrid Ward Papers, printed in Mary Jo Weaver, *Letters from a "Modernist": The Letters of George Tyrrell to Wilfrid Ward, 1893-1908* (Shepherdstown, WV: The Patmos Press, 1981), 12.

21. A letter from Tyrrell to Maude Petre, [7 March] 1905, suggests a reason for no further Williams papers: "It is a good rule of the Synthetic that each pays for the printing of his own paper—a tax on loquacity, tho' of course it keeps some poor devils like me & Williams from writing altogether" (Petre Papers, British Library, Add.-Mss.5237.111).

22. Von Hügel to Tyrrell, 19 October 1897, Petre Papers, Add.Mss.44927.6.

23. Typical entries in von Hügel's Diary are "Long walk with Williams" and *"Long important talk with Williams"* (10 and 12 December 1898, Von Hugel Papers, St. Andrews University Library).

24. Williams to Ward, [February-March 1899], Wilfrid Ward Papers.

25. Von Hügel to Ward, 6 June 1899, Wilfrid Ward Papers. See William Gibson, "An Outburst of Activity in the Roman Congregations," *Nineteenth Century* 45 (May 1899): 785-94.

26. Von Hügel to Tyrrell, 18 June 1899, Petre Papers, Add.Mss.44927.40.

27. Tyrrell to von Hügel, 20 November 1899, Petre Papers Add.Mss.44927.91.

28. Nigel Abercrombie, *The Life and Work of Edmund Bishop* (London: Longmans, 1959), 301.

29. Maisie Ward, *Insurrection versus Resurrection* (London: Sheed and Ward, 1937), 121.

30. Announcement of a series by W.J. Williams on "The Philosophy of Cardinal Newman," *New Era*, 4 November 1899, p.4.

31. Tyrrell to Ward, 4 February 1900, in Weaver, *Letters from a "Modernist,"* 25.

32. Ward, "Cardinal Newman," *Weekly Register*, 15 February 1901, p. 196.

33. J.H. Williams, "Mr. Ward and Cardinal Newman," *Weekly Register*, 22 February 1901, p. 247.

34. Williams had written to Ward: "Have you seen Mr. Herbert Williams' letter in the 'Weekly Register'? It is so curiously like the writing of a clear headed romantic old lady—with eyes shut to all that lies beyond a trim garden & the village street. . . . They say he is obscurantist to the last degree" [February 1901], Wilfrid Ward Papers.

35. W.J. Williams, letter, *Weekly Register*, 1 March 1901, pp. 279-80.

36. J.H. Williams, letter, *Weekly Register*, 15 March 1901, p. 343.

37. W.J. Williams, letter, *Weekly Register*, 29 March 1901, p. 395. J.H. Williams quickly published a more complete statement of his conservative interpretation of

Newman, citing the "perverse" consequences of his being transformed into a prophet of Liberalism. See "Development," *Dublin Review*, 4th ser., 19 (April 1901); 293-304.

38. Ward to Halifax, 21 April 1901, copy, Wilfrid Ward Papers, VI/13/1(71i).

39. Tyrrell to Ward, 28 January 1902, in Weaver, *Letters from a "Modernist"*, 72.

40. Tyrell to von Hügel, 12 April 1902, Petre Papers, Add.Mss.44928.11.

41. Clement Webb described the mysterious illness as "Grain Fever," *Webb Journal*, (20 February 1903), Bodleian, MS.Res.e.127.

42. As late as May 1905, there apparently was some concern over Williams's mental stability. Tyrrell wrote to Maude Petre: "I hope Williams is not really losing his mind. It would never do to associate myself publicly with a lunatic. . . . But, joking apart, it is my own deepening suspicion" [2 May 1905], Petre Papers, Add.Mss.52367.129.

43. Von Hügel to Lilley, 27 January 1905, Lilley Papers, St. Andrews University Library MS 30522.

44. Tyrrell to Lilley, 10 July 1904, Lilley Papers, MS 30786. Earlier von Hügel had recommended that Tyrrell not send a copy of *The Church and the Future* to Williams. Letter of 22 June 1903, Petre Papers, Add.Mss.44928.103.

45. Tyrrell to von Hügel, 11 January 1905, Petre Papers, Add.Mss.44928.145.

46. *Demain* I, no. 1 (27 October 1905): 102. The communication was dated 15 October 1905.

47. *"Lettre d'Angleterre,"* *Demain* I, no. 5 (24 November 1905): 8-9.

48. Tyrrell to Dora Williams, 1 December 1905, in Petre, *George Tyrrell's Letters* (London: T. Fisher Unwin, 1920), 168. Petre wrongly dates this letter as 1904.

49. See Tyrrell to Petre, [7 March] 1905, Petre Papers, Add.Mss.52367.111; Petre Diary, 2 and 17 May 1905, Petre Papers, Add.Mss.52373.43-44; and Tyrrell to Robert Dell, 4 May 1905, in Petre, *Von Hügel and Tyrrell* (New York: E.P. Dutton, 1937), 46. Petre did not think much of the plan.

50. Tyrrell to Bremond, 25 January 1906, copy in Univerity of San Francisco Library.

51. Petre, *Autobiography and Life of George Tyrrell,* 2 vols. (London: Edward Arnold, 1912). 2:262.

52. Petre Diary, 10 June 1906, Petre Papers, Add.Mss.52374.5; Tyrrell to Bremond, [November-December, 1906] copy, University of San Francisco Library.

53. Tyrrell to Lilley, 14 July 1904, Lilley Papers, MS 30787.

54. Tyrrell to Bremond, 27 July 1904, copy, University of San Francisco Library.

55. Williams, *Newman, Pascal, Loisy and the Catholic Church* (London: Francis Griffiths, 1906), 18-19. Succeeding page references are incorporated in the text.

56. Ibid., 172-73. A contemporary commentator, making no reference to Williams's book, stated that "to contrast Pascal and Newman is to probe the very depths of the spirit of the age." Charles Sareola, *Cardinal Newman and His Influence on Religious Life and Thought* (Edinburgh: T. & T. Clark, 1908), 125.

57. Ibid., 222-23. This is only the second mention of Loisy's name in the book, and the first in connection with Newman.

58. Ibid., p. 259. Earlier Williams had written to Ward: "I think that you will find that Loisy's distinctions about faith and history are taken, word for word, out of a Sermon of Newman's and the Preface to the Via Media"; and that "Loisy is but imitating (in his tone) Pascal, Mabillon and a host of others." Letter, [c. 1902], Wilfrid Ward Papers .

59. Tyrrell to Dora Williams, 2 December 1906, in Petre, *George Tyrrell's Letters*, 180. Tyrrell welcomed news of the publcation of Williams's book, telling Henry Clutton: "His is a very fine & delicate mind, related to W. Ward's as a lancet to a pickaxe." Letter, 21 October 1906, Katherine Clutton papers, copies provided by Dr. David Schultneover.

60. Wilfrid to Josephine Ward, [January 1907]. Letter in private hands.

61. Ward, untitled review, *Dublin Review*, 4th ser., 31 (January 1907): 178-79.

62. Michael de Vito, *The New York Review (1905-1908)* (New York: United States Catholic Historical Society, 1977), 150, 169-70,222. The Italian version appeared as "*Una nuova apologia cattolica," Il Rinnovamento* I (May 1907): 567-76. It was Tyrrell who suggested that Petre send her article to the two reviews. Petre Diary, 17 and 24 January 1907, Petre Papers, Add.Mss.52374.15-16.

63. F. W. Orde Ward, untitled review, *Hibbert Journal* 5 (January 1907): 462. Williams may have known Orde Ward, who also lived in Eastbourne.

64. Ward, "Two Views of Cardinal Newman," *Dublin Review*, 4th ser., 32 (July 1907): 1-2, 9.

65. Tyrrell to Bremond, [15 July 1907], copy in University of San Francisco Library.

66. Ibid. The anonymous letter appeared as "*Angleterre—Autour de Newman*," *Demain* (19 July 1907): 605.

67. Wiliams, untitled review, *Hibbert Journal* 6 (October 1907): 215.

68. Tyrrell to Bremond, 24 January 1907, copy in University of San Francisco Library.

69. Tyrrell to Bremond, 24 June 1907, copy in University of San Francisco Library.

70. Williams, "The Divinity of Christ and Modern Criticism," in *Lux Hominum: Studies of the Living Christ in the World of To-day*, ed. by F.W. Orde Ward (London: Francis Griffiths, 1907), p. 113.

71. Williams to Ward, [Summer 1907], Wilfrid Ward Papers.

72. Tyrrell to Clutton, 2 October, 1907, Clutton Papers. Shortly after this, Tyrrell wrote to Mrs. William Gibson: "Little Williams has given up God and is reading law under his brother's tuition; and in general the whole world is upside down" (13 October 1907, in Wilfrid Ward Papers VII/294h(2i).

73. *The Times*, 30 September 1907, 4; and 1 October 1907, 5.

74. Ward to Norfolk, 10 October 1907, copy, Wilfrid Ward Papers, VII/24(36).

75. Merry del Val to Bourne, 17 October 1907, Archives of the Archdiocese of Westminster, Roman Letters.

76. *The Times,* 2 November 1907, p. 10. Letter dated Eastbourne, 26 October 1907. This and subsequent letters led the *Catholic Times* to dub their author "the revolting Mr. Williams." Michael de la Bedoyère, *The Life of Baron von Hügel.* (London: J.M. Dent & Sons, 1951), 90.

77. Ward to Norfolk, 2 November 1907, copy, Wilfrid Ward Papers VI/24(37).

78. Ward to Norris, 2 November 1907, copy, Wilfrid Ward Papers IV/L(6i).

79. *The Times,* 4 November 1907, p. 10. Letter dated 3 November 1907.

80. Ibid., 5 November 1907, p. 18. Letter dated 2 November 1907.

81. Ward wrote to W.S. Lilly of the English Catholic Union: "Merry del Val is, I take it, the high authority alluded to by Norris." (5 November 1907), copy, Wilfrid Ward Papers.

82. The *Osservatore Romano* article appeared on 5 November 1907 and was translated in *The Tablet* of 16 November 1907, 784-85. The quotations above are taken, however, from a curious document, handwritten in Italian, entitled "Il modernismo e il Card. Newman," Dated 5 November 1907, and included with the Bourne Papers in the Archives of the Archdiocese of Westminister. I wish to thank Mr. Tim Redman for the English translation. *The Tablet* of 23 November 1907, 821, concluded that only "the mutinous Modernists" see the enclyclical as aimed at Newman.

83. *The Times,* 6 November 1907, p. 13. Letter dated 5 November 1907.

84. Ibid., 7 November 1907, p. 4. Both letters dated 6 November 1907. The chronology of events makes Norris's claim disingenuous.

85. Tyrrell to Ward, 6 November 1907, in Weaver, *Letters from a "Modernist,"* 116. Tyrrell repeated these words in a printed letter to Bishop Amigo, early in November, responding to his excommunication. Copy in Bourne Papers.

86. Tyrrell to Clutton, 15 November [1907], Clutton Papers; Tyrrell to Bremond, 14 November 1907, copy in University of San Francisco Library. Tyrrell was upset by the silence of Ward, the timorousness of von Hügel, and because he felt that "little Williams went to bed with annoyance & refused to play anymore." Tyrrell to Lilley, 12 November [1907], Lilley Papers, MS 30840.

87. [Tyrrell], "The Condemnation of Newman," *Guardian,* 20 November 1907. Tyrrell wrote to Lilley, 28 November 1907: "I learn that little Williams' letter (to *The Times*) frightened the Vatican more than anything—more than . . . my antics. If they only *saw* Williams!" Quoted in Vidler, "Modernists in Sussex," pp. 387-88.

88. Norris to Ward, 6 November 1907, Wilfrid Ward Papers VII/233a(5).

89. Ward to Norris, [7 November 1907], copy Wilfrid Ward Papers IV/L(6vi). Ward wrote to Lord Edmund Talbot: "If Tyrrell with his brilliancy and Williams with his knowledge of Newman combined, they could utterly defeat the conventional defender of Newman from charges of 'Modernism' as expounded in the Encyclical. And they know it" (Letter, [November 1907], Wilfird Ward Papers VI/31/1[10a].

90. Norfolk to Ward, 20 November 1907, Wilfrid Ward Papers, II/5(26); Norris to Ward, 21 November 1907, Wilfrid Ward Papers VII/233a(6).

91. Vaughan to Ward, 28 November 1907, Wilfird Ward Papers, VII/298/1(1). Vaughan reported the results of the papal audience in *The Times,* 2 December 1907, p. 8.

92. Vaughan to Ward, 12 December 1907, Wilfrid Ward Papers VII/298/1(2).

93. Maisie Ward, *Insurrection versus Resurrection*, 270, 272; Williams to Ward, [November 1907], Wilfrid Ward Papers. Williams's letters to Ward are mostly undated. In what follows, I have attempted to arrange them in chronological order, based upon internal evidence.

94. Ward to Williams, 18 November 1907, in Maisie Ward, Ibid., 270-72.

95. Williams to Ward, [c. 18 November 1907], Wilfrid Ward Papers.

96. Williams to Ward, [November 1907], Wilfrid Ward Papers.

97. Petre Diary, 16 November 1907, Petre Papers, Add.Mss.53374.28.

98. Von Hügel told Tyrrell that Ward likely would end up with no friends or allies. Letter, 28 November 1907, Petre Papers, Add.Mss.44930.102.

99. Ward to Fawkes, 28 November 1907, copy, Wilfrid Ward Papers VI/12/1(b).

100. Fawkes to Ward, 1 December [1907], Wilfrid Ward Papers VII/97(12i-ii). Fawkes hoped that if Ward felt he must submit he would state carefully his grounds for doing so. Letter, 4 December [1907], Wilfrid Ward Papers VII/97(13).

101. Ward to Williams, 14 December 1907, copy, Wilfrid Ward Papers.

102. Williams to Ward, [c. 20 December 1907], Wilfrid Ward Papers.

102. Ward to Williams, 24 December 1907, copy, Wilfrid Ward Papers.

104. Williams to Ward, [c. 25 December 1907], Wilfrid Ward Papers.

105. Tyrrell to von Hügel, 25 December 1907, Petre Papers, Add.Mss.44930.110. Tyrrell reported to Bremond that "Ward is in a great fright & writing twice a day to Williams for support" (Letter, 29 December 1907), copy in University of San Francisco Library.

106. Tyrrell to Clutton, [c. 15 January 1908], Clutton Papers.

107. Tyrrell to Clutton, 12 May 1908, Clutton Papers; von Hügel to Lilley 20 July 1908, Lilley Papers, MS 30549.

108. *Hibbert Journal* 6 (July 1908): 886-93. London Society for the Study of Religion paper of 5 May 1907.

109. Petre Diary, 12 and 28 April 1909, Petre Papers, Add.Mss.52374.49-50. This manuscript apparently was not published. Tyrrell mentions it submission to publishers, but that all felt the market was glutted with "modernism." Tyrrell to Clutton, 17 June [1909], Clutton Papers.

110. Williams to Young, n.d., quoted in Vidler, "Sussex Modernists," 388. The fact of Wiliams's presence at Tyrrell's funeral was made known to Cardinal Merry del Val and Bishop Amigo. G. Wadham to Merry del Val, 27 July 1909, Archives of the Diocese of Southwark, Tyrrell/Petre File, #64. Wadham described Williams, along with Petre and von Hügel, as "modernists [whose] disloyalty to the Holy See is notorious."

111. The Herzog Letter appeared in the *Guardian* for 20 October 1909, Wliams's in the number for 27 October.

112. Bedoyère, *Life of von Hügel*, 241; von Hügel to Petre, 28 June 1910, Petre Papers, Add.Mss.45361.129.

113. *Spectator*, 24 December 1910. Maude Petre's "Open Letter" appeared in *The Times* of 2 November 1910.

114. Untitled review, *Irish Journal of Education*, (March 1914): 28.

115. Powys to Llewelyn Powys, [3 July 1913], in Malcolm Elwin, ed., *Letters of John Cowper Powys to His Brother Llewelyn*, 2 vols. (London: Village Press, 1975), 1:122. Powys's letters contain frequent references about Williams's heavy drinking.

116. Powys to Llewelyn Powys, [7 February 1925], ibid., 1:367.

117. Powys, *Autobiography*, 342.

5

"Frustration, disillusion and enduring, filial respect": George Tyrrell's Debt to John Henry Newman

Nicholas Sagovsky

In the months after *Pascendi* it suited George Tyrrell to argue that the Modernists were clearly the offspring of Newman. He "might have shuddered at his progeny, but it is none the less his."[1] In his own case there was a significant amount of truth in the statement, but there was also an element of special pleading, for none of the Modernists pinpointed more clearly the points at which he diverged from Newman. Like a son learning to make his way in a changing world, Tyrrell first tried Newman's path, found that it brought him to a dead end, and then, not forgetting all he had learned in coming to that point, he struck out on his own. It would be a complex undertaking to determine how much Tyrrell *understood* Newman. The aim of this essay is more limited: to show the extent of his debt to him.

Of the Modernist writers, none appeared more like Newman. Tyrrell's writing has a similar vigor and grace; it springs from the same literary tradition; and though he has not the same delicacy and stamina in marshalling a complex argument, he shares Newman's ability to persuade and convince by a style of consummate flexibility, suggestiveness, and grace. When his writings first appeared, the most natural comparison to make was that with Newman. Maude Petre noted how people thought that a successor to Newman had now appeared,[2] and in one sense it was so. The two men shared a common concern to resist the dominance of rationalism in the religious philosophy of their day. They were concerned to present an account of believing which was true to the experience of the whole man. They shared a common love of Catholicism and an imaginative response to the antiquity and richness of teaching in that tradition. Much of this Tyrrell learned directly from Newman.

Very broadly, Tyrrell's lasting debt was to the Newman of the *Grammar of Assent*, that single work of Newman's to which he was most permanently and deeply indebted; the *Essay on Development*, the method of which he embraced, but the presuppositions of which he repudiated; the *University Sermons*; the *Letter to the Duke of Norfolk*; and the *Apologia*. In 1906, when Raoul Gout inquired about his reading of Newman, he was inclined to play it down. Tyrrell claimed that he had "never read him very much" and went on to say, "I have read *most* of his writings at least once; except the 'Plain Sermons,' the volume of the 'Via Media,' that on 'Athanasius' and that on 'Justification.' I have never read 'Tract 90.' But I have read the 'Grammar of Assent' three times, and the 'Essay on Development' about as often. The former did effect a profound revolution in my way of thinking just when I had begun to feel the limits of scholasticism rather painfully."[3] This, however, was not quite the whole story. In 1904 he told Wilfrid Ward that he had "carefully (very) studied" the last of Newman's *University Sermons* as he suspected that the concept of "the deposit of faith" differed from that in the *Essay on Development.*[4] In 1901 he told Maude Petre that he had "gone back to the *Apologia* for the seventh time."[5] When Wilfrid Ward's books on his father arrived for review, in 1893, Tyrrell had recently embarked on his "fourth re-reading" of *The Grammar of Assent.*[6] It is clear that throughout his life Tyrrell was engaged with the work of his great predecessor, and what looked like a process of steady disillusion could also be seen as one of growing discrimination.

Tyrrell came to Newman because he offered help with a range of questions that Aquinas could not answer. In time Tyrrell found questions that Newman could not answer, but he never lost his respect for either Newman or Aquinas. He admired Aquinas, not because he was an officially approved teacher of Catholic doctrine, and still less because there had been built about him a body of commentary and exposition that worked out the detailed application of his system with minute logical consistency, so that the church offered a theoretical answer to virtually any question the believer or unbeliever might (or might not) want to ask. Aquinas thrilled Tyrrell in the way that Dante thrilled him. Through Aquinas he began "the inevitable, impossible, and yet not all-fruitless quest of a complete and harmonious system of thought"[7] "inevitable," because the need of human beings to order their experience is perennial; "impossible," because our reasoning and our logic always move behind our experience; "not all-fruitless" because we always learn when we go to school with great thinkers. Tyrrell believed in Thomas "studied critically as *a* system; but not delivered dogmatically as *the* final system."[8] It was the slavish, scholastic devotion to the theological system which had been raised upon the tomb of Aquinas's "essentially liberal-minded and sympathetic"[9] spirit which distressed Tyrrell. The Aquinas that he knew and loved was lost among the learned, rationalistic commentaries. He was the victim of uncritical adulation combined with a deadening rationalism. If he did not answer the questions of a later age, so much the worse, the church seemed to think, for the questioners—but so much the worse, said Tyrrell, for the real Thomas,"whose distinctive spirit was an elastic sympathy with contemporary culture."[10] It was at this point that Tyrrell turned to Newman.

The question with which Aquinas could not help was precisely that of the status of his whole dogmatic theology. It was Newman who explored for Tyrrell the meaning of dogma, the nature of believing in the contemporary world. If Thomas offered a marvellously rich answer to the question, "What should I believe?," Newman complemented this by probing the question, "What am I doing when I believe these things?" At first there appeared to be no conflict. It was Newman who would "unbarbarise" the church, enabling her "to pour Catholic truth from the scholastic into the modern mould without losing a drop in the transfer."[11] Newman's principle of development showed how the same truths could be expressed (and perhaps believed) in a new way. His *Grammar of Assent* carried the battle against rationalism into the very heart of the rationalist camp, showing that the most commonly held beliefs are based on testimony, tradition, assumption, and practice, rather than logical proof. This was a different world from that of the manuals in which students for the priesthood were drilled.[12]

Tyrrell was always more interested in believing than beliefs, but in the last decades of the nineteenth century Roman Catholic theologians maintained an obsessive concern with the refutation of rationalistic objections by rationalistic argument. This attitude of mind was summed up by a Jesuit contemporary of Tyrrell's in a textbook of logic, where he praised the Catholic church for her inalienable possession of the truth: "To her all arts and all sciences minister, but none more than the Art and Science of Logic, since the Catholic Church alone can challenge the world to point out a single inconsistency in her teaching, or a single weak point in the perfect system of Divine philosophy which God through her has given to the world."[13] When discussing faith, apologists like this stressed the part of the intellect to the virtual exclusion of that played by the will. The common line was that, since it was possible to prove the existence of God by reason, and since the Christian revelation had been historically attested by miracles and the fulfillment of prophecy, there would be no difficulty in overcoming any objection to Christianity that might be forthcoming. Once the intellect had been convinced, the will would obviously be mobilized to give assent to the truths that had been demonstrated. So clearly was this conceived as a series of logical steps that the role of grace in enlightening the mind and moving the will was all but overlooked. It remained "extrinsic" to the process.

This was not at all how Newman approached the problem, as Tyrrell explained in a review of Wilfrid Ward's books on his father, W. G. Ward.[14] In the first of his two articles, he indicated very clearly what Newman offered him at this stage, "the conception . . . of conscience as the echo of God's voice, of the Church as the exponent of conscience and of the Christian revelation."[15] Where Tyrrell's teachers had practically made reason "the echo of God's voice," Newman's emphasis on conscience restored an emphasis he had found in Aquinas.[16] It brought back the moral and mystical dimensions to the act and to the life of faith. Purity of heart, not clarity of mind, was the essential prerequisite for the grace to believe. Assent came as the product of an internal "reasoning" far deeper than the superficial processes of the logicians. Tyrrell never lost this emphasis, and he learned it, as he learned the importance of conscience, from Newman.

Tyrrell also accepted Wilfrid Ward's assertion that Newman (and W. G. Ward) were acutely aware of the threat that Kantianism and biblical criticism offered to the received mode of Christian apologetic. Since the Aristotelian arguments for the existence of God, and the historical testimony to miracles and prophecy, were under threat, Newman and Ward worked to free "the preamble of faith" from vulnerability to the fluctuations of critical opinion. Tyrrell notes with satisfaction that "the two great principles which the Oxford philosophers insisted on—in stemming the sceptical current—were the necessarily changeable aspect of all science, and of historical science inclusively on the one hand; and on the other, the existence of a permanent basis in truly religious men for theism."[17] When they are described as seeking "a Christianity outside and beyond those traditional arguments which could be thrown into confusion or destroyed in their single-handed effectiveness by modern criticism,"[18] so far as this refers to the *historical* attack this is wishful thinking on the part of a later generation much more deeply unnerved by the problems. Tyrrell *thought* that when he sketched just such an approach to Christianity, primarily in *Lex Orandi* and *The Church and the Future,* he was being true to the spirit of Newman.

Tyrrell found in Newman still further ammunition against the rationalists. His review commends Newman because, "in opposition to Whately's school, which exaggerated the importance of exact deductive reasoning as a condition of assent to the disparagement of other modes of proof," he "laid great stress on the complex inductive inference in favour of Christianity, drawn from the history of the human heart and of the Jewish and Christian religions considered together as parts of the whole." In Tyrrell's case, the enemy is not the school of Whately, but the scholastic teachers who hold sway in the church. Newman's "complex inductive inference" has the

100

double advantage that it refutes them *and* cannot be impugned by historical criticism; hence Tyrrell's enduring respect for the *Grammar of Assent.* In that essay Newman reminded his readers how difficult it is to account logically for those things of which we are most certain, like the identity of a friend or the existence of an external world. Theologians, in particular, need to remember that "men spoke before grammars were written, and reasoned before logic was formulated. If logic cannot justify all our certainties, so much the worse for logic."[19] Christianity is a practical religion, a life to be lived, before it is a body of dogma. For Newman the impossibility of tension between the life and the dogma was axiomatic, for Tyrrell the tension became well-nigh unbearable.

The influence of Newman on Tyrrell's early writing is unmistakable. It helps to explain the freshness of *Nova et Vetera,* for Tyrrell defers to both his scholastic teachers and to Newman when he writes, "Natural reason and conscience convey to us the will of God. . . . When enlightened by Catholic faith, the voice of conscience is none other than the voice of Christ."[20] With respect to "intuition," he writes, "Our clearest moments of insight are often those when, through weakness and weariness, our mind is least under control, when concentration and voluntary attention is least possible; when reason slumbers, but spiritual vision is still awake and alert."[21] These are the thoughts of Coleridge's Xanadu (which influenced Newman more than he cared to admit), not those of the scholastic classroom. Sometimes, Tyrrell explicitly adopts Newman's scheme of "real" and "notional" assent: "Charity is knowledge; not any knowledge, but 'real' as opposed to 'notional'."[22] When he writes of one's name as "an idea whose content is ever growing and modifying,"[23] he uses the term "idea" exactly as it is used in Coleridge's *On the Constitution of the Church and State According to the Idea of Each* and in Newman's *Essay on Development.*

As Tyrrell's concern in his first two books was devotion, he could still afford to be uncritical of Newman. "I have been always a devout disciple of Newman," he told Ward in 1898,[24] and in 1899, when they were discussing the Synthetic Society, he commented, "Let us get now to the feet of Pope Conscience and God may look to the rest,"[25] which was not quite what Newman said, but sufficiently close to pass for it.[26] He even identified with Newman in his rejection by Rome. When Tyrrell's article "A Perverted Devotion" was passed by the English censors, but heavily and ignorantly criticized by the Roman, he wrote, "Poor Newman! I sometimes wonder what his *inmost* thoughts were; and I read 'Who's to blame?' yesterday. No one ever understood England and the English as he."[27] That is to say, like Tyrrell, Newman suffered at the hands of Rome because the merits

101

of his peculiar sensitivity to English life, thoughts, and modes of expression were lost on ignorant, scholastic curial theologians. Did the same tragedy have to be repeated in every generation?

Despite his identification with Newman and his debt to his fundamental theology, Tyrrell was moving away from Newman. This process was masked by his need to bring together the best of his published essays and, in publishing them as *The Faith of the Millions*, to demonstrate his orthodoxy to the world. In these essays the spirit of Newman was pervasive. He stated in the introduction that "the appeal of faith to reason and intelligence must be put in its proper place, which is secondary and conditional, not primary and causal."[28] Before that there had to be the appeal to the affections and the will. Nothing, says Tyrrell, stirs the "wish to believe" as much as "the visible fruits and advantages of belief shown in the lives of the faithful."[29] It is his settled conviction, following Ambrose and the epigraph to the *Grammar of Assent,* that "God has not willed to save His elect by logic."[30] These are some of the principles that, on his own admission, lay behind the essays of the previous five years—of which, for our purposes, three are particularly important: "Rationalism in Religion," which is explicitly indebted to Newman's essay of the same title; "The Relation of Theology to Devotion," where the debt is implicit but fundamental; and "The Mind of the Church," in which Tyrrell first began to think carefully about the issue of development.

As with a number of early essays, "Rationalism in Religion" has a certain ironic interest, because in it Tyrrell protests against some of the very positions he later espoused. His adversary here is a writer in the *Westminster Gazette,* who attacks the compulsory use of the Athanasian Creed on the novel ground that, since it describes deep and mysterious truths about the Trinity in outdated language, it is a hindrance to those whose devotion transcends the inappropriate words. Tyrrell sees this as an attempt "to dress out latitudinarianism in the clothes of Catholic orthodoxy."[31] In opposing it, he places himself on the shoulders of Newman, alluding to his essays on "Rationalism in Religion."[32] Four important points are made, all of them central to Tyrrell's approach in all his writings and all of them derivative: (1) In speaking about the Trinity we are speaking about a mystery. (Newman writes "A Revelation is religious doctrine viewed on its illuminated side; a Mystery is the self-same doctrine viewed on the side unilluminated;"[33] Tyrrell expresses the same thought succinctly in *External Religion,* when he calls mysteries "truths fringed with darkness."[34]) (2) There is no direct and unmediated knowledge of the Trinity, but all such knowledge is conveyed by means of inadequate and analogical human language. (Newman talks of "doctrine *lying hid* in language;"[35] in "Authority and Evolution, The Life of Catholic Dogma," Tyrrell writes that "we apprehend eternal truths, not in their separate distinctness, but as it were in solution, in as far as they can be fused into finite and human ideas, forms of thought and expression."[36] Both Newman and Tyrrell were reminding their readers that, although it may be a theological commonplace to see religious language as analogical, it is often forgotten that this implies a certain proper inadequacy of expression.) (3) Because of this inadequacy, we dare not alter the "form of sound words" by which revelation comes to us. (Newman says, "We should religiously adhere to the form of words and the ordinances under which it comes to us, through which it is revealed to us, and apart from which the Revelation does not exist;"[37] Tyrrell quotes these words approvingly, and underlines the last phrases.[38]) (4) The language of revelation does not refer to concepts and constructs, but to living realities. (Newman writes, "Rationalism takes the words of Scripture as signs of Ideas; Faith, of Things or Realities."[39] Tyrrell says "It is just because the language of Scripture and traditional dogma is not scientific and abstract, but natural and concrete . . . that we need a providential determination of points of development which reason alone cannot determine."[40] This distinction and this plea for a teaching church Newman would have heartily endorsed.)

Nevertheless, a major shift was coming. Indeed, it was first evident in "The Relation of Theology to Devotion." Such was the importance of this paper that when Tyrrell republished it in *Though Scylla and Charybdis* he wrote, "I am amazed to see how little I have really advanced since I wrote it; how I have simply eddied round and round the same point."[41] Once more, Tyrrell stressed the analogous or symbolic character of religious language and the fact that in talking about God we are dealing in mysteries. Rationalism is attacked with characteristic overstatement: "Men are influenced through their imagination and their emotions; and in nowise through their abstract ideas."[42] The main point of the essay was one for which Tyrrell was deeply indebted to Newman: devotion is to be seen as a "first-order" activity, theology as "second-order." Taking a favorite analogy of Newman, he wrote, "Devotion and religion existed before theology, in the way that art existed before art-criticism; reasoning, before logic; speech, before grammar."[43] This is what the rationalists and the theologians forget. Oblivious of the fact that Christianity is a life before it is a doctrine and that the point of the doctrine is to promote the life, they naturally undervalue *the lives* of the saints. For Tyrrell in particular the life of the saint can be indirectly revelatory because he now wants to say that the responsibility of the church with respect to revelation is to "preserve the exact ideas

103

which [the] simple language conveyed to its first hearers,"[44]—not the language, as before, but the ideas. How are we to disentangle these from their linguistic packaging, except by reference to the continuity of experience in the church, in the saints, and in ourselves?

Tyrrell was becoming increasingly frustrated with Newman's failure to explore these lines of thought, suggested by his work but ruled out by his tendency to flinch at the very moment when Tyrrell wanted him to press forward. "How far away even Newman seems to one now!" he wrote to Maude Petre in December 1900.[45] "His method and spirit are an everlasting possession; but of his premises and presuppositions hardly one has escaped alive." This was written just before Tyrrell tested some of Newman's "premisses and presuppositions" to the limit. Those in the area of ecclesiology (at the level of theology, not that of history) served him excellently; Newman's idea of "the deposit of faith" rapidly fell apart, and in leaving that Tyrrell departed from Newmanism forever.

On 29 December 1900 the bishops of England and Wales published a Joint Pastoral Letter entitled "The Church and Liberal Catholicism." It was based upon an ecclesiology that Tyrrell cordially loathed: "Two orders of persons, therefore, constitute, by the design of Christ, the visible Church. The small body of chosen men, assisted by the Holy Ghost, who represent the authority of Jesus Christ; and the large body of the faithful taught, guided and guarded by the Divine Teacher, speaking through the audible voice of the smaller body. Theologians call the one the *Ecclesia docens,* the other the *Ecclesia discens.*"[46] Already, Tyrrell had written and spoken against this divisive understanding of the church, which bolstered the authoritarian mentality of the clergy and encouraged a dumb submissiveness in the laity. It would not do to "distinguish the *Ecclesia docens* from the *Ecclesia discens,* the Church teaching from the Church taught . . . the Church active and militant, from the Church passive and quiescent; the former body being identical with the clergy and the latter with the laity." The laity were not "so much ballast in the bark of Peter."[47] When the Joint Pastoral letter was published, Tyrrell immediately set about a vigorous campaign of denunciation.[48]

The real affront was to the organic unity of the church, to a vision of Catholicism as a living and growing whole, to the doctrine of the Mystical Body. Tyrrell complained that the Joint Pastoral "would destroy the organic unity of the Church by putting the Pope (or the *Ecclesia docens*) outside and over the Church, not a part of her, but her partner, spouse, and Lord, in a sense proper to Christ alone."[49] John Coulson notes how, "from his earliest Anglican days, Newman's emphasis had always been on the fullness

104

of the Catholic idea," and how he had written of there being "something in the 'pastorum et fidelium *conspiratio*," which is not in the pastors alone."[50] It was because Newman had imparted this vision and theology of the church to Tyrrell that Tyrrell was able to react so strongly and speedily to the Joint Pastoral letter. He told Ward that the view of the bishops could no more blend with Newman's than oil and water. If one is all right, the other is all wrong,"[51] and he wrote to Raffalovich,"The Joint-Pastoral, now approved by the Pope, makes me question whether I have ever rightly understood the Vatican Council at all. . . . If I am wrong it is Newman who deceived me."[52]

At precisely the time of the controversy over the Joint Pastoral, Tyrrell's thinking on the "deposit of faith" and development was shifting away from Newman in a much more radical direction. In 1899 he described revelation as "a supernatural instruction of the mind" (a phrase of considerable ambiguity, explored only gradually by Tyrrell). Such "instruction" is the means by which God communicates with man.[53] It involves divine accommodation to the weakness of human understanding: Tyrrell talks of revealed "mysteries," which "defy adequate expression in any form of human thought and language."[54] He follows Newman in his belief that the words which express God's revelation are not to be tampered with: "To the Catholic, the language and symbolism in which Christ clothed His revelation was divinely chosen and approved. . . . Every letter of that deposit is . . . treasured."[55] The linguistic deposit does not change, but it is important to see that the church can in principle penetrate *the meaning* of the deposit more deeply and formulate the results of this improved understanding in officially enunciated dogmas. The mind (i.e., the understanding) of the church grows as she meditates upon the deposit.

The beginning of Tyrrell's major shift can be seen in "The Relation of Theology to Devotion" as first published in 1899.[56] (In later reworkings of the paper Tyrrell adjusted what he said to keep pace with his changing views.) He described "the deposit of faith" as "not merely a symbol or creed," but "a concrete religion left by Christ to his Church," that is to say a way of life. "Formularies are ever to be tested and explained by the concrete religion which they formulate."[57] In the last remark there creeps in the possibility of *a clash* between the formularies and the substance of the faith—something Newman, and Tyrrell, in his former devotion to Newman, did not envisage because they could see no other yardstick by which to judge spiritual experience or life than the formularies themselves. As yet, though, Tyrrell's main concern was the application of Newman's notion of development in place of the logical model of development that still governed the teaching of the theologians. The mind, he learned from Newman, does not develop by the application of logic, nor does "the mind of the Church" grow in this fashion. In his essay of that name[58] he endorsed the conclusion of Newman that there had been real development in the mind (i.e., understanding) of the church, though the deposit ("the form of sound words") remained the same. He talked of "the history of an *idea* gradually unfolding itself in the 'mind of the Church'."

In October 1900, Tyrrell acknowledged to Ward that he had changed his view on "the deposit." It was the first stage of a double shift. He first rejected the idea that "the deposit" referred to a "form of sound words," whether written down or in the minds of the first believers, and argued that it referred to "the present-day expression of the faith in which that former expression is at once lost and preserved as the child is in the man."[59] However, he was quickly dissatisfied with this and told Ward that he now believed "the deposit" referred to "those identical truths and realities which were expressed and seen less perfectly (relative to me) through the earlier forms, more perfectly through the later and more transparent forms."[60] This was Tyrrell's crucial step away from Newman, who never dreamed that our understanding of religious truth could lead us to criticize the sacred forms that mediated that truth to us. There was now the possibility, for Tyrrell, who was rapidly learning from critics like von Hügel and Loisy, of a radical historical critique of scripture, something Newman never embarked upon. Tyrrell had moved from conservatism to liberalism.

He explained to Ward that what he was concerned to accommodate was "the growth of the power of mental vision which should be allowed for in the Church as in the individual"—by which "the primitive expression becomes, as it were, a more transparent medium for us."[61] He illustrated this by the picture of a history book that means much more to the author, or the grown man, than the schoolboy for whom it was written, because the experience of the schoolboy is limited. He goes on, "And now we must make the violent hypothesis that Tommy though otherwise advancing in all branches of education has no other access to that period of history for the rest of his life. He has probably lost the work long ago, but remembers the substance of it quite faithfully though not the words. Let him every ten years sit down and write an essay on that period and I think you will have a very strict parallel to the development of ecclesiastical dogma. The facts dealt with are the same throughout *in substance,* but more clearly and fully seen; not only more clearly . . . but more *fully,* as real development requires."[62] Behind the shift is Tyrrell's growing awareness of the power of biblical and historical criticism, threatening the integrity of the scriptural "deposit." If criticism were to lead him to reject the miraculous (as it shortly did) this would not matter because he had shifted the emphasis from "the form of sound words" to the truths those words were intended to express.

It was clear that Tyrrell could no longer in any sense call himself a follower of Newman and in October 1902 he wrote an article called "The Limitations of Newman."[63] In this he pleaded against the canonization of Newman's works, so that the letter remained but the liberal and flexible spirit was lost. As Tyrrell saw it, "many of his quiet assumptions have become pressing difficulties for us. We no longer ask how the Catholicism of today grew out of the Church of the Fathers or out of the Bible, but how these grew out of beginnings immeasurably more difficult to trace and define." What Newman offered in response to the questions of Tyrrell's day was not an answer but "a method of search." He simply had not faced the new situation created by biblical and historical criticism. To Tyrrell, it had become urgent to "put religion high above all scientific, historic and even ethical uncertainties, and free it from that 'body of death' to which theologians and apologists have tied it."[64] This he now tried to do, as did Loisy, by distinguishing sharply between the sphere of religion and the sphere of science (including historical science) in a way that would have horrified Newman.

Tyrrell's thoughts about Newman were further sharpened when he came to review Wilfrid Ward's *Problems and Persons*. Ward attempted to follow Newman, showing that Catholicism and modern science could be reconciled by a doctrine of development which satisfied the demands of both. In a first article, "Semper Eadem,"[65] Tyrrell feigned a conservative attack on Ward, distinguishing sharply between liberal theology and "school theology," which were irreconcilable, because the principle of development was "all-dominating" in the first, and in the second "it was dominated and brought under that of authority."[66] Newman had been thought by some to offer a way through this dilemma. Tyrrell showed that it was not so. In a second article[67] he tried to remove the impression that he had returned to the conservative fold, which many had received from the first article, and to show that Newman wobbled at this point.

In this second article, Tyrrell examined the last of Newman's *University Sermons* and found that the "object of Revelation" was understood as "continually presented to our apprehension,"[68] and therefore our ways of speaking about the object were always open to testing against that continual experience. This was tantamount to "liberal theology" and similar to that espoused by Tyrrell after his shift of 1900. This was not the case with the

Essay on Development, where Newman is speaking *ad hominem* to the Tractarians, who held the conservative, propositional view of revelation. Newman here accepts the Tractarian view that the deposit of faith is "the communicable record and symbolic reconstruction of a revelation accorded to the Apostles alone."[69] This totally alters the application of the theory of development common to both essays. It tames and restricts it. In the first case, that of "liberal theology," the formulations of the past are to be tested by present experience and, if found wanting, to be restated in a way more conformable to our present understanding of God. In the second case, present restatements are to be tested for their conformity to the privileged apostolic "form of sound words." Tyrrell knew where he stood, and was disappointed to find that he was in the opposite camp to Newman, who "used the liberal method in defence of the conservative position. . . . He was a liberal in intellect and conservative in sentiment."[70]

Tyrrell could no longer be called a liberal in the sense that Newman was a liberal. He was now a revolutionary, a "Modernist" in the making. As he put it to von Hügel, "Something like a theological revolution is needed. There it is that I feel Newman cannot help us any more. It is not the articles of the Creed, but the word 'Credo' that needs adjustment."[71] The nature of this revolution could be expressed in a number of ways. It could be seen, as Tyrrell suggests, as one in which the principle of development comes to dominate the dogmatic principle (in Newman's sense). It was also one in which Tyrrell ceased to see religious language as referential in anything but the loosest sense. He now saw it as primarily expressive, and therefore akin to "poetic" or "literary" language, "thrown out," as Matthew Arnold would say, "at a vast reality." It was not to be equated with scientific language, which denoted processes and objects in the world and which could be verified by physical experiment. It was unashamedly symbolic (though open to verification by the experiment of living the Christian life). The great confusion of the theologians was to take symbolic language and treat it as though it were scientific. Tyrrell took this point from Matthew Arnold and turned it against Newman, who "may have insisted more explicitly than other theologians on what is universally allowed as to the inexact and analogous character of inspired utterance, whose form is literary and imaginative rather than scientific; he may have felt more distinctly the fallacy of making such loose utterances the premises of deductive arguments . . . but he would have cordially anathematised those conclusions which the author of *Literature and Dogma* endeavours to draw from such admissions, and which seem to punish the aggressions of theology by a wholesale denial of its rights."[72] Tyrrell was concerned for "*the rights* and limits" of theology. He stood between Newman and Arnold. He was a revolutionary but not an anarchist.

In Tyrrell's last years he sought both to claim and to repudiate Newman. When *Pascendi* was published he worked to prove that Newman, like himself, was caught by the condemnation. Tyrrell argued in *The Times*[73] that while the Encyclical "tries to show the modernist that he is no Catholic, it mostly succeeds only in showing him that he is no scholastic." Newman being no scholastic, the absurdity of *Pascendi* could be shown by demonstrating how this man, who had influenced so many others precisely because he expounded a reasonable, attractive, and nonscholastic Catholicism, was caught in the net. As Tyrrell told Houtin, "It is important in England to insist that Newman, and the more moderate 'Modernism'[74] has been condemned. Personally I believe Newman was an incurable ecclesiasticist, fighting for ecclesiasticism with modern weapons and that these weapons (i.e. his *Grammar of Assent* etc.) were of use to Modernists in their war against Scholasticism. . . . So far as Newmanism means, not his scope and motive, but his method, Newman is the father of Modernists; and that method condemned in the Encyclical is undoubedly his."[75] Thus Tyrrell, attacking *Pascendi* in *The Times* refers to "the modern, and Newmanistic, notion of development," "the spirit that breathes in a certain letter of a certain Cardinal to a certain Duke;" he refutes the condemnation of the tenet that God reveals himself in the voice of conscience and quotes Newman "who drinks first to conscience, and then to the Pope;"[76] he notes that *Pascendi* teaches that "laymen do not, by their learning, modify the collective mind of the Church, and so help (as Newman supposed) in the imaginary 'development' of dogma." In a letter to the Bishop of Southwark, written after his excommunication, he claimed, somewhat archly, to have been "brought into, and kept in, the Church by the influence of Cardinal Newman and of the mystical theology of the Fathers and the Saints."[77] Although it was claimed "on the highest possible authority" that Newman was *not* condemned by the Encyclical, it did not suit Tyrrell's case to be convinced. He challenged Rome to declare that "the 'most characteristic positions' of Newman as presented in the *Essay on Development* and the *Grammar of Assent*" were "untouched by the Encyclical."[78] There was, of course, official silence.

An article called "The Prospects of Modernism"[79] took much the same line. Tyrrell argued that Newman was "the founder of a method which has led to results which he could not have forseen or desired. The growth of his system has made its divergence from scholasticism clearer every day. If scholasticism is essential to Catholicism, Newman must go overboard."[80]

In two respects Newman had committed himself to modernity: in his notion of development as an "organic" rather than a dialectical process, and in the conviction that revelation consisted not only in certain statements which were susceptible of development, but in an animating "idea" which remained the same. The notion of the "idea," not in the sense of an intellectual concept, but of an animating principle, which came from Coleridge, was "the weapon that Modernists have taken from him and turned against much of that system in whose defence he had framed it."[81] Tyrrell is concerned to show that, since it is rooted in first-century apocalyptic, the "idea" of Catholic Christianity is quite different from that of Liberal Protestantism. The Modernist is the Catholic who seizes on the "idea" and looks to express it in the contemporary world. Whatever else he might be, like Jesus, he is no liberal Protestant.

In taking this line, Tyrrell knew that he was *using* Newman, who would have repudiated the conclusions that he, or Loisy, came to—just as Ward did. The Newman whose spirit he deferred to all his life was, he told Raoul Gout,[82] well depicted in Bremond's book *The Mystery of Newman,* for which he wrote an introduction. The most important point that the book has to make is that the key to understanding Newman lies not on the surface of his theology but in his inner life. Tyrrell felt himself to be, despite the divergence of their theological conclusions, a sharer of that inner life. This is Bremond's real interest, but in a final chapter he does discuss Newman's religious philosophy, and the three points that he seizes on are all ones of particular importance for Tyrrell. Bremond picks out the primacy of conscience, the communion of saints, and dogma as a composite whole as the three most important aspects of Newman's religious philosophy. They are three of the most important in Tyrrell's.

It would not be unfair to describe Tyrrell's whole theology as a theology of conscience. In 1908 he wrote that "for me, religion stands or falls with the divine character of conscience. If I have learnt this from Newman I have verified it by my own experience and reflection; and it is a conviction that grows stronger every day."[83] When Tyrrell dived into the crypt church of St Etheldreda's, Ely Place, in flight from the Anglo-Catholic charade of St Alban's, he was thrilled to find just that sense of the communion of saints which Newman loved: "Oh! the sense of reality! here was the old business, being carried on by the old firm, in the old ways; here was continuity, that took one back to the catacombs."[84] On the unity of dogma Tyrrell was no less forthright: "The mind, indeed, may abstract, and analyse, and dissect; it may give a fictitious completeness to what are really fragments;

but it is only the unbroken unity of the living whole which appeals to the heart."[85] The whole person needs to be drawn into the wholeness of Catholicism to experience the "living" unity of dogma.

In his *Autobiography,* Tyrrell contrasts himself with Newman, whose Catholicism was "the outcome of his theism, practical and speculative."[86] Newman had shown how to be a theist was to be drawn, step by step, into being a Catholic. Tyrrell claimed that for him the process was entirely different. He was attracted first by the ritual and mystery of Catholicism and forced, step by step, to a genuine theism that would support "a system that hung mid-air save for the scaffolding of mixed motives which made me cling to it blindly, in spite of a deep-down sense of instability." Not until Newman showed him how to ground the system in his heart, through his conscience, did the instability go. This was what, at root, he owed Newman: a deep stability in his faith. He gave his assent to the Catholic faith, and Newman expounded to him the grammar of his action. However, Tyrrell was also forced to integrate new and potentially devastating questions into his life and thought. The Newmanite synthesis was broken, the meaning of dogma changed, but his faith remained, on the whole, secure. Tyrrell told Bremond that in Newman "the head of a sceptic, the heart of a theologian, brought forth a faith that was wilful blindness."[87] It was a verdict born of frustration, disillusion, and enduring, filial respect.

NOTES

1. G. Tyrrell, "The Prospects of Modernism," *Hibbert Journal* 6 (1908), 243.

2. M.D. Petre, *The Autobiography and Life of George Tyrrell* (2 vols., London: Edward Arnold, 1912), 2:207.

3. Ibid., 209.

4. Tyrrell to Ward, 4 January 1904 (M.J. Weaver, ed., *Letters from a "Modernist"* [Shepherdstown, WV: Patmos Press, 1981], 92.

5. Tyrrell to Petre, 15 February 1901 (Petre, *Life of George Tyrrell* 2:208).

6. Tyrrell to Ward, 12 December 1893 (Weaver, *Letters from a "Modernist,"* 3).

7. Petre, *Life of George Tyrrell* 1:248.

8. Tyrrell to Bremond, 22 August 1900 (Petre, *Life of George Tyrrell* 2:46).

9. Tyrrell to von Hügel, 6 December 1897 (Petre, *Life of George Tyrrell* 2:45).

10. *Weekly Register,* 30 March 1900 (Petre, *Life of George Tyrrell* 2:44).

11. Tyrrell to Ward, 12 December 1893 (Weaver, *Letters from a "Modernist,"* 3).

12. For an account of the "manuals," see G. Daly, *Transcendence and Immanence: A Study in Catholic Modernism and Integralism* (Oxford: Clarendon Press, 1980), chapter 1.

13. R.F. Clarke, *Logic*, Manuals of Catholic Philosophy, Stonyhurst Series (London, 1909), 483.

14. Review of W. P. Ward, *William George Ward and the Oxford Movement* (London: Macmillan, 1889), and *William George Ward and the Catholic Revival* (London: Macmillan, 1893), *The Month* 79 (1893): 560-8, 80 (1894): 59-68.

15. Ibid., 562.

16. Ibid., 567.

17. Ibid., 564.

18. Ibid., 564.

19. Ibid., 565.

20. *Nova et Vetera,* fourth edition (London: Longmans, Green, 1905), 349.

21. Ibid., 213-4.

22. Ibid., 174-5.

23. Ibid., 170.

24. Tyrrell to Ward, 22 September 1898 (Weaver, *Letters from a "Modernist,"* 5).

25. Tyrrell to Ward, 6 September 1899 (Weaver, *Letters from a "Modernist,"* 18).

26. Newman wrote in his *Letter to the Duke of Norfolk* (London: Longmans, Green, 1875), 66: "Certainly, if I am obliged to bring religion into after-dinner toasts (which indeed does not seem quite the thing) I shall drink,—to the Pope, if you please, —still, to Conscience first, and to the Pope afterwards."

27. Tyrrell to Ward, January 1900 (Weaver, *Letters from a "Modernist,"* 24).

28. *The Faith of the Millions,* First Series, third edition (London: Longmans, Green, 1904), vii.

29. Ibid., xi.

30. Ibid., xv.

31. Ibid., 88.

32. *Essays Critical and Historical,* ninth edition (London: Longmans, Green, 1890), vol. 1, 30-101.

33. Ibid., 41.

34. *External Religion* (London: Sands, 1899), 113.

35. *Essays Critical and Historical* 1, 41.

36. *Faith of the Millions* 1, 147.

37. *Essays Critical and Historical* 1, 47.

38. *Faith of the Millions* 1, 96. This was written in 1898. Subsequently, Tyrrell's view of revelation was quite altered. In this essay he stresses the importance of determining "the human ideas, the human sense, intended in the original words of revelation" (p. 107). Tyrrell soon came to identify revelation with these "ideas" rather than "the original words."

39. *Essays Critical and Historical* 1, 35.

40. *Faith of the Millions* 1, 111-12.

41. *Through Scylla and Charybdis* (London: Longmans, Green, 1907), 85.

42. *Faith of the Millions* 1, 239. In the *Grammar of Assent* Newman wrote, "it is in human nature to be more affected by the concrete than by the abstract" (Christian Classics reprint, Westminster, MD, 1973, p. 37).

43. Ibid., 252. cf. *Newman's University Sermons* (London: S.P.C.K., 1970), 184, 260, 321-22.

44. *Faith of the Millions* 1, 239.

45. Tyrrell to Petre, 26 December 1900 (Petre, *Life of George Tyrrell* 2:144).

46. *The Tablet,* 5 January 1901, 9.

47. *External Religion,* 123-24.

48. See M.J. Weaver, "George Tyrrell and the Joint Pastoral Letter," *Downside Review* 99 (1981), 18-39.

49. *The Pilot*, 2 March 1901, 282 (Petre, *Life of George Tyrrell* 2:154).

50. J. Coulson, *Newman and the Common Tradition* (Oxford: Clarendon Press, 1970), 117, quoting J. Coulson, ed., *On Consulting the Faithful in Matters of Doctrine* (London: Geoffrey Chapman, 1961), 104. See also *Newman and the Common Tradition*, 229-30.

51. Tyrrell to Ward, 28 January 1901, (Weaver, *Letters from a "Modernist,"* 62).

52. Tyrrell to Raffalovich, 11 April 1901 (ms. at Blackfriars, Oxford).

53. *Faith of the Millions* 1, 124 ff.

54. Ibid., 128.

55. Ibid., 142.

56. This analysis is indebted to J. Laubacher's excellent *Dogma and the Development and Dogma in the Writings of George Tyrrell* (Louvain/Baltimore: Watkins Printing Co., 1939).

57. *The Month* 94 (1899), 473.

58. *The Month* 96 (1900), 125-42, 233-40; *Faith of the Millions* 1, 158-204.

59. Tyrrell to Ward, 2 October 1900 (Weaver, *Letters from a "Modernist,"* 54).

60. Ibid.

61. Ibid.

62. Ibid., 55.

63. *Monthly Register* 1 (October 1902), 264-65.

64. Tyrrell to Bremond, 17 February 1902 (M.D. Petre, ed., *George Tyrrell's Letters* [London: T. Fisher Unwin, 1920], 10.

65. *The Month* 103 (1904), 1-17. Reprinted as "Semper Eadem 1" in *Through Scylla and Charybdis*, 106-32.

66. *Through Scylla and Charybdis*, 135.

67. "The Limits of the Theory of Development," *Catholic World* 81 (September 1905), 730-44. Reprinted as "Semper Eadem II" in *Through Scylla and Charybdis*, 133-54.

68. *Through Scylla and Charybdis*, 140.

69. Ibid., 147.

70. Tyrrell to Ward, 28 January 1902 (Weaver, *Letters from a "Modernist,"* 72).

71. Tyrrell to von Hügel, 19 February 1905 (Petre, *Life of George Tyrrell* 2: 220).

72. Introduction to H. Bremond, *The Mystery of Newman*, translated by H.C. Corrance (London: Williams and Norgate, 1907), xiv.

114

73. 30 September, 1 October 1907.

74. I.e., what Tyrrell called "Wilfridwardianism."

75. Note on the back of Houtin's copy of Tyrrell's "Letter to the Bishop of Southwark," sent to Houtin 4 December 1907 (Fonds Houtin, Bibliothèque Nationale, Paris).

76. See note 26.

77. Petre, *Life of George Tyrrell* 2, 342.

78. See the note to the printed version of this letter, e.g., in the Houtin Papers, Paris, or the Clutton Papers, Oxford.

79. See note 1.

80. Ibid., 243.

81. *Christianity at the Crossroads* (London: Longmans, Green, 1909), 33.

82. Tyrrell to Gout, 26 May 1906 (Petre, *Life of George Tyrrell* 2: 209).

83. Petre, *George Tyrrell's Letters,* 228.

84. Petre, *Life of George Tyrrell* 1: 153.

85. *Lex Credendi* (London: Longmans, Green, 1906), ix.

86. Petre, *Life of George Tyrrell* 1: 112.

87. Tyrrell to Bremond, 28 November 1905 (Fonds Bremond, Bibliothèque Nationale, Paris).

Part Three

FRENCH MODERNISTS
AND
NEWMAN

6

Bremond's Newman*

Roger Haight, S.J.

During the first decade of this century the figure of John Henry Newman generated considerable interest. And Henri Bremond (1865-1933), more than any other single person, was the interpreter of Newman for France. This essay studies the view of Newman that Bremond purveyed in France around the turn of the century.

Referring to the years just prior to the Modernist movement, Bremond wrote that very few people in France read Newman or were influenced by his thought.[1] Yet in 1907 one finds a review article critically surveying a whole host of publications concerning Newman.[2] This sudden interest in Newman was due partly to the emergence of religious and theological controversy and the congeniality of Newman's ideas to the issues at stake. It was said of Bremond that no one in France knew Newman better,[3] and certainly no one wrote more on him in France during this period.

I shall deal exclusively with Bremond's Newman, which, along with the use to which Loisy put Newman's theory of the development of doctrine, was the most significant image of Newman in France between 1900 and 1910. It is not my intention to judge the historical accuracy of Bremond's portrait of Newman.[4] Rather I shall deal with Bremond's Newman as an autonomous subject so that the reader will constantly see double, so to speak, with the "real" or historical Newman remaining a mere shadow. The subject matter of this essay, then, is really the interpreter and his interpretation of Newman.

As for the procedure suitable for such a project, I propose the following scheme as at least workable for this occasion. In the first place, I shall consider the situation in which the interpretation was made since this has considerable bearing on Bremond's Newman. Secondly, I will look at Bremond's method of interpretation since the issue of method, understood as that which generates understanding, is decisive for understanding itself. Only then shall I sketch the sketch of Bremond's Newman specifically in those details that are theological.

---

*An earlier, expanded version of this article appeared in the *Journal of Theological Studies* in 1985.

Bremond began to develop his interpretation of the religious philosophy of Newman and publish it in 1897, four years after the dismissal of Loisy from the Institut Catholique and the publication of *L'Action* by Blondel in 1893. This date may be considered the beginning of at least a significant phase of the emergence of the Modernist movement. Modernism is understood here as an historical movement of thought within the Roman Catholic church which sought to reinterpret Christian doctrine theologically into terms comprehensible to intellectual culture at the end of the nineteenth century.

If the genetic and consistent underlying logic of the Modernist movement is to be seen as apologetic in the classical sense of the Apologists, that is, as interpreting Christianity in terms of a new culture, still there is a second dimension that is equally important for understanding its dynamics. At first and more profoundly a confrontation between Catholicism and modernity, this dialogue quickly became a debate between a Modernist interpretation of Christianity and the position represented by Roman Catholic authority as expressed in the language of neo-scholastic systematic theology.[5] More explicitly than in the writings of liberal theologians, Roman Catholic Modernism appears as an inter-Christian and intra-church controversy; indeed, Modernism was an intra-Catholic struggle between two different interpretations of Catholicism. This makes it understandable why Modernists will appeal back to models or precursors within the tradition of the church. Blondel will appeal to Cardinal Deschamps; Laberthonnière will appeal to Augustine and Pascal; Loisy and Bremond, for different reasons, will appeal to Newman.

The Modernist movement and controversy is also described as a crisis, and a description of the elements of the crisis will help to illumine Bremond's interpretation of Newman. It has been suggested that a way of understanding this crisis is in terms of a paradigm shift and all that goes with such a shift.[6] In the case of such a genuine change in the fundamental structure for understanding data, there will be two parties or groups who share basically different assumptions, principles, and axioms for understanding the same phenomena. In short, they will be speaking two different languages, one not intelligible or no longer intelligible to the other. When one adds to this the fact that theology often shares in the absolutism of the religious imagination, one has the grounds for genuine crisis, for often abusive polemics, and for condemnation.

The two parties or positions in the Modernist crisis were of course the modernizing interpretation of Catholicism and that of the neo-scholasticism which was embraced by Roman authority in the church and which consequently shared in that authority.[7] It may be said that there were two general problems that arose out of the eighteenth and nineteenth centuries which also underlay the Modernist crisis, the first concerning religious knowledge and faith and the other concerning the integration of theology with the findings of critical history. On the former question, the one that was ultimately addressed by Bremond, the position of neo-scholasticism stressed the objectivity of revelation, the rational credibility of an assent of faith, an objective and intellectually argued apologetics, the truth of Christian dogma in its propositional form, and an authority of the church which preserved this tradition intact and required Christian obedience.[8] The Modernists for their part stressed revelation as a form of, or as based on, religious experience, the impossibility of establishing the truth of revelation by rational argument, the necessity of beginning apologetics with anthropology or an account of the religious a priori within existence, the impossibility of concepts or propositions being adequate to the transcendent object of faith, the necessity of mediating between the authority of doctrine or the church, and the meaning which Christian doctrine bestows on religious life and morality.[9]

This is the context in which Bremond interpreted Newman, a religious and theological context in which a turn to religious experience in the understanding of apologetics, faith, theological method, and doctrine was pitted against extrinsicism and doctrinal authoritarianism. And Bremond's penchant for probing religious experience would obviously enough carry him in the direction of his newly found Modernist friends. A brief look at Bremond's method will provide another preliminary note before presenting his interpretation of Newman.

Bremond's Method

Besides his historical situation, Bremond's method of interpreting Newman is very significant for the interpretation itself. Although I shall focus on Bremond's presentation of Newman's doctrine or religious philosophy, still Bremond himself insisted that he arrived at this through a consideration of Newman's life. Bremond was not a professional philosopher or theologian. He was, rather, a biographer or historian of the interior, spiritual, and religious dimensions of specific people. And the methods he employed in charting this history has direct bearing on his interpretation of Newman.

Some historians or biographers may limit themselves to recreating as accurately as possible the empirical side of events, or to the explicit significance borne by their sources or texts. Bremond was not one of these; he did not stop there, but rather used texts and events as windows to the interior life of a person. He sought the religious psychology of a person in the sense of the dynamics of a particular person's religious experience. Later on he described his method in the following way: "There are two ways of writing history. One is to enumerate the principal religious writers of a country, describe their works, discuss the originality of each of them and his literary and philosophic value. The other way is that followed by Newman and Saint-Beuve, to seek to penetrate the inner soul of the persons they are studying with the nuances particular to each. That will be our method."[10] One has the impression that Bremond works from a general familiarity of the whole life of a person on whom he is writing, in the case of Newman from a great deal of reading of him and about him. But at the same time, he is able to see behind or within specific events and texts to find a whole world of meaning and disclosure. "Henri Bremond has an uncanny power of seizing on any detail which reveals a touch of humanity."[11] Either by conjecture or intuition or projection, or by a sensitivity generated out of the dialectic between holistic impression and particular text, or finally by all of these together, Bremond was able to draw maps of the unique, personal, interior, and religious experience of his subjects. In the case of Newman, Bremond read, reread, and meditated on him with great patience. What he sought was an interior knowledge or communion with him so that, finally, he could analyze, extract, and make a judgment on those elements of him that were most precious and useful for his context.[12]

Bremond did not take a picture of Newman but painted a portrait. He did this by gradually sketching in lines, traits, and qualities that contributed to the whole. Each detail must be taken in conjunction with other qualities which counterbalance them. The many details are all held together in tension so that many characteristics, if taken by themselves, would prove to be inaccurate.[13] Whether or not Bremond's method, acclaimed for its use in his later, more famous writings, was equally successful in his portrait of the religious and psychological biography of Newman is debated. His brother, André, who also knew Newman, considered it Henri's finest work in a rather large corpus.[14] Wilfrid Ward found it such a distortion that he felt obliged to attack it publicly, at least as much for its biography as for its doctrine.[15] In any case, this method of Bremond is one of the keys to his interpretation of Newman's doctrine.

The Doctrine of Bremond's Newman

We are now in a postion to look at the doctrine of Newman as Bremond portrayed it to the French public. Personally, Bremond was interested in other aspects of Newman, especially his interior and religious life, more than his doctrine. But he did deal with what he called Newman's religious philosophy and consciously drew Newman's ideas into the apologetic and theological discussions that were part of the Modernist movement in France. In what follows I shall deal principally with Bremond's main statement concerning Newman's religious philosophy, which is contained in the conclusion of his biography of 1906, but I will also chart some of his writings on Newman both before and after this statement.

Bremond's first significant article representing the religious philosophy or theology or doctrine of Newman was written as early as 1897.[16] The article concerns the foundational issues of the process of coming to faith and thus the nature of faith and the structure of apologetics, all of which were lively issues at the time. Bremond's premise is that the term *irrational* when applied to faith and religious knowledge contains an ambiguity; it can have two distinct and different meanings. *Irrational* may refer to "every act coming from a faculty other than reason" and hence what is strictly not rational. Or the term may be used in a looser sense to mean what is not strictly or purely rational in the sense of cool intellectual and weighed logical argument of a scientific, mathematical, or syllogistic kind. But in this case, the so-called irrational can still mean something reasonable and reasoned, indeed rational, even though it rests on the basis of a wider logic.[17] Newman's teaching on implicit reasoning from the *Oxford University Sermons* and on natural inference and the illative sense from the *Grammar of Assent* are brought to bear on this second kind of "irrational" rationality in the domain of religious knowledge. "The whole goal of this essay is to draw attention to the existence and the value of a certain natural logic that will never be restricted or reduced to the rules of Aristotle."[18]

Thus as early as 1897 Bremond related Newman to the incipient Modernist movement dealing with the apologetic question. This can be said in spite of the fact that in republishing the article in 1901 he said that the epistemology and psychology of faith of Newman is not to be confused with what was then called "the new apologetic" of Blondel and Laberthonnière.[19] In his exposition of Newman, Bremond consistently contrasts it to an intellectualistic view and points to the moral dimension of the religious question and the moral basis of religious faith and conviction. One is led to the truth by "doing the truth."[20] One arrives at religious truth from moral attitudes and a sound moral life.[21] At the end of the article, Bremond comments that this moral dimension has not been developed enough in this essay, but that the mere translation of Newman would suffice to illustrate it.[22]

In 1904, Bremond published Newman's fifteenth university sermon, "The Theory of Developments in Religious Doctrine," together with an edited version of *An Essay on the Development of Christian Doctrine.*[23] Bremond's comments on the sermon are most significant. In the introduction where they are found, he asserts that Newman, in this work, shows "the intimate connection between the Christian life and dogma, and how the latter is nothing more than the *explicitation* of the former."[24] The point of the theory of development is to resolve the seeming antinomy, or to explain the continuity, between the current vast theological system and the evident simplicity of Christian experience. And this is done by explaining dogma as expressions of religious experience: ". . . if on the one hand, dogmas only have value on the basis of the experience which they render explicit, then this experience, on the other hand, tends toward becoming explicit and being described, explained and commented upon by dogma."[25] Precisely on the question of the relation between religious experience and dogma, Newman often affirms the priority of experience, according to Bremond. "In this point, perhaps, one finds that which is most original and most important in the sermon."[26] At least this is the most striking feature when compared to present-day positions in religious philosophy. According to Newman, both in the origins of Christianity and today, the "religious impression" within the believer is primary, and it alone can legitimize dogmatic formulas.[27]

The following year Bremond published his second volume on Newman which dealt with the psychology and philosophy of faith or religious knowledge.[28] Its principal sources are *The Grammar of Assent* and the *Oxford University Sermons* from which long passages and whole sermons are simply translated. Since it would be impossible to summarize this work here, I shall merely describe it. Bremond's own summary of it will appear in the next work to be considered.

La Psychologie de la foi is more interpretive of Newman than Bremond's first volume. In this book Bremond interjects more of his own comment. The texts are arranged synthetically into six chapters of Bremond's design. Moreover, there is a logic to them as the themes begin with philosophical and epistemological considerations and follow an argument to a conclusion concerning the role of the "moral" and conscience as the keys to religious knowledge or assent, and hence to Newman's apologetic. Also, Bremond's own text plays a greater role in the presentation. In some sections he organizes, guides, and explains the thread of Newman's argument to such an extent that Newman's texts are mere illustrations. In short, he assumes more interpretative responsibility in this anthology because of the impossibility to reproduce the whole of his sources, especially the *Grammar,* in a single book.

But this work is still an historical representation of Newman and much less interpretive than what will follow. Or better, his interpretation is very closely tied to the texts of Newman, to exegeting them or explaining in other words what they are saying. There are a few lapses from this historian's point of view, especially in his Preface and Introduction, but in general, it is an attempt to present Newman in Newman's words.

With this book one is introduced to a polar tension in Newman's thought. In his Introduction, entitled, "Le Dogmatisme de Newman," Bremond stresses Newman's dogmatic bias, his Roman Catholic insistence on a deposit of faith, an infallible authority to say what it is, and his integralism over against any form of liberalism. But against this background the whole book emphasizes Newman's anti-intellectualism and his existential approach to faith through a method of phenomenological description of the personal dynamics of how a concrete person comes to believe. This is the meaning of the phrase "psychology of faith," which actually appears very rarely in the text. It does not mean "a merely psychological" approach to faith.[29]

In all, while this is a fairly objective work on Newman, it shows at the same time Bremond's definite bias of interpretation. It presents the existential side of Newman and emphasizes the personal, "subjective," and a priori qualities of faith, and especially the moral predispositions and prerequisites that underlie faith. I think it is safe to say that the drawing of a parallel between Newman and Blondel at the conclusion of the work expresses one of its intentions and guiding ideas from the beginning:

> It is in this way that it (the Newmanian apologetic) prepares, announces and sanctions that which is called somewhat improperly the new apologetic. If I understand this latter, it would be nothing more than another way of explaining the theory of the *illative sense* and showing that every formal apologetic supposes and demands an anterior adaptation in which the arguments themselves in some way draw the major part of their convincing force. This basic identity of two doctrines is even more remarkable in that the philosopher of *L'Action* has not, as far as I know, made any special study of the *Grammar of Assent.*[30]

Bremond's most famous study of Newman was published the next year and was entitled *Newman: Essai de biographie psychologique.*[31] The book was immediately successful. Four editions of it were published within a year, and it became available to an English audience through the translation in 1907.[32] The book is indeed a psychological study. Ranging over the whole corpus of Newman, but with less emphasis on his theological works, Bremond tries to dissect the elements of the inner life of Newman and to distill its essence. Only at the end, as a kind of epilogue, and explicitly as a function of the inner life of the man, does Bremond synopsize Newman's doctrine or religious philosophy. "The best, the only way of setting forth accurately Newman's religious philosophy is to give an account of his inner life."[33] The reason for this is that Newman was not a systematic thinker; he did not arrive at conclusions by abstract reasoning. The germ of Newman's whole religious philosophy rests in the surrender of faith itself to whatever it leads.[34]

Yet for all that Bremond does try to reduce Newman's religious philosophy to three principles. These are, in the order of their importance, the following: the primacy of conscience, the communion of saints, the infallibility of the church or integral dogmatism.

Conscience, according to Bremond, "is the great principle upon which rests, in whole and in detail, the philosophy of Newman."[35] For Newman, "the whole religious edifice rests on the conscience."[36] The function of conscience is related not just to natural religion, but also to revealed religion and specifically to Christianity. It is not merely a moral consciousness of right and wrong; it is as well a religious sentiment. A moral experience is also religious; and the religious awareness expressed by dogmas has a moral dimension and is a moral principle for life. "For him, to listen to the voice of conscience is to hear directly the voice of God; and not the God of natural religion, but the God of revelation."[37] "The *Grammar of Assent* has for its object to show us that the conscience is the only means of arriving at a religious knowledge of religious truth."[38] The illative sense is conscience in quest of religious truth. Conscience then is a principle and the end of all religious knowledge, natural or revealed. "Dogma and practice, all that which is, properly speaking, religious, necessarily regulates itself by it."[39]

Conscience then is the kernel or dead center of Newman's religious philosophy. Bremond even sees in Newman a parallel to the work of Schleiermacher in "putting conscience, Christian experience, and personal realisation of the Divine, at the base of the whole religious structure."[40] Newman reverses the view that religion is the "foundation of conscience."[41]

But at the same time, conscience is not an isolated faculty in Newman; Newman believed in informing his conscience, in consulting, in "taking the advice of others."[42] But in the end, Newman stands for the primacy of "his personal experience of religion."[43] And on this basis lies Newman's "anti-intellectualism, the ruling idea of his psychology of faith."[44]

The second principle of Newman's religious philosophy Bremond calls "the communion of saints," and it is linked to Newman's conversion to Catholicism. The logic of this conversion is depicted thus: Newman had a great love for the Fathers and the church of the Fathers. And in the comparison of the Anglican and Roman churches with the patristic church, he saw closer parallels in Rome. To which church, he implicitly asked, would the Fathers, if resurrected, gravitate and feel at home? The point, then, is that it was Newman's feeling and love for the sanctity and the vitality of the patristic church which he saw paralleled in the Roman Catholic church, through an idealization of its external discipline and holiness, that led to his conversion.[45] Thus here too Bremond finds in Newman a primacy of inner religious experience and anti-intellectualism, or at least a relegation of intellectual argument to a secondary position. "All that which is purely intellectual and systematic had never in his eyes more than an accessory value."[46] He converted to Catholicism because of its ethical life and holiness which he recognized by instinct or a religious experience. The theory of development was built up to account for this fact.[47]

The third of Newman's basic principles Bremond calls "Integral Dogmatism" or dogma as a complete whole, unity, system. Newman accepted with a firm faith "the whole theoretical system of doctrine and—let us not shirk the word—scholasticism taught by the Roman Church."[48] Everyone knows that Newman was no minimizer, Bremond would say again later: he would defend the last scrap of revealed truth against every sort of liberal.[49]

Moreover, Bremond puts forward texts showing that, in accepting the whole of it and in each detail, Newman also displayed a very traditional and even scholastic type of understanding of revelation and dogma. "Ordinarily, theology represents dogma as a mass of assertions revealed by God once for all, and confided, as a deposit, to the infallible keeping of the Church. Whence it follows that faith is an act of submission, of adhesion to the truth of this teaching, and that theology, the systematic study of these same doctrines is, like mathematics, a science of logical and rigorous deductions. Newman formally admits this first principle with all its consequences."[50]

In reflecting on these three principles of Newman, Bremond finds a certain contradiction or antinomy stretching between the first and the third. On the one hand, there is the primacy of conscience, the existential principle of religious experience, which is central to Newman and to which he was faithful to the end of his life. On the other hand, there is the dogmatic principle of integralism which required submission or obedience to an extrinsicist notion of revelation, authority, and dogma. "This same antinomy breaks out, it seems to me, in all that Newman has written on the development of Christian dogma," he notes.[51] Newman can write: "To conscience first, and to the Pope afterwards!" Yet he submits to the dogmatic principle. He has conflicting notions of faith, one experiential, the other a submission to authority. On one side, everything offered by authority will be criticized from the point of view of conscience; on the other, the dogmatic principle calls for obedience.[52]

However, Bremond proposes this antinomy in Newman with an important nuance. Existentially, in Newman himself, in his actual life and thought, this antinomy was nonexistent because in fact his conscience led him to dogmatic submission. In Newman himself then the first and third principles are not in conflict; they merge and are one; they harmonize. It is only when these two principles are seen abstracted from his actual life, that is, isolated as autonomous axioms "in principle," so to speak, that the antinomy appears.[53] But this is what Newman never did because he was not an intellectualist or systematic thinker. Thus Bremond comments that "it is possible, indeed, that Newman succeeded but imperfectly in reconciling logically the principle of the primacy of conscience with that of dogmatic Catholicism."[54]

Finally, Bremond concludes this synopsis of Newman's doctrine by drawing him even closer into the Modernist fold through a consideration of his apologetics. Apologetics, it will be recalled, was one of the main formalities under which Blondel and Laberthonnière approached the issues of faith, dogma, and implicitly revelation.[55] Newman's method is contrasted with that of scholasticism, the sanctioned apologetics of the Catholic Church, which tries to meet rationalism by proceeding rationalisticly. It unfolds on the basis of pure reason and objective abstract argument, prescinding from faith to meet its audience. Newman's method is completely different. It does not appeal to pure reason or the "demonstrative cogency" of argument. He never suspends personal conviction and his own faith. "He explains, he describes his faith, he never attempts to demonstrate it."[56] And this is so because "his own faith does not rest on arguments."[57] His was a certainty of a certain experience. Newman presupposes in his audience "a beginning of holiness, a cetain intimate realisation of the truths of faith, a first experience of God."[58] And, having come full circle, Bremond insists again that, for this reason, before looking at his doctrine, one must consider Newman's life and devotion out of which his doctrine emerged and which it reflects.

Thus did Bremond draw Newman into the problematic of Modernism as at least a precursor and ally of the Modernist movement. Newman, he says, was a pioneer. "He did not say the last word on the controversies which fill the Christian thought of today, but he foresaw the problem of modern times, and his books help to state it clearly."[59] The antinomy between religious experience and the submission to external authority "exercises the wits at this very time, of the elect of Catholic thinkers."[60] For Newman, "the necessity of solving these apparent antinomies, induced him to open new roads to Catholic thinkers or to give new life to old ideas. Newman's psychology of faith is like an introduction to 'pragmatism' and the philosophy of 'Action'."[61] In presenting Newman thus, Bremond was aware of "the seriousness and force of the objections which scholastics may raise against Newman's philosophy."[62]

Object they did, principally in the person of Jules Lebreton, a Jesuit teaching at the Institut Catholique in Paris. In an article in early 1907, to which Bremond responded, and in a further argument with Bremond's reprisal, Lebreton took exception to Bremond's portrayal of the primacy of conscience in Newman, especially in matters dealing with revealed religion, and hence Catholic faith.[63] We may look briefly at Bremond's apology for the French Newmanists who were principally but not exclusively himself.[64]

The issue raised by Lebreton's criticisms, Bremond says, is whether or not the Newman which he proposes and which scholastics object to is the real Newman or a product of the imagination of those in love with modern ideas.[65] And the kernel of this issue is the primacy of conscience in Newman as he presented it. In response Bremond intensifies his claim. Newman held, he says, that conscience had both a negative and a positive primacy in matters religious. It is a power of investigation or inquiry, of illumination, and of supreme jurisdiction. This was his express and consciously held doctrine.[66] In fact, the primacy of conscience is almost the unicity of conscience as the criterion in dogmatic matters. In effect, Newman said "I would not believe in the truth of (a) principle if I did not find in it a benefit for my moral life." For him a dogma would not be a dogma, not an object of faith at all, "if that truth was not before all else a moral principle, *an ethical principle.*"[67] For much of his evidence, Bremond appeals to the *Grammar of Assent*. The purpose of this book is "to show us that the conscience is the sole means of arriving at a religious knowledge of religious truths."[68] The core of the book is Newman's defense of the illative sense, and "this illative sense is the name which conscience assumes in the search for religious truth."[69]

Bremond concludes with many of the same reflections he made earlier. If the principle of the primacy of consciousness were taken by itself and dealt with as an intellectual axiom, *more scholastico,* it would lead to error and one would end up condemning him. But for Newmam, this was an existential principle, always balanced with the principles of the communion of saints and integral dogmatism. It never occurred to Newman to apply to each dogma the principle or criterion of the primacy of conscience.[70] As for the idea that Bremond was falsifying Newman by making him a precursor of the philosophy of action, Bremond insists again: "If Newman were born sixty years later, he would have written neither the *University Sermons,* nor the *Grammar;* he would have written *L'Action* (of Blondel). This philosophy (of action) furnishes Newmanian thought with the harmonic notes and the explicit justifications which it certainly needs in the light of criticisms of Baudin and de Grandmaison."[71]

Bremond took up his pen again the following year to address doctrinal issues in Newman. His article of 1908, "Autour de Newman," however, is written after the condemnation of Modernism and strikes a different tone than those considered thus far.[72] One of the issues now is whether some of the ideas of Newman were touched by the condemnation. In response Bremond falls back on a now familiar distinction. Some of Newman's ideas, isolated from his life and writings, taken by themselves and with a logic of their own, might lead or come close to the doctrines condemned as Modernist. But in fact Newman was not a systematic theologian; his was not an abstract doctrine but always envisaged the individual, the contingent, the concrete, and the living situation. As a result, all his ideas were proposed with nuances, corrections, and limitations found throughout his large corpus.[73]

As to Newman's relation to the philosophy of action of Blondel, Blondel did not know Newman when he wrote *L'Action*; nor did Laberthonnière when he wrote his early articles. If some of his principal articles cite Newman, these were added afterward on the basis of remarks from a friend, presumably Bremond, who was struck by the similarities between the thought of these two men and introduced Laberthonnière to the *Grammar of Assent.*[74] In general, Bremond plays down the influence of Newman on French thought, at least as regards the apologetic question.[75] It is impossible, he says, to attribute to Newman any direct influence on the evolution of the so-called "new apologetic" and the philosophy of action.[76] "Newman did not dictate *L'Action,* but he sent those loyal to him to the school of Père Laberthonnière and M. Blondel."[77]

Summary of Bremond's Interpretation of Newman

Having surveyed historically how Bremond portrayed the religious thought or philosophy of Newman, we can now summarize that interpretation. There is no doubt that Bremond *interpreted* Newman; he did not undertake an objective historical research project that would have as its goal a precise representation of the meaning and role of conscience in Newman's writings. Rather, he interpreted Newman very broadly and not just implicitly but explicitly brought him into relation with the Modernist movement in France. More specifically he linked Newman's religious thought to that of Blondel and Laberthonnière, and not to that of Loisy.

Several themes run through of the essays of Bremond on Newman, and an enumeration of them may serve to define Bremond's Newman. First and most important of all, I believe, is that Newman is portrayed as an existential thinker. The focus of this thinking itself is the concrete and particular, the individual life lived in quest for truth within a particular situation. Negatively expressed, he was anti-intellectualist, completely at odds methodologically with scholasticism. To remain faithful to this point of view, Newman turned within himself and his own experience and employed a phenomenological method that explored how the human mind, or the whole subject, moved toward religious truth. The quest itself presupposes an openness and desire for religious truth. This openness characterizes the whole of a person, so that the movement toward faith is eminently moral, both in the sense of responsible and in the sense of upright, good, or self-transcending. This moral dimension of the quest for religious truth is a condition for the quest itself and thus part of the structure of religious truth-finding and truth itself.

Bremond sees the existential and moral dimensions of Newman's doctrine as symbolized in the primacy of conscience. In fact, Bremond finds it impossible to exaggerate the claims for the centrality and scope of conscience in Newman. The conscience is a faculty that inquires; it is a power of knowing or recognition; and finally it is both a moral and religious power. Conscience is the supreme judge of both right and wrong, and of religious truth, natural and revealed. Once again, this flows from and reinforces the characterization of Newman as a thinker whose thought focuses on the concrete individual person. It is obvious that Bremond generalizes Newman's view of conscience; he depicts it as conflated with implicit reasoning and the illative sense. The result is that Newman is presented as an experiential theologian, one who saw religious truth resting on experience, but an experience which nevertheless has an inherent and implicit reasonable structure. Conscience really encompasses the whole person and includes instinct, taste, and attention to the good, true, and holy. In the end, conscience becomes so generalized that it is equivalent to the whole anthropological ground for religious experience.

In apologetics, Newman is seen as arguing from faith experience, not prescinding from it and arguing toward it on the basis of reason alone. It is an apologetic that turns first to the interior dynamism of human interiority in order to describe how interiorly human beings move toward religious truth to finally experience it and know it. Consequently, dogmas in Bremond's Newman are expressions of religious experience just as conscience is the basis of religion. Newman is seen reversing the view that would see religious experience and conscience depending on dogma.

But all of this is only one side of Newman, for he also held an extrinsicist notion of dogma and his conscience led him to submit in obedience to the whole of and every single dogma presented to him by Roman Catholic authority. However, this apparent antinomy is merely a tension in Newman's actual life because, as a concrete existential thinker, he did not isolate these elements as two autonomous principles in conflict with each other. They cohered into one. Newman's method of immanence, to speak in French Modernist terms, led to transcendence by an acceptance of church authority. This is Bremond's Newman.

NOTES

1. Henri Bremond, "Autour de Newman," *Annales de Philosophie Chrétienne* 155 (January 1908): 359-60.

2. Jules Lebreton, "Autuor de Newman," *Revue Pratique d'Apologétique* 3 (15 January 1907): 488-504. See p. 488 for a list of authors surveyed.

3. Victor Giraud, in his review of *Newman: Psychologie de la foi* by Henri Bremond, *Annales de Philosophie Chrétienne* 151 (October 1905): 101.

4. This has been done by Maurice Nédoncelle, "Newman selon Bremond ou le procés d'un procés," *Entriens sur Henri Bremond,* sous la direction de Maurice Nédoncelle et Jean Dagens (Paris: Editions Mouton, 1967), 43-59.

5. This shift of "fronts" actually occurred for Blondel and Loisy and Tyrrell. But more generally and symbolically, this double audience or debating partner is important for understanding what is going on in the writings of the whole movement.

6. The category of a paradigm shift is developed by Thomas S. Kuhn, *The Structure of Scientific Revolutions* (Chicago: University of Chicago Press, 1970). An application of the category to this period may be seen in T. H. Sanks, *Authority in the Church: A Study in Changing Paradigms* (Missoula, MT: Scholar's Press, 1974), 103-77. The usefulness of the category is shown by Schillebeeckx's taking it up again to illustrate the changes in perspective that are ocurring in christology. See Edward Schillebeeckx, *Jesus: An Experiment in Christology,* trans. by Hubert Hoskins (New York: The Seabury Press, 1979), 576-82.

7. Gabriel Daly, in his *Transcendence and Immanence: A Study of Catholic Modernism and Integralism* (Oxford: Clarendon Press, 1980), shows the radical difference between the two languages of Roman theology and the Modernist movement. Although it may be said that the two parties did not comprehend each other, still it is also true that most of the Modernists did understand neo-scholasticism since they were brought up on it and moved away from that position.

8. This position was labeled extrinsicist and intellectualist by the Modernists, and it is generally accepted today that this pejorative description was correct.

9. Although this position was labeled subjectivist and immanentist by its opponents, this claim is generally untrue and requires specific testing in each Modernist thinker.

10. Henri Bremond, *Histoire littéraire du sentiment religieux en France,* Vol 1 (Paris: Bloud et Gay, 1929), v-vi. The paraphrase of Bremond's passage in the text is cited from Hogarth, *Henri Bremond: The Life and Work of a Devout Humanist* (London: Society for the Propagation of Christian Knowledge, 1950), 41. A fuller translation of the pertinent elements is the following: "Newman in England and Sainte Beuve in France have brought into vogue another method, moral and religious rather than merely literary. Their main object is to penetrate into a soul's Holy of Holies . . . and the particluar *nuances* of its secret. What such historians would above all know of their Christian poets, preachers, or devotional writers, is the truth of their inner lives, their methods of prayer, their personal individual experience of the realities of which they speak. Of these two methods, I have chosen to follow the second."

11. Hogarth, *Henri Bremond,* 159.

12. André Bremond, "Henri Bremond," *Etudes* 217 (October 1933), 39-40.

13. Nédoncelle, "Newman selon Bremond," 48-49. The specific reference here is to Bremond's work, *Newman: Essai de biographie psychologique* (Paris: Bloud et Gay, 1906). This work was translated into English as *The Mystery of Newman*, trans. by H.C. Corrance and introduction by George Tyrrell (London: Williams and Norgate, 1907). References to this work will be to the English translation. An example of Nédoncelle's observation is Bremond's initial description of Newman as auto-centric, which, Bremond cautions, must be taken in conjunction with other qualities that will be described later on in the work. *Mystery,* viii. Another case in point is the primacy of conscience in Newman's religious philosophy, which we shall discuss at length further on.

14. "I don't think he wrote anything more penetrating, more intelligent, with more strength" (André Bremond, "Henri Bremond," 40).

15. Wilfrid Ward, "Newman through French Spectacles," *The Tablet* 108 (21 July 1906): 86-89. In this article Ward attacks Bremond for failing to cite a text of Newman on the development of doctrine correctly and thus for misinterpreting him. The work in question, on the development of doctrine, will be considered further on. Along the way he says that Bremond as a foreigner did not understand the subtlety of Newman's style and use of English. Bremond failed "to understand the man of whom he writes" (89). The whole motive of the outburst is the explicitly confessed fear that Newman will be associated with a group of so-called "Liberal Catholics" who stand apart within the church. He is afraid that Newman's theory of development will be construed as impugning "the unchangeableness of God's truth" (89). George Tyrrell responded to Ward in "Newman Through French Spectacles—A Reply," *The Tablet* 108 (4 August 1906), 163-65, under the pseudonym Francophil. In it he takes Ward to task in his ironical way and defends Bremond by arguing that his interpretation of Newman is substantially correct. A year later, in "Two Views of Cardinal Newman," *Dublin Review* 282 (July 1907): 1-15, Ward again attacks Bremond, this time regarding the biographical accuracy of his portrait of Newman in *The Mystery of Newman* which had just appeared in England.

16. References to this article will be to its republication as "La Logique du coeur: M. Brunetière et 'l'irrationnel' de la foi," *L'Inquiétude religieuse* 1 (Paris: Perrin et Cie., 1901): 91-130.

17. Ibid., 109.

18. Ibid., 116.

19. Ibid., 91, n. 1. Thus the association is here made by a denial of one.

20. Ibid., 103.

21. Ibid., 130.

22. Ibid., 128, n. 1.

23. Henri Bremond, *Newman: Le développement du dogme chrétien* (Paris: Librairie Bloud et Cie., 1904). References here are to the second edition, 1905.

24. Ibid., 3.

25. Ibid., 4.

26. Ibid.

27. Ibid.

28. Henri Bremond, *Newman* Vol II (*Psychologie de la foi*) (Paris: Librairie Bloud et Cie., 1905).

29. Ibid., esp. 35-36, 40-41.

30. Ibid., 356-57, note 2.

31. Cf. Note 13. Bremond published two articles at the end of 1905 preparatory to his psychological biography of Newman of 1906. These are "La Première conversion de Newman," *Annales de Philosophie Chrétienne* 151 (November 1905): 160-179; "Mémoire et dévotion: Etude sur la psychologie religieuse de Newman," *Annales de Philosophie Chrétienne* 151 (December 1905): 259-70.

32. Hogarth, *Henri Bremond*, 6.

33. Bremond, *Mystery*, 329.

34. Ibid., 330-31.

35. Ibid., 336.

36. Ibid., 333.

37. Ibid., 334.

38. Ibid., 333.

39. Ibid.

40. Ibid., 332. Bremond even conjectures that Newman read Schleiermacher (334, n. 20). It should be noted that for Bremond, Schleiermacher symbolizes "personal" in the direction of "individual" experience, and thus wrongly, since for Schleiermacher doctrine is based on the experience of the church community.

41. Ibid., 333.

42. Ibid., 335.

43. Ibid., 336.

44. Ibid., 337.

45. Ibid., 337-45.

46. Ibid., 344.

47. Ibid., 343-45.

48. Ibid., 329.

49. Henri Bremond, "Apologie pour les newmanistes français," *Revue Pratique d'Apologétique* 3 (1 March 1907): 659.

50. Bremond, *Mystery*, 348-49. This thesis of Bremond is followed by a series of texts from Newman illustrating its several points.

51. Ibid., 352.

52. Ibid., 350-52. Bremond sees the first two of Newman's principles governing the *Oxford University Sermons* while the third is dominant in the *Essay on Development* (*Mystery,* 352. n. 1). A similar analysis was seen and proposed by Tyrrell in 1905 in "The Limits of the Theory of Development," *Catholic World* 81 (September 1905): 730-44, and reprinted in *Through Scylla and Charybdis* (London: Longmans, Green & Co., 1907), 133-54.

53. Bremond, *Mystery,* 350-52.

54. Ibid., 332. But they were reconciled existentially.

55. Apologetics deals with the structure of one's coming to religious truth and faith. Its significance lies in the faet that this structure or logic of argument is in turn a hermeneutical principle for interpreting the kind or nature of the turth involved.

56. Bremond, *Mystery,* 356.

57. Ibid., 357.

58. Ibid., 358.

59. Ibid., 327.

60. Ibid., 350.

61. Ibid., 332. Tyrrell published an article on pragmatism in the journal on which Blondel (owner), Laberthonnière (editor), and Bremond collaborated: "Notre attitude en face du pragmatisme," *Annales de Philosophie Chrétienne* 151 (December 1905): 225-32. Reprinted in *Throught Scylla and Charybdis,* 191-99. Tyrrell refers to W. James and F. W. Schiller. But Blondel also referred to his philosophy as pragmatism.

62. Bremond, *Mystery,* 327.

63. Jules Lebreton,"Autour de Newman," 488-504; Henri Bremond, "Apologie pour les newmanistes français," *Revue Pratique d'Apologétique* 3 (1 March 1907), 655-66; Jules Lebreton, "Le Primat de la conscience d'après Newman," *Revue Pratique d'Apologétique* 3(1 March 1907), 667-75. These last two articles are followed by an exchange of letters, pp. 676-78. The fourth book on Newman, edited by Bremond, is *Newman: La vie chrétienne* (Paris: Bloud et Gay, 1906). It is not relevant to this theological study.

64. Another was Ernest Dimnet, who wrote *La Pensée catholique dans l'Angleterre contemporaire* (Paris: Librairie Victor Lecoffre, 1906) which contains a chapter on Newman entitled "Le Voyant," pp. 73-129. Also Emile Baudin published *La Philosophie de la foi chez Newman* (Montligeon [Orne]: Librairie de Montligeon, 1906) which collects his series of articles of the same title in *Revue de Philosophie* 6 (June-October 1906). Also the article of P. de Grandmaison, "John Henry Newman considére comme maître," *Etudes* (20 December 1906), was taken by Bremond as favoring his interpretation of Newman.

65. Bremond, "Apologie pour les newmanistes français," 655.

66. Ibid., 660.

67. Ibid., 662. This is stated relative to a specific dogma, that of apostolic succession.

68. Ibid., 663-64.

69. Ibid., 664.

136

70. Ibid., 664-65.

71. Ibid., 665, n. 2. The criticisms were of Newman.

72. Bremond, "Autour de Newman," 337-69.

73. Ibid., 342-47. A case in point was proposition 25 condemned by the syllabus of errors, *Lamentabili:* "Assensus fidei ultimo innititur in congerie probabilitatum." *Enchiridion Symbolorum,* edited by Denzinger and Schönmetzer (New York: Herder, 1963, 671.

74. Ibid., 359 and n. 1.

75. Bremond does not mention Loisy's use of Newman's ideas, especially regarding development.

76. Bremond, "Autour de Newman," 364.

77. Ibid., 365.

7

Was Loisy Newman's Modern Disciple?

Ronald Burke

There was great difference between the faith of John Henry Cardinal Newman (1801-1890) and that of Alfred Firmin Loisy (1857-1940). From the time of Newman's "inward conversion" at fifteen, he developed increasing trust in a personal creator and strong affirmation of the Catholic ecclesiastical tradition. Loisy, on the other hand, developed a more "mystical" faith in a less personal God[1] and practical trust in a scholarly historical-critical method quite independent of the church's authority.[2] Such differences, in the respective historical settings they occurred, helped one to be named a cardinal of the church and the other to receive its most severe excommunication.

Although convert Newman was the subject of considerable mistrust and ecclesiastical opposition, the cardinal's hat seemed to lift from his head previous clouds of suspicion.[3] The ideas of the priest-critic from the farmlands of France, on the other hand, were more insistently opposed by authorities in the church. He was made a *bête noir* of Catholicism: his books were forbidden, his "modernism" was condemned, and he was himself finally excommunicated as *vitandus*—"to be avoided by faithful Catholics under threat of their own excommunication."[4] Prima facie, Loisy and Newman were unrelated opposites.

Though different in many ways, the greatest difference between these two theological giants of the nineteenth and twentieth centuries was that they stood on opposing sides of an "attitudinal divide" in Catholic history. Despite his independence and innovations, Newman was "pre-modern." A man of intense traditional piety, he was not at all infatuated with the idea of progress in history and evolution. He idealized not the future church but the church of the ancient past. Admitting change but not encouraging it, he was thoroughly submissive to the hierarchically organized authority of the church. Loisy, to the contrary, was quite "modern." He did idealize progress, the future, and personal responsibility. He struggled doggedly against (excesses in?) ecclesiastical authority. Champion of scientific freedom, he protested the calcification and procrustean use of ancient dogma.

Because of their differences and because of the previous dearth of hard evidence, there have heretofore been no extended studies of the relationship between Loisy and Newman.[5] There have been only passing comments on the topic, originally from persons attempting to defend or attack one or other of the men.

Originally there was controversy as to Newman's orthodoxy. In France, soon after the publication of Newman's *An Essay on the Development of Doctrine*, some shared the opinion of Englishman James Mosely that the new convert was a rationalist. Philosopher Emile Saisset wrote in 1848:

> We should be very sorry to cloud the joy of those who are now hailing the conversion of Mr. Newman, but we advise them not to be too triumphant. That Rome should receive with honor a theologian of such worth and virtue is worthy of her policy and her maternal indulgence, but whether she knows it or not, in absolving Pusey's disciple she is granting an amnesty to rationalism.[6]

The majority opinion, however, opposed the accusation of rationalism in Newman. This opinion was reflected in the words of a future archbishop of Paris, Abbé G. Darboy. He found the *Essay* to be a fine work of faith, basis for an appropriate philosophy of church history, and bringing new light to the understanding of Catholic dogma.[7]

Of later importance was the question of the Newman-Loisy relationship. Accepting the majority view of Newman, the moderate Jesuit, Leonce de Grandmaison (1868-1947) himself feared Loisy "deviated a bit from the ideas of Newman."[8] Much more radical was the opinion of a one-time friend of Loisy, Albert Houtin, who had become an atheist. He claimed Loisy only used Newman's respected name to hide the rationalistic character of his own ecclesiastical ideas.[9] Loisy's enduring friend and defender, however, Henri Bremond (1865-1933), emphasized that Loisy had been authentically "inspired by Newman's work."[10] This notion of a fundamental sameness between the views of Newman and Loisy is more recently repeated by Bernard Holland in his claim that in Loisy's life Newman's work "fell in with and accelerated the line of thought that Loisy was already pursuing."[11] Similarly, Heinrich J. Holtzmann found Newman's idea of development (or "germination") crucial to explaining why people like Loisy continued their apologetical efforts and their allegiance to Rome.[12] Emile Poulat reminds us, however, that if Loisy did come into general accord with Newman, it was not because he always had been there. As

Loisy himself had pointed out, his favorite reading, previous to Newman, had been the apostate orientalist Ernest Renan (1823-1894).[13]

How great was the similarity and how close the relationship between Loisy and Newman? Was one, both, or neither properly criticized for rationalism? The supposition of this paper is that the most important evidence in judging Loisy's similarity to Newman is his theological *magnum opus*, the largely (and regrettably) unpublished apologetic *Essais d'histoire et de philosophie religieuses*.[14] This document, read in the context of Loisy's other writings, the story of his life, and his later condemnations by the church, is very informative. From it three hypotheses can be offered in explanation of the relationship of Loisy to Newman.

1. From the time he was eighteen years of age, Alfred Loisy sincerely struggled to overcome modern challenges to the legitimacy of Catholic faith.
2. Newman's writings offered Loisy models of illative faith and doctrinal development, with which he could explain Christian revelation in ways more suited to modern questions and experience.
3. Loisy's theory of revelation was more decisively "modern" than Newman's work, but nonetheless authentically Roman Catholic.

I

Loisy read the English cardinal's writings and got to know them well during a telling time in his life. As is evidenced in correspondence with his friend, Baron Friedrich von Hügel, in September 1896 he asked that seven of Newman's books be brought to him. They were within six weeks.[15] Two years later, on 1 December 1898, Loisy published an article on one of these ground-breaking books, "Le Developpement chretien d'apres le Cardinal Newman."[16] In this commentary on Newman's *Essay on Development*, Loisy showed a lucid and balanced grasp of Newman's thought, one "far superior to that of many subsequent commentators."[17]

Loisy not only understood well the idea of development in Newman's work. He also evaluated it very highly. There is no Catholic author to whom Loisy ever gave higher praise. He found Newman to be the most "open" theologian since Origen, open to the facts of history, reality both inside and outside the church.[18] Newman realized the developmental character of religion, saw the datedness of many scholastic categories, and criticized the illusory character of Protestant individualism.

Only two things were lacking to Newman in Loisy's view. First of all, he applied the model of development only to the history of doctrine and not to its origin in revelation. He seemed too willing to see revelation as an extraneous reality, something which broke violently (i.e., supernaturally) and fully developed into human history.[19] Newman saw revelation this way even though his notions of doctrinal development and of the "illative sense" of moral certitude provided basis for a more developmental and intuitive model of revelation.[20]

The second thing lacking to Newman, the only thing "truly lacking," Loisy wrote, was that he "had no disciples."[21] Was Loisy now to assume this role?

It has already been stated that Loisy read Newman's works at a time of crisis in his own career. Although almost forty years old, he was at an important turning point in his life. The child of French peasants, headed for the seminary by the time he was sixteen, he was ordained to the priesthood at age twenty-two (with a special papal dispensation required because of his young age). Even before his ordination, in the early seminary days of 1875 (eighteen years old), he claimed to have been thrown into prolonged "intellectual disturbance" by some of the teachings of the church. He was unwilling or unable to accept the church's teachings based simply on traditional authority. Because he wanted some further confirmation of these teachings, he was haunted with the question of whether there was any reality at all which corresponded to the church's doctrines.[22]

Loisy's intelligence allowed him to be sent on from the local seminary, at age twenty-two, for higher studies at the Institute Catholique in Paris. There he met the Institute's historian, Abbé Louis Duchesne, and, even more important, he met a surprisingly new way by which to approach the authority of traditional doctrines: through the historical and critical examination of the Bible.

Loisy discovered the human and historical character of the Bible. He found historical and geographical errors, unavoidable contradictions, and developing ideas. These discoveries contradicted the view of the Bible Loisy had been given in his childhood and seminary days, a view that claimed the Bible to be perfect and unchanging. Enthusiastically he employed the new, historical perspective on the Bible.

At twenty-six he proposed a dissertation to explain in an affirmative way the concept of scriptural inspiration. His idea was that inspiration is always history-dependent, always culturally "relative." Inspiration does not extract the author from the vocabulary and world view, the grammar and shortcomings of the times. Yet in this milieu, inspiration *does* allow the

142

author to express the best and highest moral and theological ideas then possible. These ideas would demand in later times further clarification and correction, but that was the task of later days and exemplified the developmental character of the Catholic tradition.[23]

The Institute's director convinced Loisy the dissertation was too dangerous to submit: the affirmation of historical relativity in inspiration contradicted the scholastic emphasis upon the ahistorical and supernatural truthfulness of scriptural propositions. In this encounter, Loisy's struggle to introduce the church to a more modern and history-conscious view of the past met an early defeat.[24]

Loisy remained at the Institute for another nine years, teaching the noncontroversial subjects of Hebrew and Assyriology and publishing extensively.[25] Another controversy arose regarding the historical character of scripture. Loisy became involved and this time he was cursorily dismissed. As a result, in 1894, Loisy was reassigned or, better, "demoted." He was appointed chaplain at a girls' high school in a suburb of Paris (Neuilly). A decisive period in his life thus began.

What was Loisy's faith? At this time of demotion and defeat, prior to studying Newman's work, he was still celebrating daily Mass, teaching catechism and scripture to the girls, delivering homilies, and hearing confessions of the nuns. Yet the questions of early seminary days had matured and his faith was quite different from that of his early youth:

> I never regained the simple faith of my childhood, nor could
> I accept literally a single article of the creed, unless it was
> that Jesus was 'crucified under Pontius Pilate.'

These are surprising words to comprise the self-described faith of a Catholic priest! Three explanations have been proposed. First, some such as Albert Houtin claim the words to reflect clearly the fact that Loisy was an imposter as priest.[26] Gabriel Daly, in a conflicting opinion, claims that here Loisy is "reading back" into earlier days a more skeptical attitude that in fact developed only after his excommunication.[27] Allowing for much accuracy in Daly's claim, this author would argue a third possibility: read in the full-life context of this faith-practicing priest, these words accurately depict only a *portion* of Loisy's faith. For he goes on immediately to write:

> Religion appeared to me more and more in the light of a
> tremendous Force (*la grande puissance*) that had dominated,
> and still was dominant in, the whole of human history. All its

143

manifestations had their abuses; still they represented practically the summed-up moral endeavor of the human race. The Christian religion, a continuation of that of Israel, was distinguished among all others by the loftiness of its ideas. The Catholic church was the spiritual mother of the European peoples, fallen indeed from her former estate, but still influential, and still potentially mistress of her future. If she could only *learn to speak intelligibly to the modern people* [italics added], no hostile power could prevail against her. To that Church, in spite of all she made me suffer, I remained sincerely attached.[28]

It is not impossible that all these words came from an historian of considerable genius who had recently been demoted and yet remained authentically Catholic. He had strong faith in some inexplicable "Force" in human history. Like all saints and mystics of the tradition, he saw the sinfulness in all of history's religions, shortcomings in all doctrines and understandings of God. He found not only a human sinfulness but also a historical relativity in Catholic scriptures and in the Catholic creed. And despite all the flaws and weaknesses in the Roman Catholic church, he wished to help that church speak the gospel intelligibly to people of modern times.

Already familiar with the Enlightenment and with liberal Protestantism,[29] he was disenchanted with tradition's Hellenistic-scholastic formulations of faith in the "supernatural." He described his own inchoate faith in 1893 as a kind of "evolutionary pantheism." But in that still-developing faith he remained seriously dedicated to a church that was to aid the morality and evolving history of humanity. His lament, intensified by his own demotion, was that the church refused to speak in ways intelligible to educated people of the day.

It was at this time of crisis that Loisy requested and read the writings of Cardinal Newman. "I studied them exhaustively. Newman's type of mind attracted me far more than did that of Protestant theologians."[30]

At the heart of Cardinal Newman's work Loisy found the notion of divinely intended historical development. The fact of development, previously denied in the church, here was admitted and more officially affirmed. Within three months of receiving Newman's works, in January 1897, Loisy was jotting down daily notes with which to compose a new defense of Catholicism. In this apologetic (*Essais d'histoire et de philosophie religieuses*) and in the books which followed immediately upon it (*L'Evangile et l'Eglise* and *Autour d'un petit livre*)[31] Loisy changed. He moved away from Renan's type of "evolutionary pantheism" and toward an "incarnational theism" more like Newman's. He pictured the "tremendous Force" in human history not as accidental but as intentional, transcendent, and present to human life. At least on the basis of circumstantial evidence, Newman's writings were responsible for a turn in Loisy's path. Both the timing and the content of the apologetic suggest, as Bremond put it, that Loisy was "inspired by Newman's writings." He changed from an evolutionary to an incarnational perspective.

II

There can be little doubt that Loisy found affinity with Newman. Houtin claims the affinity was but a facade, Loisy claiming Newman as a patron only so that under the authority of the cardinal's name the tactician at Neuilly could conceal his own atheistic ideas.[32] Yet this interpretation conflicts with a number of points. Although anti-dogmatic, Loisy was not atheistic. He retained a "mystical faith." He did not hide behind Newman, but criticized directly his failings (e.g., his supernaturalistic idea of revelation).[33] The judgment of Loisy's friend, Henri Bremond, seems more accurate, that Loisy was inspired by Newman. Most important evidence is Loisy's own consistent testimony and his writings of the time.

In his *Memoires* Loisy claims to have been influenced philosophically by only two men, Renan and Newman.[34] In a substantiating note from twenty-eight years before,[35] he describes 1881-1893 as years in which he was in an ongoing mental debate with things Renan had written. Then, from 1894 to 1900, it was with Newman, "appropriately expanded" (*passablement elargi*), that he struggled against the excesses of modern atheism and (liberal) Protestant theologians.

Loisy felt he had found a true ally in Newman, one who offered the church an improved way to speak to people of the day. Even though Newman himself needed further to be modernized (*passablement elargi*), he was an aid to Loisy and an influence upon him in articulating his Catholic faith to Protestants, the Holy Office, and unbelievers alike.[36] The alliance continued until the spring of 1904 when Loisy was finally overwhelmed by hierarchical opposition, ceased his Modernist efforts to reform the church, possibly suffered a nervous breakdown,[37] and terminated the Roman Catholic segment of his lengthy academic career.

As already suggested, before his excommunication, Loisy turned his notes on Newman into a lengthy, important, and largely unpublished defense and correction of Catholicism, the apologetic entitled *Essais d'histoire et de philosophie religieuses* (1898-1899).[38] The first section

145

of the *Essais* was soon published (note 16) as commentary on Newman's idea of the development of Christianity.

As Loisy emphasized in comparing Newman to Origen, Newman realized that the church developed in history. Christianity and its doctrines, Newman had claimed, develop like an idea in the mind of a community. It was this hypothesis of development, in contrast with traditional emphasis upon *semper eadem,* that provided Loisy with a way of understanding and articulating his own idea of the fundamental theological concept, revelation.

Revelation, like inspiration, had been a problem for Loisy. The notion of a "supernatural" God who occasionally intervened in "natural" human history to bestow special knowledge upon selected members of the race seemed inconsistent with the data of history and with the demands of an acceptable (modern) philosophy. What Newman provided with his ideas of the "development" of dogma and an "intuitive sense" at the foundation of morality and faith was a new model for understanding revelation.

The importance and difficulty Loisy had found to reside in the concept of revelation is presented early in his *Essais.* He wanted to preserve the "dignity" of revelation, but knew that could not be done by describing it in terms that would be dismissed by educated people of the day:

> The dignity of revelation does not demand we make of it an artificial mechanism that cannot be conceived philosophically. . . . Just as scientific doctrines originate from previous notions and progress results from new combinations of old ideas (perceived by the scientific genius who lights up the relationship of things more satisfactorily), so also the fertile truths of religion, constituting the substance of revelation, are formed through the conjunction of preexistant ideas and images.[39]

Previously such a developmental explanation of revelation was at most implicit and perhaps impossible in the Catholic church. But Newman's work with doctrine had shown that "development" was a historical reality, one that was *compatible* with faith.

Loisy felt that Newman had known, like himself, that new ways had to be found in which to address the people of modern days:

> It never occurred to him [Newman] that he was acting rashly in offering traditional theology assistance which it had not requested. He only knew that 'Catholicism ran the risk of

146

having a new world to conquer without possessing weapons for the warfare.'[40]

Newman wanted to provide theology with the wisdom and weapons of modern sciences, sciences that recognized change. Yet the challenge of scholarship had intensified since Newman's time. Great progress had been made in the scientific and historical knowledge of Christian origins, as well as of the origins and history of all humanity and religions. That was why Loisy felt that Newman's theory of development needed now to be expanded. It had to consider not only the later development but also the very origins of religions and, particularly, the concept of revelation.

Loisy's effort was not to contradict Newman's work, but to be its continuation. It would be thanks to Newman, after all, that the model of development and intuition could be used to speak more intelligently of religion's origin in revelation to people of the modern world.[41] But was the notion still Catholic?

Was Loisy's explanation of revelation only Renan's Enlightenment immanentism ("evolutionary pantheism") or was it comparable to Newman's constant and foundational affirmation of a transcendent God who identified himself with humanity (an "incarnational theism")?

Newman's language offered Loisy the beginnings of an alternative to scholastic vocabulary with which to articulate revelation and faith. Not presented in the context of university dialogue, not systematically developed, the intuitive and developmental model of revelation is inchoate in the *Essais*. The *Essais* contained an idea, Poulat has said, "in possession of itself," but not yet in possession "of its own expression."[42]

Loisy wanted to return to a biblical worldview—prior to any notion of "nature *vs.* supernatural." He spoke of the history of religions and of Christian revelation in developmental terms: religions evolve, important revisions are honored as "revelations," and great religions slowly "increase their vitality" and "broaden their influence." As in the biblical worldview, God is a Mystery intimately involved in all of this development and life.[43]

For Loisy, enlightenment rationalism is inadequate to explain revelation and faith. There is more than an immanent power or human reason at work.

> The truths of revelation are alive in faith long before they are analyzed into the speculations of doctrine. Their native form is a supernatural *intuition* [italics added] and a practical affirmation, not an abstract consideration and systematic definition. On the intellectual side, revelation does involve notions and judgments

that the supernatural action of God has *suggested* [italics added] to those God has chosen as organs of his manifestation to humanity. These notions and judgments do not result from a purely rational work or human thought of religious subjects. . . . They are not a fruit of reason alone. They would be unintelligible if they did not take the form of human concepts, but the concept is not simply the logical conclusion of reasearch and reason. It is proposed as the symbol of eternal truth which surpasses all created intelligence and a superior light penetrates even this symbol to render it somehow clear and effective.[44]

Loisy tried not to abandon either reason or faith, modernity or tradition. He settled for neither rationalism nor fideism. He spoke of the supernatural in more subtle terms, suggesting its influence as *intuition* and *suggestion.*

Loisy attempted to speak a modern language of faith. He did not want to speak of God as a world-interrupting Force. But neither did he claim that revelation was the result of a godless evolution. He wanted to say that there is a Force at work, perceivable with the eyes of faith in the human community and its history, a Force more potent than things cosmic, finite, or human. Hence he wrote of the presence of "la grande puissance," a transcendent power in which humans somehow are allowed to share.

In their minds and hearts, in thoughts and deeds of faith, people participate in something higher than their "natural" selves. It is this participation in something transcendent which is the source of revelation, as it is of doctrine, dogma, morality, and religion.

Loisy claimed there is intimately present to all humanity a transcendent Mystery. With an undeveloped christology, Loisy claims this presence was best manifest in the life and teachings of Jesus. It is a presence and mystery that offers to all humanity an ability for self-transcendence and an intuitive, "primitive revelation."

This primitive revelation has never been fully specified in a formal doctrine. It is a revelation that mankind bears in depths of its religious consciousness, written in indistinct characters. The sole article that constitutes this unexplained revelation is that God reveals Himself to man in man, that humanity enters with God into a Divine association *(rapport).* Jesus manifested this reality in Himself in his life and teachings.[45]

It is this association with God, this presence of the transcendent, that Loisy claimed to be the foundational revelation. This presence allows people to trust in reality despite the apparent dearth of reward, to exercise the gift of self-transcendence despite the risk of change. It is this same presence which gives birth, then, to faith in a God of love and to faith's expression in worship, doctrine, polity, and in propositional revelation.

> It is God and not man that is the source of revelation: revelation is realized in man, but as the work of God in him, with him, and through him. . . . It is man who searches, but God who incites; man who sees, but God who enlightens.[46]

These are not the words of atheist, rationalist, or heretic. Historian Loisy finds a gift and direction in human life which cannot be explained by chance and natural evolution. There is something more at work:

> The perception of religious truth is not a fruit of human reason alone. It is a work of intelligence, but executed under pressure (so to speak) of the heart. This whole work which ends in a more and more perfect result of Israelite and Christian religion, . . . This revelation is not so much the work of *man* regarding God as the work of *God* on and with man.[47]

Reason alone does not suffice to explain revelation. There is something more, something like Pascal's *espirit de finess,* something more than historical and human. Revelation develops, not by accident but by design. It develops in humanity. It develops from the experience of God's empowering presence. This powerful presence in human life cannot be reduced to chemicals, chromosomes, or any other measurable quantity. The power is God, and God as present to and transcendent of man.

> It is necessary, if we do not wish to renounce both sound philosophy and fundamental principles of religion, to maintain the essential distinction of God and man. Retaining this distinction and looking to revelation's origin, it is the action of God, transcendent and immanent to the soul, ... The purely rational conclusions that man can draw by his intelligence from contemplation of the universe are *not* revelation. They are but facts, impressions, and vehicles that prepare or accompany revelation.[48]

Roman Catholic Loisy was not a rationalist. He had faith in a force that made his *Essais*, like the writings of Newman, an instance of "incarnational theism." A transcendent power, explainable in no better terms than "God," is experienced as present in human life.

Even well-qualified and recent authors have given too little space to this "transcendent force" in Loisy's *Essais*. In his few words regarding Loisy, Roger Aubert gives him credit for bringing attention to Newman in France. But he suggests Loisy failed to consider the critical difference between an outwardly determined "evolution" and an inwardly predetermined *developpement vital*.[49] In fact this was not overlooked in Loisy's *Essais*. Thought it was difficult for Loisy to answer the problem in the language of the times, without returning to supernatural violations of the natural causal continuum, he tried to solve this problem with words regarding the transcendent's presence in humanity: an incarnational theism.

Loisy did more than assert this incarnational theism. He attempted to substantiate his claim in human experience. With references to peoples' ability for maturation and growth, their capacity for self-sacrifice and purity of heart, he attempted to evoke an aesthetic and experiential confirmation of Mystery's presence. In his *Essais* he sought to show that the one world religion which claimed God's incarnation was also the one religion whose doctrine was most explanatory of human experience. By using developmental language, pressed back to the very beginnings of religions, Loisy wanted to elicit from modern people both a faith in revelation and a renewed appreciation of their own capacity for duty, heroism, self-transcendence, and honor. Both were to be explained by the reality of a transcendent God incarnate to human life.

Almost everything else in the lengthy *Essais* is an implication of Loisy's idea of revelation. All legitimate morality, religion, theology, and revelation are *developing* expressions of the *illative* human experience of God's fundamental presence at the core of human existence. Although Newman's terms are not often cited, the model comes from his work.

Because of the value of development, true religion must always be open to change, seeking always and anew to "raise man above himself, to uproot his passions, egotism, and adoration of his own reason." For if a religion became too enamored with its own particular form of piety, truth, and justice, it would constitute an obstacle to religious and moral progress for its members.[50] Indeed, excessive conservatism does not preserve the value of Christianity but can become a most subtle and threatening kind of heresy.[51] Although he was an historian, Loisy's fascination and hope lay not with the past. His theological confidence in God's presence to humanity guaranteed a better future.

We must look to the past only to ensure that nothing worth saving is lost. . . . We must look toward the future and prepare for it because the future will achieve what we regret is absent in the present.[52]

III

Loisy's idea of revelation was not a discardable aberration in the Catholic tradition. It was a precursor of Vatican II and of a prominent theology in contemporary Catholic thought, transcendental Thomism. Karl Rahner, S.J., (1904-1984) has written an incarnational, intuitional, and developmental theory of revelation. The self-communication of God empowers all human hearts with a capacity for self-transcendence. This incarnational presence also offers to human reflection an indistinct, intuitive revelation. What Loisy called "primitive" revelation, Rahner called "transcendental." From this single experiential basis, Rahner proposed, develops a variety of religions and—with historical correlations—the Bible and dogma of the Catholic tradition, called "categorical" revelation.[53]

Despite the strong similarity, it would be excessive to suggest Loisy's primitive intuitional revelation was a direct precursor to Rahner's idea of transcendental and categorical revelation. Neither Rahner nor any of his students has ever assigned any credit for the idea of transcendental revelation to *vitandus* Loisy (or to Cardinal Newman). Indeed the idea may well have come to Rahner from other sources.[54] The idea of "primitive" revelation may be a ready blend of modernity's intellectual atmosphere and the continuation of the Catholic tradition. If this is so, neither can there be claim that Newman's influence upon Loisy was exclusive. Yet the timing and the content of what Loisy wrote in his ultimate effort in Catholic apologetics is sufficient to show Loisy attempting to be, for a time, Newman's modern disciple.

One question lingers. Did Loisy faithfully extend or in fact defile the faith of the Oratorian genius? Did not Loisy embody the very liberalism Newman opposed throughout his life?

Newman reverenced the past, the ancient church, and the Fathers. Loisy reverenced more the future, the process and movement born in the past but promising a finer day. Both did oppose the excesses of scholasticism, its penchant for abstractions and definitions, its distance from experience and history. Whether he intended it or not, Newman began a revolution in theology, but with only a *willingness to take seriously the changes* that had occurred both inside and outside the Catholic church. In his willingness

151

Newman retained worship of a personal, triune, and intervening God, reverence for a sacred moment in the past, and strong commitment to the historical moment in which a living idea was first conceived, the "idea" and revelation of Christianity.

Newman was at most willing—if need be—to accept change in the Christian tradition. In his reflective religious quest he sought the church which had experienced the *least* change since the time of antiquity. And even in the Roman Catholic church he found change to be a difficulty which required a book-length hypothesis to serve for an explanation. For Newman, change could at best be tolerated.

Much more than Newman, Loisy affirmed the value of change. With more of the spirit of the Enlightment, he thirsted for change, finding it long overdue in the (Post-Reformation) Catholic tradition. The responsibility of the church was not merely to tolerate change as a necessary evil. With God-assisted human effort, the church must seek with passion and patience the most honest form of truth available at the time, trying always to "disengage the substance of truth from its superannuated forms." Development and change were the story of the church, from the first moment that the presence of God was experienced and then expressed in human history. Though Newman might have seen absence of change as a blessing, Loisy saw it as a fault. With Newman's example, he saw development as not only tolerable but essential in a church too militantly dedicated to being "forever the same."

Loisy's faith, then, was not the same as Newman's. A generation apart, they stood on opposite sides of the shift from classical to modern times. Struggling for a viable modern theology. Loisy claimed that God is active in the world through natural causes. As he wrote early in the *Essais:*

> At the source of everything there is a secret and all powerful
> Force that reason can neither discern nor examine, one that
> only faith knows and decisively affirms. Eyes of faith are
> essential to the revelation of God.

Loisy learned much from Newman but was indeed—for praise or blame —more modern and more alone. For personal or church's fault, his ideas were left incomplete. He did not develop in his theory of revelation the strong christology which confirms the orthodoxy of Rahner's idea of revelation. Yet in his struggle to articulate in modern form a viable theory of Christian revelation, Loisy did maintain a profound reverence for the mystic's God, an abiding distinction between God and man, and a

152

fundamental assertion of God's presence in human life. It was the presence of God which founded his confidence in change. As such, and despite their differences, Loisy was himself a modern Catholic "development," a modern disciple of Cardinal Newman.

1. See Raymond de Boyer de Sainte Suzanne's *Alfred Loisy: Entre la foi et l'incroyance* (Paris: Centurion, 1968).

2. Was Loisy ever a person of sincere and authentic Roman Catholic faith? If so, when and for how long? For a survey of judgments on these questions, see Ronald Burke, "Losiy's Faith: Landshift in Catholic Thought," *Journal of Religion* 60 (1980): 138-64. Even more recently, Emile Poulat points out the controversy is not so much about "the facts" as a question of what subtle and almost indecipherable attitudes and feelings were in the minds and hearts of Loisy and his opponents. See Poulat's *Modernistica* (Paris: Nouvelles Editions Latines, 1982), 292. See also Poulat's *Critique et mystique. Autour de Loisy ou la conscience catholique et e'espirit moderne* (Paris: Editions du Centurion, 1984).

3. Wilfrid Ward, *The Life of John Henry Cardinal Newman*, vol 2 (London: Longman's Green, 1912), 438.

4. The two most important books regarding Alfred Loisy are both by Emile Poulat: *Histoire, dogme et critique dans la crise moderniste* (Paris: Casterman, 1979, orig. 1962) and *Alfred Loisy. Sa vie, son oeuvre, par Albert Houtin et Felix Sartiaux* (Paris: Éditions du Centre National de la Recherch Scientifique, 1960). Also very important are Alec Vidler's *A Variety of Catholic Modernists* (Cambridge: University Press, 1970) and Thomas Loome's *Liberal Catholicism, Reform Catholicism, Modernism* (Mainz: Matthias-Gruenewald-Verlag, 1979), Loome's criticisms of Loisy are sometimes more personal than clearly professional.

5. See, for example, *The Rediscovery of Newman: an Oxford Symposium*, ed. by Johannes Artz (Mainz: Matthias-Gruenewald, 1975); and B.M.G. Reardon's "Newman and the Catholic Modernists" in *Church Quarterly Review* 4 (1971): 50-60.

6. "De l'origine et de la formation du Christianisme, a l'occasion du livre de M. Newman," in *La Liberte'de penser* 15 (March 1848): 337-57.

7. "Comment y a-t-il progres doctrinal dans le catholicisme?", *Correspondant* 23 (1848): 281-93.

8. "L'Evangil et l'Eglise," in *Etudes* 94 (1903): 155.

9. The scholarly world still awaits a more definitive judgment on Loisy's faith and Houtin's disparagement of it. The leading authority on the topic is Emile Poulat. See notes 2 and 4 above.

10. Newman, *Le Développement du dogme chretien* (Paris: Librairie Bloud et Cie, 1907), xxvii. In other writings, Bremond goes on to affirm Loisy's positive influence upon his own faith. See André Blanchet's "L'Abbe Bremond: quelques traits pour un partrait futur," in *Entretiens sur Henri Bremond*, ed. Maurice Nédoncelle and Jean Dagens (Paris: Mouton, 1967): 15, and the *Bremond-Blondel Correspondance*, ed André Blanchet, 3 vol. (Paris: Aubier Montagne, 1970-71), 1: 386-87.

11. *Baron Friedrich von Hügel: Selected Letters* (London: J.M. Dent and Sons, Ltd., 1928) 16.

12. "Thus we arrive at the famous theory of germination, which since Cardinal Newman's *Development of Doctrine* (1845) forms the first and last means of understanding the great enigmas of history, but also and especially forms the philosophical justification for the continued allegiance which Reform Catholicism—so often disavowed by Rome—pays and will pay to this same Rome." *Protestantishche Monatschefte* 7 (1903): 186-87. For this reference see Hans Rollman's "Holtzmann, von Hügel, and Modernism—1," *Downside Review* 97 (1979): 142.

13. "Loisy a découvert Newman et a crû que dans le moule de la pensée newmanienne il purrait coulet ses idées. Au contraire, il a été tout de suite un adversaire de Renan." Emile Poulat in *Revue historique* 230 (1963): 264.

14. The first draft of this work was titled *Essais d'histoire et de critique religieuses* and was completed by the spring of 1898. Loisy later labeled this *tres insuffisiant* and rewrote it between the summer of 1898 and the spring of 1899. He crossed out on the manuscript the original title of the revision, *La crise de la foi dans le temps present* and replaced it with *Essais d'histoire et de philosophie religieuses.* Both manuscripts, as well as a typewritten version (1,134 pp.), prepared by the executor of Loisy's estate, Lois Canet (1883-1958), are available at the *Bilbliotheque nationale* in Paris and, in photocopy, at St. Michael's Library, University of Toronto. Later page references will be to the Canet edition.

15. Much of the basic data in this essay regarding Loisy is drawn from his three autobiographies, *Choses passées* (Paris: Emile Nourry, 1918); the three-volume *Mémoires pour servir a l'histoire religieuses de notre temps* (Paris: Emile Nourry, 1930-31); and *Un myth apologétique* (Paris: Emile Nourry, 1939). Reference here is from the *Mémoires* 1: 415, which shows Loisy requested Newman's *Grammar of Assent, Idea of a University, An essay on the development of Christian Doctrine, Via Media, I, Anglican Difficulites, II, Essays Critical and Historical, II,* and *University Sermons.*

16. *Revue du Clergé français* 17 (1898): 5-20. The author, with a successful pseudonym, signed the article "A. Firmin," his first initial and middle name. Loisy published five other articles in the same journal, using the same name. The last, "La Religion d'Israel," appeared in the 15 October 1900 issue. It was condemned by Abp. Cardinal Richard of Paris, terminating Loisy's plans for further publications in the *Revue.* It is not clear that the author's identity was ever discovered during the Modernist crisis.

17. This high evaluation comes from one of the finest interpreters of Newman, Nicholas Lash. See his *Newman on Development* (London: Sheed and Ward, 1975): 147. Likewise Jean Guitton found the article *fort remarquable* and an *etude tres intelligent* in representing Newman's thought. *La philosophie de Newman* (Paris: Boivin, 1933), 122 and 224.

18. Loisy, *Mémoires* 1: 426, 432, 448, and 551-2.

19. Ibid., 551-52.

20. Ibid., 432.

21. Ibid., 426.

22. Used here is the translation of *Choses passées* (note 14) by Richard W. Boynton, *My Duel With the Vatican* (New York: Greenwood, 1968 [original New York: E.P. Dutton, 1924]) 58-71.

23. Ibid., 97-98.

24. Ibid., 168.

25. See the "Bibliographie Alfred Loisy" in Poulat's *Alfred Loisy*, 303-24, slightly expanded in his *Critique*, 322-27.

26. See note 9.

27. Daly suggests "anachronistic retrojection" on Loisy's part. See this and his outstandingly fine analysis of Modernism in *Transcendence and Immanence* (Oxford: Clarendon Press, 1980) 53.

28. Loisy, *My Duel*, 168.

29. Loisy, *Mémoires* 1: 426.

30. Boynton, *My Duel*, 168.

31. For an article that accurately places these two books in the developments of Loisy's life, see Normand Provencher's "Une tentative de renouvellement de l'hermeneutique biblique: le modernisme d'Alfred Loisy," in *Eglise et theologie* 7 (1976): 341-66. Like any valuable investigation of Loisy, this one too has been aided by Emile Poulat's work.

32. Poulat, *Alfred Loisy*, 86.

33. See note 19.

34. Loisy, *Mémoires* 2:560. See Daly's comments on the incongruity of these two influences, in *Transcendence*, 61.

35. *Revue d'histoire et de littérature religieuse*, (November-December 1918): 570.

36. Loisy, *Mémoires* 1: 438-44.

37. See, for instance, Daly's *Immanence* 60, and the author's "Landshift," 160.

38. See note 14.

39. Loisy, *Essais*, 152-53.

40. "Le Developpement chretien d'apres le Cardinal Newman," *Revue du Clergé français* (1898): 15. Further on in the *Essais* (p. 722) there is another paragraph of strong praise for Newman: "perceptive and learned historian, profound theologian, sensitive psychologist, insightful philosopher . . . all the gifts of Origen—and perhaps even more." Loisy probably identified with what he said next: "Because Newman affirmed the necessity in the Church of change, the Church opposed him in all his endeavors."

41. "Le Developpement," 17.

42. *Histoire, dogme et critique dans la crise moderniste* (Paris: Casterman, 1979—original 1962), 74.

43. Loisy, *Essais*, 327-64; 173-4.

44. Ibid.,141-44.

45. Ibid., 146-47.

46. Ibid., 154; 160-64.

47. Ibid.

48. Ibid., 144.

49. Roger Aubert, "Les etapes de l'influence die Cardinal Newman. Un precursor longtemps meconnu," in *Wissen Glaube Politik. Festschrift für Paul Asveld*, by Winfried Gruber et al. (Graz, Wien, Koln: Verlag Styria, 1981): 125-38.

50. Loisy, *Essais*, 145-46.

51. Ibid., 146.

52. Ibid., 413.

53. For analysis of Rahner's concept of revelation, see the author's Yale dissertation, *Rahner and Revelation* (Ann Arbor, MI: University Dissertations, 1974). See also Gerald McCool, *A Rahner Reader* (New York: Seabury, 1974).

54. The source is usually presumed to be Joseph Maréchal, S.J., as in "Abstractions ou intuition," *Mélanges Joseph Maréchal* (Bruxelles: Edition Universelle, 1950), pp. 102-180.

Part Four

NEWMAN
AND THE
VATICAN

8

Newman: The Roman View

Gary Lease

Ignaz von Döllinger, one of the few scholars of the nineteenth century to stand as an equal to Newman in his knowledge of church history, remarked upon hearing that Newman was to be made a cardinal that such an act was only conceivable because the Romans did not read English, and thus did not really know Newman's true position. "If Newman had written in French, Italian or Latin," he wrote, " then his books would have landed on the Index long ago."[1] This laconic observation points toward a problem which haunted Newman throughout the latter part of his life, and indeed has clouded his role and place in his chosen church community long after his death: The Roman authorities of the Catholic church, to which Newman had converted in 1845, were invariably ambivalent toward him, often suspicious and frequently mistrusting. At times there was even talk of "heresy." Despite the cardinal's hat in 1879 and even following his death in 1890, Newman has continued to be claimed by a wide variety of directions and factions within—and without—the Roman church. This tantalizing possibility of using Newman to support quite divergent theological and institutional programs has caused the Roman authorities endless headaches. At no time did this difficulty create greater confusion than during the so-called Modernist crisis during the first decade of our century.[2]

The world of competing authoritative claims over the content and formulation of the Christian faith, which filled the nineteenth century, formed the backdrop both for Newman's life and thought, and for Rome's judgment of him. Indeed, Newman's first major appearance on the stage of theological and ecclesiastical battle, the so-called Oxford Movement, was marked profoundly by the fight over what the genuine Christian message was and above all who had the authority to proclaim it. In his efforts to force through a unique understanding of the Anglican church's position in the Christian cosmos, "Newman divided Oxford."[3] In essence, he called for a second Reformation, a revolution which would settle where the authority for defining and proclaiming the Christian gospel lay.[4] For Newman the culmination of this revolution took its form in the *Essay on the Development of Christian Doctrine* and his formal conversion to the

Roman church in 1845. His decision as to where the source of authoritative decisions about what one must believe to be a Christian was located, had been reached: It was not one's Anglican bishop, much less the English Parliament, but rather the Church of Rome through its pope, maintaining continuous witness to Christianity's beginnings.

Thus began for Newman a stormy second half of his life. While Newman enjoyed a certain trust on the part of the English hierarchy, his status in Rome was never the firmest. Charges from the English press, such as those of the early fifties when Newman was accused of building dungeons beneath the Birmingham Oratory, kept his name in an unfavorable light.[5] Even more troublesome, however, was the now infamous *Rambler* affair. For a brief period in 1859 Newman assumed the editorship of this periodical, which had been under fire from Catholic authorities both in England and in Rome.[6] Newman's editorship was viewed as a safeguard against the journal's slipping into doctrinal hot water. Unfortunately, the contrary proved to be the case.

One of Newman's first acts as editor was to publish an article of his own, "On Consulting the Faithful in Matters of Doctrine," basically a historical study demonstrating his long-held conviction that it was the entire church, in all its members, which through its testimony to its living faith, provided the basis for binding doctrinal definitions.[7] The result of controversy over whether the "laity's" opinion on matters of doctrine could and should be of interest to the episcopacy, the article immediately raised eyebrows and was delated to Rome by an English bishop. George Talbot, one of the oddest appearances in nineteenth-century English Catholicism and one of four private chamberlains to Pius IX, had already established himself as a mouthpiece for the English hierarchy in Rome; his later unsavory intrigues in the selection of Manning as Wiseman's successor in Westminster (1865) confirmed that position.[8] And it was Talbot who made it clear to Newman (through his friend Ambrose St. John), some eight years later, that Rome had been highly disturbed over Newman's utterances in the *Rambler*; at least in some quarters his ideas were viewed as disruptive of the hierarchical control in the church.[9] Though the matter was basically cleared up in 1867, Talbot could write later that "it is perfectly *true* that a cloud has been hanging over Dr. Newman" since the *Rambler* article, and that none of Newman's work since then had effectively removed it.[10] Here then was the beginning of that famous "cloud" which Newman himself felt over his life and role in the Roman church, and which he saw as lifted only with the cardinalate twenty years later.[11]

There is ample evidence that Manning, still upset over the *Rambler* affair as well as Newman's struggle for Catholic university education and his stance during Vatican I,[12] worked hard to block Newman's reception of the red hat.[13] There is little doubt that, at least in Newman's mind, he had certainly been suspected of heresy by certain Roman circles.[14] However, the offering of the cardinal's hat came to him as a great relief, indeed a genuine "acquittal" from the uncertain and often nebulous charges which had circulated against him ever since the late fifties. Any doubts he may have had were removed by Leo XIII's personal reception of him in Rome: Kind and affectionate, Leo treated him so specially as to make it clear even to Newman that, as far as the highest circles of the Roman church were concerned, he enjoyed the fullest degree of trust and approbation.[15]

And there is no doubt that not only the initiatives of some of England's leading Catholic laity, above all of the Duke of Norfolk, led to this official and public avowal of Rome's acceptance of Newman; Leo XIII, long in opposition to the policies and conduct of Pius IX, said later that he had wished to honor the church by honoring Newman, someone he had always honored himself.[16] Newman himself wondered how Leo had come to think of him,[17] but evidently had forgotten that Dominic Barberi, who had received him into the Roman community in 1845, reported soon thereafter to the papal nuntius in Brussels: Gioacchino Pecci, later Leo XIII![18] Cardinal Nina, Leo's secretary of state, wrote Newman that the pope was particularly impressed with Newman's genius, his learning, his piety and zealousness in the exercise of his ministry, his devotion and attachment to Rome, and his general services to the cause of religion; these were the traits and accomplishments which the red hat was designed to honor.[19] Thus, after more than twenty years of suspicion and seeming exile, the pope sought to express Rome's approval and acceptance of Newman and his life's work by crowning him with one of the church's most public honors. Even Cardinal Manning, an implacable foe for so many years, confessed at Newman's death, just eleven years after the awarding of the red hat, that the church had lost its "greatest witness to the faith."[20]

In the famous address delivered at his reception of the cardinal's hat in Rome, Newman had stressed the fact that, whether in the Anglican or the Roman church, he had stood in the forefront of the battle against "liberalism" in religion all his life.[21] Yet shortly after his death, a movement which had been in formation for some time in the Roman church gathered strength and broke upon the public light. Composed of scholars, historians, theologians, and concerned laity, the so-called Modernists sought a way whereby one might remain a rational, critical member of the emerging twentieth century while at the same time also remaining an ardent and faithful member of the Catholic church. These "Modernists" found it natural to seek aid and comfort from the writings of Newman and from the example of his life. Had he not seen "the intellectual problems facing Christians in the modern world: Christian education; faith and intellectual assent; the development of the Christian tradition; the place of the laity in the Church"?[22] Since, however, the Modernist movement, together with many of its most prominent representatives, were eventually condemned by Rome, there gathered a new "cloud" over Newman, the suspicion that he, too, was condemned along with the "Modernists."[23]

Certainly, at first glance, this would seem to have been the case. Though Newman decried "liberalism" in religion, many of the Modernists' key tenets and positions, as cataloged by Rome in its Encyclical of condemnation *Pascendi* (1907), appeared to stem from Newman's writings: The historical "development" of doctrine, the primacy of an individual's conscience over the authority of Rome, the arational foundations for assent to matters of religious faith. All of these ideas were labeled "liberal" and consigned to the fire. A great struggle for Newman's imprimatur arose, as first one side and then the other attempted to enlist him for their cause, some trying to demonstrate that Newman, indeed, had been long ago the champion of the very ideas which they were now trying to advance, while others sought to show that Newman had never thought any such thing and would have rejected these "new and liberal" ideas with the same clarity and vehemence with which he had proclaimed, in 1879, his life-long battle against "liberalism." What precisely occurred?

As far as the Roman authorities were concerned, Newman himself gave no cause for concern. In 1902, for example, the young Archbishop Merry del Val, assigned to the Roman Index, found himself embroiled in a controversy over papal claims with the Anglican F.N. Oxenham. Merry del Val stated in a series of sermons that, among other writings well qualified to teach the truth of papal claims, certainly Newman's *Apologia* was admirably suited.[24] Eventually Merry del Val published these sermons in a small book designed for English converts to Catholicism.[25] The volume closed with Merry del Val quoting directly from Newman's *Apologia*, citing his abandonment of the Anglican church for the Roman faith.[26] Some years later Merry del Val warned a friend against Wilfrid Ward, charging that he is "unsafe" and teaches "unsound doctrine," but nevertheless always manages to wriggle out of it by saying that it is really Newman whom he is presenting: "Poor Newman" is Merry del Val's laconic comment.[27] If, then, Rome's use of Newman as late as 1902 was one of approval, one can only wonder whether it was Newman himself or the uses to which his writings and ideas were put by others which caused his posthumous involvement with the Modernist movement.

Certainly it was not the adoption of Newman's thought by Protestant historians which brought him into the Modernist camp. Of all such scholars, one would have expected Harnack to have made extensive use of Newman's "development" of doctrine. Yet one finds him mentioned only briefly in the fourth edition of Harnack's history of dogma, and then only in connection with a short note on the crisis of "modernism" and the effects of the papal condemnations of 1907.[28] Harnack determined that the unique point of departure for the Catholic Modernists was their use of the modern developmental schema in analyzing primitive Christianity and the history of Christian doctrine. While doing so, the Modernists rejected sharply any connection with Protestantism and considered themselves completely and fully members of the Catholic church. It was clear to Harnack, however, that they were, in fact, one with Protestantism: The pope had made it clear to them that they were no longer Catholics, and quite properly so, since despite their own misgivings they belonged to Harnack and his colleagues. Harnack concluded that one of the major influences on this movement was the consequences to be drawn from the historical works of Cardinal Newman! Since this note appeared some two years after the condemnations and arguments of 1907, it is difficult to view Harnack's conclusion as the cause for viewing Newman as a source of Modernism. On the contrary, it is likely that he first drew that conclusion upon reviewing the discussions which swirled about *Pascendi*.

Equally certain is the fact that the deep-seated respect for Newman by such left-wing German Catholics as Franz Xaver Kraus also did not garner for the cardinal a membership in the Modernist group. Kraus, a church historian and all-around gadfly in German church affairs during the last quarter of the nineteenth century, was one of the few Continentals still living who had actually met Newman. Invited to the Birmingham Oratory during a visit to England by Sir Rowland Blennerhessett, he was absolutely overwhelmed with Newman's presence, his deep piety and his power of mind.[29] Years later he remembered that Newman impressed him, like no other, as being someone who, while having his feet on the ground, already had his spirit in heaven.[30] Newman was, he said, the highest embodiment of the Christian spirit he had ever encountered. And while his life's work should be considered one of the greatest and most blessed evolutions of a religious spirit available to us, we must also realize that this was tempered, but made all the more valuable, by the over forty years of evil designs, pain, and suffering he had to endure in the Catholic church.[31] Kraus remembered Newman telling him personally how Pius IX and his curia had "tyrannized" the faithful, and Blennerhessett reported that upon Newman's trip to Rome for the red hat, he had become an even more decided opponent of the curia than before.[32]

With great feeling, Kraus closed his memory of Newman with the recounting of Blennerhessett's conversation with Bishop Clifford after Newman's burial. According to Blennerhessett, Clifford said to him: "Well, at least we've had the good fortune for once of being able to bury a priest who was a great mind (*Geist*) and who had not been censured." Whereupon Blennerhessett answered: "Yes, but let's just wait." Kraus commented that evidently Blennerhessett thought it quite possible that what was attempted some four times during Newman's life (i.e., censure) would finally happen after his death. Presumably Newman's letters contained criticisms of Rome and the curia far stronger than anything Kraus and his fellow strugglers had ever said. And Kraus can report the rumor that Manning even had copies of some of these letters and tried to use them in Rome to stop the cardinalate, but that Leo XIII had responded that he knew full well what Newman's opinion of the curia was and that he did not see any problem in that to naming him a cardinal.[33] While Kraus certainly would have been able to envision Newman being condemned along with the Modernists, neither his diary entries (unknown at the time) nor his newspaper article of 1901 stand as sources able to explain the linking of Newman with the Modernist movement.

Erich Przywara, the German Jesuit, advanced the theory almost two decades later that Newman had ended up in bed with the Modernists, and indeed was celebrated in some circles as the "father of Modernism" due to studies of him by Alexander Whyte and Dean Church.[34] Taking as his point of departure Whyte's *Appreciation of Newman*,[35] Pryzwara cited his use of remarks made by Whateley, one of the chief influences on Newman after his arrival at Oxford and later Anglican archbishop of Dublin. For it was Whateley who lashed out at the Oxford Movement, and its leader Newman, as representing a flight from reason in the service of religion, "a desire to believe based only on feelings." Pryzwara saw in this charge the basic thesis for Modernism: Whatever reason might protest against, that is precisely the substance of faith because it corresponds to the believer's "feelings" and because it is "needed."[36] And it is precisely this view of Newman which Przywara found in Bremond's psychological study of Newman; since he made use of Whyte and Dean Church, this should come as no surprise.[37]

On the one hand Whyte maintained that Newman's theology was never a New Testament theology; in the eyes of the Calvinist, Newman had never been able to break away from the Old Testament theology of terror.[38] And on the other, it was Dean Church, writing at Newman's death, who asked the question, How was it possible that Newman had left the church of his fathers and gone over to Rome? The answer was not at all clear for Church, once such a close and intimate friend of Newman, but at least he could report that what had captured Newman's heart and his imagination was one thing, but what had justified the move to his reason, another.[39] Out of this, Przywara argued, Bremond was able to construct a psychology of Newman's faith in which anti-intellectualism played the key role, Newman's famous youthful "conversion" experience was the foundation for his belief in the Catholic church, and the acceptance of particular doctrines was dependent upon their correspondence with personal emotional needs.[40] For Bremond, according to Przywara, Newman is the "precursor" because his theory of belief is that of a religious consciousness which reveals itself to the believing person.[41]

The only apparent explicit trace of Bremond's theories is to be found in the study of Newman by Charles Sarolea (1870-1953),[42] an ex-Catholic from Belgium who spent many years in Edinburgh, first as Belgian consul-general and later as a professor of French at Edinburgh University. Using both Bremond and Newman himself, Sarolea reached the conclusion that Newman knew nothing of a mediator between God and humanity, such as a priest: For Newman there is but God and himself.[43] And no priest, so no church. The circle was complete, and Newman emerged as a champion of religious subjectivism without par: Faith, for Newman, was completely an act of the will and of love, while reason does not partake in it at all.[44] Yet, in a final chapter on "Newman and Modernism," Sarolea appeared confused; confronted with Newman's *Development of Doctrine* ("more a logical process than an organic growth") and with his *Difficulties of Anglicans,* Sarolea confessed that Newman was basically a scholastic and a rationalist. In fact, many of his teachings might well appear to smack of Modernism; systematically and consciously, however, he was a reactionary. Indeed, Sarolea maintained that Newman's influence in the future would grow in the measure that he continued to be misunderstood![45]

We may be arriving near the heart of the matter. Loisy had quite explicitly placed his own theory of doctrinal development under the protection of Newman's *Essay on Development,* while Bremond, hardly without suspicion after leaving the Jesuits in 1904 and his continued close contacts with Loisy and Tyrrell, seemed to cite Newman as the source for some of the most infamous ideas on religious knowledge and the nature of faith associated with the Modernist movement. Loisy, of course, had been excommunicated, but his use of Newman was not mentioned in the Roman statements; Bremond's being censured was, to judge from its timing and nature, the result of his attendance at Tyrrell's burial and not of his book on Newman.[46] If Rome would not react to such applications of Newman's name and writings, what would it take to prompt the headquarters of Roman Catholicism to express its judgment on him?

The list provided by the Holy Office in July of 1907, condemning a series of citations from so-called Modernist authors, and the papal encyclical in September of the same year, which outlined in systematic fashion the "doctrines" of the new heresy and their opposition to orthodox Roman Catholic thought, had above all four major problems in view. First of all, the papal condemnations were directed at attempts to understand and analyze the act of faith as exercised by the individual human being, and thus the relationship between faith and knowledge. Closely connected with this problem was the additional concern of whether human reason is capable of knowing anything beyond the natural sphere, i.e., whether human reason can achieve knowledge of God and divine workings outside of the act of revelation. These two questions dealt together with the problem of religion's origins: Were they "objectively" available to human reason, or only "subjectively" produced by human feelings and need? The final two points were directed toward a different sphere of worries in Rome: The first touched upon the authority to be granted to an individual's conscience, and thus, in consequence, the second concerned the authority to be granted the teaching organs of the Roman church, and in the main to the pope. Thus while earlier possible uses of Newman in support of Modernist causes had not occurred in direct opposition to Rome, even though their authors might well have been censured, or even excommunicated on doctrinal ground, such uses after the appearances of *Lamentabili* and *Pascendi* fell into a much different category. Using Newman to protect oneself against action by Rome meant a direct challenge to Roman authority, and, as we will see, finally provoked a judgment on Newman and his thought.

Romolo Murri (1870-1944), ordained in 1893, was a leading Italian agitator for the "new" ideas.[47] In 1907, the year of *Pascendi*, he published an Italian translation of Newman's *Essay on the Development of Doctrine.*[48] At the same time, the Italian professor Domenico Battaini published an Italian translation of Newman's *Essay in Aid of a Grammar of Assent.*[49] In the accompanying notes and introductions, the two translators made no bones about Newman's "involvement" in Modernism. Battaini found in Newman's work the "bulwark of the new ideas"; indeed, he was their "precursor and father."[50] Murri, on his side, constantly referred to

Harnack, Loisy, and Tyrrell for further elucidations of the points made by Newman in his *Essay on Development*. While Battaini claimed that the Modernists were doing nothing more than applying strictly the ideas of Newman, Murri drew the consequences and reported that since Newman admitted only two realities—God and himself—could it be surprising that "there was little room for an external church"?[51] The inference was clear: If Newman did not admit of a visible church, certainly he would not have held that any such claimant had any authority to demand obedience. Thus when Newman appeared to allow for such authority, pointing out that obedience to an ecclesiastical superior may, in fact, be an aid to one's spiritual development, Murri corrected the remark by noting that, of course, the very notion of authority disappears when its action would seem to the religious conscience to be hurtful to the life of the spirit.[52] Here, then, Newman was claimed in support of those contesting the second set of questions with which *Pascendi* and the Roman authorities were concerned in dealing with Modernism: the existence and validity of Rome's teaching authority. There would seem to be little doubt that if Newman were to be understood as presented in these Italian translations, he would have to be reckoned as a posthumous member of the Modernist movement.

Within the year Rome provided an answer. Calling on an auditor of the Sacred Rota, Monsignor John Prior of the English College in Rome, to meet the challenge, an essay was published in Italian in the *Civiltà Cattolica* and an English translation in *Rome;* the whole was finally published as a separate pamphlet for wider distribution.[53] Prior took great pain to point out that his rebuttal of the charges made in the Italian translations of Newman's works was in strict agreement with the pope's own judgment: Newman had been misrepresented, and shabbily, too.[54] Quoting mainly from Newman's own works, primarily from the *Apologia,* Prior attempted to show that Newman stood in clear opposition to the ideas paraded under the banner of Modernism. Not only did the said translations give a false picture of what Newman actually thought and taught, but, so Prior tried to prove, there had even been falsifications and omissions in the frenzied effort to enlist Newman for an unholy cause.[55] It is quite clear, in this first Roman position on the issue, that Newman cannot be seen as having quarters in the Modernist camp.

But the real struggle was yet to come. As might be expected, it broke out in Newman's home country, England. The opening salvo was fired by George Tyrrell, long recognized as a critical follower of Newman. In fact, a year before the appearance of *Pascendi*, Tyrrell had supplied an introduction to the English translation of Bremond's *The Mystery of Newman*.[56] While praising Bremond's study as a necessary and highly appropriate step in gaining, at last, an objective and detached assessment of Newman and his accomplishments, Tyrrell also emphasized that Newman cannot be claimed by any party; "the theologians of every colour, black, white, and grey" who have vied with one another for the right to call Newman their own must surrender those claims.[57] This was particularly true for those who would base their position on Newman's theory of a development of doctrine. In Tyrrell's view, Newman certainly did not intend that theory to be "of a liberalising or minimising character"; he had no wish to go beyond what he had found in the Fathers.[58] On the other hand, those who misrepresent him may indeed have an excuse: "Newman's incontestable abhorrence of doctrinal liberalism does not at once prove that he may not be the progenitor of it."[59]

Clearly Newman's personal position was not at question; his critique of scholasticism, so Tyrrell, had to do with its "apologetic efficacy" and thus its method, not with its teachings. It was quite clear to Tyrrell that Newman's "revolution in epistemology" heralded a new age in thought: Science is now bankrupt, and the old rationalism has been thrown out of court. It was Newman who had led religious apologetic to a higher plane where philosophy had now also repaired. Thus contemporary philosophy and science, aware as they must now be that knowledge rests inevitably on "faiths and assumptions," are working with Newman's weapons. The paradox was complete for Tyrrell: Those Catholics whom Newman would have rejected—those, who, in spite of the Syllabus really think that they can "come to terms" with the modern mind—are in fact those who "look to him and to his methods as the sole hope of their cause." Yet beyond the common theory of knowledge and the persuasion that the traditional apologetic of scholasticism simply would not work, there was really no union between Newman and his supporters.[60] While Tyrrell therefore offered an explanation of why some of the Modernists felt compelled to call upon Newman for help in their struggle, he had also made it clear that he did not view Newman as part of that movement. How quickly this would change.

On 8 September 1907 *Pascendi* was released to a world which by and large had not suspected what was afoot. By the end of the month Tyrrell had penned a two-part article for the London *Times* providing an analysis of the encyclical of condemnation.[61] In addition to excoriating the pope, Tyrrell also pointed out that the encyclical had gone so far as to condemn clearly key ideas found in Newman's thought. Certainly his claim that the individual religious conscience has primacy over hierarchical authority;

his distinction between primary and secondary dogmas; and finally Newman's proposal that the laity help "modify the collective mind of the Church and so help in the imaginary 'development' of dogma" had all been condemned by the papal statement.[62] In Tyrrell's eyes this must turn away many minds who will feel deeply this "blow struck against" not only the Modernists themselves, but "their spiritual ancestry" among whom Newman ranks highly.[63] A week later Tyrrell was joined by Robert Dell, a journalist and Catholic convert living in Paris, who wrote to *The Times* pointing out that the claim of *Osservatore Romano* that the "evolution of dogma" is now to be deemed a "heresy" proves Tyrrell right: Newman was undoubtedly aimed at by the encyclical *Pascendi*, which means that the church's leaders viewed him as a heretic.[64] At the same time Wilfrid Ward reported to his friend Lilly that he was shattered by "Newman's condemnation" in *Pascendi.*[65] The floodgates opened.

Canon John Vaughan of the Westminster archdiocese replied immediately that a clear distinction was necessary; while the encyclical condemned the idea of a development or evolution of dogma stemming from an individual's religious sense, Newman had always held to a development of doctrine from a deposit of faith. Newman would have found the first possibility abhorrent, while the second, his own position, remained untouched by the papal condemnation.[66] Back came the charge from "Eboracensis" that Newman quite clearly had taught that an individual's religious conscience is "above all dogma."[67] By the end of the month, W.T. Williams had gotten together a statement representing a number of Catholics, liberal and otherwise, who found it an "evil" that one pope would imply approval of an English Catholic's writings by naming him a cardinal, while a later pope "should reverse the decision by condemning every characteristic proposition for which that writer made himself responsible."[68]

The struggle over Newman's good name escalated with a report from John Norris, superior of Newman's old Birmingham Oratory, that on "highest" authority" he may say that the " 'genuine doctrine and spirit of Newman's Catholic teaching are not hit by the Encyclical, but the theories of many who wrongly seek refuge under a great name are obviously censured.' "[69] But the very next day Phillip Sidney protested that Newman's popular theory as to the development of doctrine "has been condemned by the reigning Pope."[70] Next to Sidney's protest, there was a vigorous defense of Newman's orthodoxy by Francis Gasquet, later to be a cardinal himself. To his mind the charges that *Pascendi* could possibly have had Newman in mind were "false, mischievous, and misleading." Of course all have known for some years now, he continued, of rumors circulating in Rome that Newman was to be condemned, but this was a smoke screen put up by those who knew the hammer would soon descend upon themselves. Norris's letter made it clear that "on the highest authority . . . no theory, no idea, no opinion even put forward by the great Cardinal has been either implicitly or indirectly set aside, let alone condemned by the late Encyclical."[71]

Gasquet found himself seconded by the *Times* Roman correspondent, who quoted from the *Osservatore Romano* of 5 November and its response to Tyrrell's articles in *The Times*. The *Osservatore* claimed that it was authoritatively authorized to reject any inference that the encyclical sought to condemn Newman; *Pascendi* had indeed aimed at some who claim to be interpreters of Newman, but it is easy to see the difference.[72] Three days later *The Times* again cited the *Osservatore* in defense of Newman. While insisting on Newman's adherence to the doctrine of papal infallibility, the *Osservatore* pointed out that Newman's view of the development of doctrine is one of progress in explicating and understanding the same doctrine, while the Modernists see that development as a process of one doctrine changing to another.[73]

Still the drumbeat kept up. Dell replied from Paris that regardless of the claims made by Gasquet and others, the clear meaning of the encyclical was to condemn Newman. If the pope did not intend to do so, then he must have signed an encyclical which he did not understand; perhaps its reputed author, supposedly an old enemy of Newman's thought, took this opportunity to crack down on him. However it may be, the result is an "incoherent infallibility."[74] Tyrrell, after remaining quiet since his first articles in *The Times*, now returned to the fray with an article in the *Guardian* on "The Condemnation of Newman." He agreed that the encyclical, in its natural sense, appeared to condemn Newman; if this were not intended, so challenged Tyrrell, then let the Vatican tell one and all that Catholics may still hold to Newman's *Essay on the Development,* to his *Grammar of Assent,* to his *Letter to the Duke of Norfolk* as well as to his views on scholasticism. If the Vatican were to do this, and assure all "Modernists" that nothing of Newman's had been condemned, then they would immediately accept the encyclical.[75]

Canon Vaughan reported, in reply to Tyrrell, that he had just had an audience with the pope; he had spoken of Newman "with greatest admiration" and especially of his "constant attitude of loyalty and submission to the Holy See."[76] Tyrrell fired back that the question at issue had never concerned Newman's obedience, but rather whether the pope had said that no idea, no theory, no opinion even of Newman's had been condemned?[77]

And here the argument began to peter out. Bremond tried to mediate between both sides without, of course, wishing to come under fire himself. He was, he wrote, "quite at one with those who defend Newman from any sympathy with Modernism, whatever weapons he may have unconsciously forged for its use."[78] But it was left to the hierarchy to have the last word.

First out of the blocks was Bishop Edward O'Dwyer of Limerick in Ireland. Considering himself long a student and follower of Newman, O'Dwyer was appalled at the linking of Newman to the Modernist movement, and above all the insinuations in the English press that Newman was equally condemned by *Pascendi*. With his pamphlet, written before December 1907, O'Dwyer set a line which would characterize Rome's view of Newman for the future.[79] From the outset O'Dwyer denied the basic premise of the previous claims: Absolutely nothing in Newman's writings suggests that those who were condemned by the encyclical might find support from him.[80] Taking his cues from *Pascendi* itself, O'Dwyer outlined three major areas in which Newman was claimed in support of Modernist ideas: (1) In distinction to the Modernists, as presented in the encyclical, Newman held firmly that human intellection is capable of knowing god; this position is fundamental to the Catholic faith. This distinction is "an essential difference in kind."[81] (2) While the Modernists are viewed as holding the source and origin of religion to be in human nature itself, and thus effectively denying the normative role of revelation, both Newman and the church hold firmly to the concept of revelation as a direct communication from god of definite truths, and not as a "religious sense."[82] Thus Newman's theory of a development of doctrine is both orthodox and sound, and is certainly not meant to be caught in the encyclical's condemnations: Newman takes as the object of such a development a revealed deposit of faith, which does not change as it develops, while the Modernists, as condemned by the pope, maintain no revelation, no objective truth, and no deposit of faith, which is why they can hold that religious truth can and does change.[83] (3) Finally, Newman was committed to the validity of the hierarchical and papal teaching authority. At question is not Newman's personal obedience, but his speculative persuasion. In O'Dwyer's view, Newman held that only the pope and the bishops "are placed to rule the Church: And they, and they alone, possess these prerogatives. From them, the laity receive their doctrines, and their legislation. The Pope and the Bishops legislate; the laity obey." Yet Newman also showed clearly (e.g., in his *Apologia*) that given this basic constitution in the church, there still remains adequate room for the use of individual gifts within that church.[84] All of Newman's admonitions concerning the place of conscience must be understood against that backdrop.

Approbation from the highest position in Rome was not long in coming. Some three months later, on 10 March 1908, Pope Pius X issued a letter of praise and commendation to Bishop O'Dwyer, congratulating him on having made such a fine and powerful defense of Newman's name and thought.[85] Pius X himself approved the bishop's effort *vehementer* and was pleased to see the harmony between his encylical and Newman so clearly presented. His works, according to Pius, were as valuable to him as they had been to his predecessor, Leo XIII, who had created Newman cardinal. Though Newman, in his works from pre-Catholic days, may well not have exercised extraordinary caution in his expressions, he is nevertheless an *optimus et sapientissimus vir* whose thought had nothing to do with Modernism; it was the Modernists who took Newman's words out of context. In fact, Pius closed, we might all be able to learn much from Newman: to hold the magisterium sacred; to preserve the tradition of the Fathers; and, the chief thing for preservation of Catholic truth, to honor and obey with the utmost fidelity the Successor of Blessed Peter. It is difficult to imagine a stronger statement of approval and support from the Roman authorities than this letter from the very man who just six months before had issued the condemnations of *Pascendi*.

By that time, however, the argument over the proper classification of Newman had shifted across the Atlantic. Writing in the *Ecclesiastical Review*, A. Vieban took the Protestant church historian Charles Briggs to task for having suggested that the encyclical intended to place all the followers of Newman among the Modernists; indeed, Briggs cited an anonymous Roman cardinal as saying that "if Newman was now living he would be classed as a heretic."[86] Against such groundless charges, Vieban simply cited O'Dwyer's pamphlet and the pope's letter on its occasion to show that "there is nothing in Newman to suggest or extenuate the doctrines of the Modernists."[87] In the same issue H.P. Russell blasted those who would "shelter their doctrines under the shadow of his (i.e., Newman's) great name."[88] Certainly the root principle of the Modernists, subjectivism, was something against which Newman had fought all his life; we need only review Newman's own words to see how his teaching on ecclesiastical authority, the development of doctrine, and his faith in doctrinal definitions differs from the Modernist positions.[89] Concluding the series of articles dedicated to Newman and Modernism, G. Lee from the Pittsburgh Catholic College protested against the calling of Newman's Catholic orthodoxy into question and against the "evil epithets" which had dragged him "into association with sowers of error."[90] Yet the propositions which Newman himself condemned in his *Apologia* and in his famous biglietto speech, echoed, in Lee's ears, almost exactly the condemnations in *Lamentabili* and *Pascendi*. There was no doubt: Those who would link Newman to Modernism have been rebutted by his very own words.

As we have seen, the "Roman" view of Newman and his work has been a most ambiguous one. His theory of doctrinal development, designed to meet important historical problems, has constantly given rise to the suspicion that it could possibly serve to undermine the persuasiveness of the Christian faith as well as to support it. Newman's call to take seriously the gifts possessed by all Christians in their service to the church and his efforts to provide a more balanced understanding of the church's teaching function, in particular the definition of ecclesiastical and papal infallibility, have made some Roman theologians more than nervous. Finally, the attempts on the part of several thinkers associated with the Modernist movement to support their own theories on the nature of revelation and human knowledge of things divine by calling upon Newman, led to a free association of his name with a direction in Catholic theology which had been formally condemned. While Leo XIII had created Newman a cardinal, thereby seeking to confirm publicly Rome's approval of his work, this gesture remained in large part a personal move on the pope's part. It was the episode of Modernism which forced Rome to take a new and official position on Newman's place in the church. Again, it was the pope himself, Pius X, who issued the final approbation.

The whole affair, however, left a smoke in the air which curled about Newman's name and writings for many years after *Pascendi*. Though officially blessed, Newman continued under suspicion, if only at the lower levels of church hierarchy and usage.[91] The slow rehabilitation of Newman which began after the First World War did not truly bear fruit until the 1950s and 1960s.[92] Some have spoken of the Second Vatican Council as "Newman's Council," and it is true that through the council the influence of his thought reached an audience and gained a church-wide stature which it had never had before.[93] The many Newman Houses scattered across Europe and North America give witness to his place in the institutional church. Recent popes, such as Paul VI, have stressed the value of Newman's inspirational influence for the church in its efforts to understand and live fruitfully in today's modern world.[94] John Paul II has claimed Newman's philosophical and theological thought, together with his spirituality, to be of particular originality and value for the church. Joining with Paul VI, he has identified Newman's "vast theological vision" as one of the foundations for the work of the Second Vatican Council, as well as for the church of the postconciliar era. According to him, Newman's thought remains a constant source of inspiration for the mission of the church in the modern world, and a key to the restoration of Christian unity.[95]

Perhaps the most striking, and in some ways startling, indication of Rome's final acceptance of Newman was a speech given by the Vicar General for the Vatican City, Archbishop Peter van Lierde, at the forty-seventh commemoration of the death of Raphael Cardinal Merry del Val, Secretary of State under Pius X, and a key moving force behind the condemnation of Modernism. During his talk, Archbishop van Lierde drew an unexpected parallel between Merry del Val on the one hand and the Cardinals Mercier, Ferrari—and Newman!, on the other: "all of them great figures of diverse activities and ministries." And just like his great predecessor, Cardinal Newman, so also Merry del Val had been dedicated to the conversion of the Anglican church to Rome.[96] If indeed Rome now considers Newman in the same breath with Merry del Val, then there can be no doubt that it no longer views him as under a "cloud" of suspicion: The process of defanging Newman is complete, he has been assimilated into the Roman world, his icon is finished.

NOTES

1. Döllinger to F. Michaelis, 1 May 1879. First in the *Guardian, Times*, and *Merkur*, now in Ignaz von Döllinger, *Briefe und Erklärungen über die vatikanischen Dekrete*. (Munich: C.H. Beck, 1890), 109-110; and (in English translation) in *The Letters and Diaries of John Henry Newman*, ed. C. Dessain (Oxford: Clarendon Press, 1976), 29:132.

2. "Theolgians of every colour, black, white, and grey, have tried to appropriate Newman," said Tyrrell, "and to forbid any interpretation of his teaching but their own": in his Introduction to the English translation of Henri Bremond's study of Newman, *The Mystery of Newman* (London: Williams and Norgate, 1907), xv.

3. Owen Chadwick, *The Victorian Church*, Part I (London: A. & C. Black, 1966), 168.

4. The Anglican Church has the "mission" to show to all that one may be Catholic but not Roman; Protestantism is unable to do so, and thus it falls to the English church, using only the "Primitive Church" as its guide: in John Henry Newman, *Lectures on the Prophetical Office of the Church* (= *The Via Media of the Anglican Church*, vol. 1) (London: Longmans, Green, 1901), 20-21.

5. Chadwick, *Victorian Church*, 509.

6. For a brief but authoritative account, see John Couson, Introduction, in John Henry Newman, *On Consulting the Faithful In Matters of Doctrine* (London: G. Chapman), 1961, 1-49.

7. See my analysis, in Gary Lease, *Witness to the Faith* (Shannon: Irish University Press, 1971), 86-93.

8. George Talbot (1816-1886) converted to Catholicism in 1842 and sought admission to Newman's Oratory in 1847; he was refused. Wiseman helped him gain his Vatican post where he remained until his commitment to an asylum in 1868. His clear role, together with Cardinal Antonelli, in blocking Ullathorne and advancing Manning in 1865 during the battle over the pope's naming of Wiseman's successor as archbishop of Westminster can be traced in the Odo Russell letters (= Ampthill Papers), and has been reconstructed in Matthias Buschkühl, *Die irische, schottische und römische Frage* (St. Ottilien: EOS Verlag, 1980), 78-80.

9. Coulson, Introduction, 40-41. Talbot to Ullathorne, 3 December 1859, in *Oratory Archives*, vol 35.

10. To Manning, in Couson, Introduction, 41.

11. See Newman's letters in *Letters and Diaries*, 29: 58, 72, 63: "this reproach" has disappeared, he has received "the acquittal" which he had always hoped for. Of course, the main source of disfavor in Rome, the *Rambler* affair, certainly was not the only one. The controversy over a school for Catholics, the ill-fated Irish University expedition, and later indisretions concerning the conduct of Vatican I all contributed their part. Talbot's judgment that from the Roman point of view Newman might well be the "most dangerous man in England" (Wilfrid Ward, *Life of John Henry Newman*, [London: Longmans, Green, 1913], 2: 147, in a letter to Manning from

1867) while not reflective of *everyone's* opinion in Rome (witness Hohenlohe, who had met Newman on his first visit to Rome), certainly was characteristic of official Rome under Antonelli and Pius IX (cf. note 9).

12. Johannes Artz, "Newmans Kardinalat," *Theologie und Philosophie* 53 (1978): 237-38. For another account, cf. Carlo Snider, "Il Cardinalato di Newman," *John Henry Newman. Saggio commemorativo nel Centenario del Cardinalato*, ed. M.K. Strolz (Rome: Gregorian University, 1979), 69-103.

13. Artz, "Newmans Kardinalat," 222-24. Manning was also suspected of having engineered the disappearance of Newman's declaration of orthodoxy in 1860 before it could reach Rome: ibid., 237.

14. Newman, *Letters and Diaries*, 29: 160.

15. See Newman's account in *Letters and Diaries*, 29: 121.

16. See the report in Roundell Palmer's (Lord Selborne) *Memorials*, edited by Lady Sophia Palmer (London: Macmillan, 1896-1898) of the audience granted him by Leo XIII in 1888: "I," said Leo, "always had a cult for him"; cf. *Letters and Diaries*, 29: 426. Herein lies the source of the often-cited word of Leo's: "My Cardinal!"

17. Newman, *Letters and Diaries*, 29: 276.

18. Urban Young, *Dominic of the Mother of God: Life & Letters of the Venerable Fr. Dominic Barberi* (London: Burns, Oates, Washbourne, 1935), 259.

19. Newman, *Letters and Diaries*, 29: 84.

20. Manning's speech at the London Oratory (He was not present at the funeral itself!), is to be found in Edmund Purcell, *Life of Cardinal Manning* (London: Macmillan, 1896), 2: 748.

21. Wilfrid Ward, *Life of Newman*, 2:460.

22. Dr. Donald Coggan, Archbishop of Canterbury, "Message from the Anglican Church," in *Newman. Saggio commemorativo.*

23. See Philip Flanagan, "Introduction," in *Newman Against the Liberals*, ed. Michael Davies (New Rochelle: Arlington House, 1978), 14: Newman was claimed as "one of themselves" by the Modernists; only in the last few decades has this "shameful misrepresentation" been refuted.

24. Oxenham, the English chaplain in Rome, sent a letter of challenge to the *Church Times*, 14 March 1902, 313; Merry del Val replied, ibid., 21 March 1902.

25. Raphael Merry del Val, *The Truth of Papal Claims* (London: Sands and Co., 1902).

26. Ibid., 128-29.

27. Merry del Val to Broadhead, 17 January 1908: Merry del Val/Broadhead Papers, *Ushaw College Archives*, 11.

28. Adolf von Harnack, *Lehrbuch der Dogmengeschichte* (Tübingen: J.C.B. Mohr, 1900, 4th ed.), 3: 46-67.

29. See an account of the visit, in May 1878, in F.X. Kraus, *Tagebücher*, ed. H. Schiel (Cologne: J.P. Bachem, 1957), 386.

30. Zenos, (= F.X. Kraus), "Fluctus feri maris" (= *Centenarbetrachtungen* V), in *Beilage zur Allgemeinen Zeitung*, Nr. 75 (Munich: 1 April 1901), 3.

31. Ibid.

32. Kraus, *Tagebücher*, 386, 450.

33. Ibid., 579 (from 25 August 1891).

34. Erich Przywara, "Zur Geschichte des 'modernistischen' Newman," *Stimmen der Zeit* 102 (1922): 443-51.

35. Alexander Whyte, *Newman. An Appreciation* (Edinburgh: Oliphant, Anderson, and Ferrier, 1901). A Calvinist in theology but a Catholic in devotion, Whyte (1837-1921) was a minister in Edinburgh for his entire ecclesiastical career.

36. Przywara: "Zur Geschichte," 444.

37. Ibid., 445-446. Przywara has in mind here Henri Bremond, *Newman: Essai de biographie psychologique* (Paris: Bloud, 1906).

38. Whyte, *Newman*, 97: "Newman's preaching . . . never once touches the true core, and real and innermost essence, of the Gospel"; 99: ". . . Newman never was, root and branch, mind and conscience, imagination and heart, completely converted and completely surrendered up to Jesus Christ, the alone Redeemer and Righteousness of sinful man."

39. Richard W. Church, *Occasional Papers* (London: Macmillan, 1897), 2: 474.

40. Bremond, *Mystery of Newman*, 396, 408-409, 414.

41. Ibid., 407, 418.

42. Charles Sarolea, *Cardinal Newman and His Influence on Religious Life and Thought* (Edinburgh: T. and T. Clark, 1908).

43. Ibid., 131.

44. Ibid., 102.

45. Ibid., 155, 170, 172.

46. On Loisy, see Przywara's observations, "Zur Geschichte," 449. On Bremond's suspension, cf. Lawrence Barmann, *Baron Friedrich von Hügel and the Modernist Crisis in England* (Cambridge: University Press, 1972), 229.

47. Often labeled a "Modernist" (e.g., *New Catholic Encyclopedia* [San Francisco: McGraw Hill, 1967], 10: 88), Romolo Murri spent the bulk of his long career occupied with the Catholic Social Movement and Italian politics. After the suppression of Opera dei congressi by Pius X, he founded the Lega democratica nazionale, which was also condemned by the Pope in 1906. He was finally excommunicated in 1909, but returned to the church in 1943, just before his death. Paul Sabatier reported that Pius X considered Murri the "Prince of Modernists," and traced the enmity back to the pope's days as Patriarch of Venice when he had forbidden his clergy to read Murri's newspapers; Murri evidently responded to this prohibiton with a strong letter to Cardinal Sarto which the later pope never forgave him: in *Modernism* (= The Jowett Lectures 1908) (New York: C. Scribner's, 1908), 118-19.

48. = *Lo sviluppo del domma cristiano*. Murri also produced an analysis of *Pascendi: La filosofia nuova e l'enciclica contro il modernismo* (1908).

49. = *Fede e ragione*. Battaini also offered translations of Newman's *Letter to Pusey*, the *Letter to Norfolk*, and his *Apologia*, all published in 1909.

50. *Fede e ragione*, xviii.

51. Ibid., 15. *Lo sviluppo*. 9.

52. *Lo sviluppo*, 95.

53. John Prior, *Cardinal Newman and the Magisterium of the Church* (Rome: "Rome," 1909).

54. Ibid., 5.

55. Ibid., 34, 40-41.

56. The English version of Bremond's psychological biography, translated by C.C. Corrance (cf. note 2). Tyrrell dated his introduction 3 October 1906.

57. Tyrrell: ibid., xiii-xiv.

58. Ibid., xiv.

59. Ibid., xv.

60. Ibid., xvi-xvii.

61. George Tyrrell: "The Pope and Modernism," Part I in *The Times*, 30 September 1907, 4; Part II in *The Times*, 1 October 1907, 5.

62. Ibid., Part I, 4.

63. Ibid., Part II, 5.

64. Letter to *The Times*, 9 October 1907, 13.

65. Ward to Lilly, 3 November 1907, in Barmann, *Baron Friedrich von Hügel*, 204.

66. Letter to *The Times*, 10 October 1907, 4.

67. Letter to *The Times*, 11 October 1907, 12.

68. Letter to *The Times*, 2 November 1907, 10.

69. Letter to *The Times*, 4 November 1907, 10. In an additional letter to *The Times*, Norris makes clear that the "highest authority" to whom he had applied was in Rome (could this have been Merry del Val?); he had only done so because of Williams's letter (note 68) since they at the Birmingham Oratory had not thought for a second that Newman had been condemned.

70. Letter to *The Times*, 5 November 1907, 8.

71. Ibid.,

72. Report to *The Times*, 6 November 1907, 7.

73. Report from the *Osservatore Romano* of 8 November, in *The Times*, 9 November 1907, 5.

74. Letter to *The Times*, 13 November 1907, 19.

75. George Tyrrell, "The Condemnation of Newman," in *Manchester Guardian*, 20 November 1907, 1896-1897.

76. John Vaughan, Letter to *The Times*, 29 November 1907, 9.

77. George Tyrrell, Letter to *The Times*, 2 December 1907, 8. He is referring to Gasquet's letter of 5 November (cf. note 71).

78. Henri Bremond, Letter to *The Tablet*, 18 January 1908, 100.

79. Edward Thomas O'Dwyer, *Cardinal Newman and the Encyclical Pascendi Dominici gregis* (London: Longmans, Green, 1908, 2nd ed.).

80. Ibid., 5.

81. Ibid., 25; also, v; 19.

82. Ibid., 22, 31.

83. Ibid., 22-23, 38-41.

84. Ibid., ix. O'Dwyer's summary of Newman's thought reminds one of Talbot's charge, "what is the province of the laity? To hunt, to shoot, to entertain. These matters they understand, but to meddle with ecclesiastical matters they have no right at all." (Talbot to Manning, 1867; cf. note 10); and Ullathornes's startling query to Newman, "who are the laity?" (in Coulson, Introduction, 18).

85. In *Acta Sanctae Sedis* 41 (1908), 200-202. An English translation was promptly published in *The Times*, 23 March 1908, 4.

86. A Vieban, "Who are the Modernists of the Encyclical?" *The Ecclesiastical Review* 38 (1908): 489-508. Cf. C.A. Briggs's article, "The Encyclical against Modernism," *The North American Review* (February 1908): 204-05. Briggs had already written Harnack in Germany, trying to drum up support for an international protest against *Pascendi* and the "persecution" by Roman officials of theologians, scholars, and professors: Briggs to Harnack, 2 October 1907, in Harnack Papers, German State Library, East Berlin, Box 28.

87. Ibid., 492.

88. H.P. Russell, "A Lesson from Newman," *The Ecclesiastical Review* 38 (1908): 514-28; here, 514.

89. Ibid., 515, 528.

90. G. Lee, "Newman's 'Probabilities'," *The Ecclesiastical Review* 38 (1908): 528-41; here 528.

91. Sabatier, *Modernism*, 96-97, noted in 1908 that the Vatican had been "warning the pontifical booksellers in Rome not to let themselves be carried away by the fashion, and not to be always giving prominence to Newman's books or to books about him." In Sabatier's experience, to be called a "Newmanist" in Vaticanese was to be placed "on the downward slope to Modernism."

181

92. The German efforts were of prime importance. Przywara, Werner Becker, and Heinrich Fries (the latter two in their *Newman-Studien)* were the key figures. Charles Dessain's magisterial editing of Newman's *Letters and Diaries*, a project only now reaching conclusion, has been of monumental importance in gaining a fuller understanding of Newman's life and accomplishments.

93. See, for example, Bishop B.C. Butler, "Newman and the 2nd Vatican Council," in *The Rediscovery of Newman,* ed. John Coulson and A.M. Allchin (London: Sheed & Ward, 1967), 233-46.

94. Paul IV's message to the Newman Symposium in 1975, cited by John Paul II in his message to Archbishop Dwyer on the occasion of the centennial commemoration of Newman's cardinalate. *Newman, Sagio commemorativo* 5-6.

95. John Paul II, ibid., 6-8.

96. Speech given 5 March 1977: Unpublished manuscript from Vatican Radio.

Part Five

EPILOGICAL CONCLUSION

9

Newman and Modernism:
A Theological Reflection

Gabriel Daly

The one indisputable reason for associating John Henry Newman with Modernism is the fact that so many Modernists mentioned him as an important influence in their intellectual and ecclesial lives. As long, therefore, as the Modernists remained the Untouchables of the twentieth-century Roman Catholic church, Newman was open to suspicion of guilt by prospective association. One of the more regrettable results of the anti-Modernist campaign is the effect it has had on Roman Catholic historical and theological scholarship during the first half of the twentieth century. It brought about an artificial and stultifying debate over who was and who was not a "Modernist." Disciples of Blondel, Laberthonnière, von Hügel, Lagrange, and Genocchi have been at pains to defend their men from the charge of "Modernism." Only thus could they win them a hearing, or at least save them from obloquy, in the church they were trying to serve. This unreal situation has amply compounded the confusion which stemmed from the unreality of the original condemnation. The encyclical *Pascendi dominici gregis* not merely claimed to be unveiling a system of logically interconnected ideas, but also alleged the existence of a sinister plot to have these ideas disseminated throughout an unsuspecting church by covert and unscrupulous means. *Pascendi*'s claim to be able to discern and define a heresy which it named "Modernism" was to have a more lasting influence than its actual condemnation of the alleged heresy. The term "Modernism" was still being intoned by the integralist minority at Vatican II in its efforts to obstruct the reforms which were being proposed at the council.[1] The sheer width and imprecision of the term allowed it to be invoked as an automatic condemnation of any idea or initiative in the church that was not consonant with the tenets of the Ultramontane scholasticism which provided Roman Catholic orthodoxy with much of its conceptual structure and apologetical methodology. Any philosophical construction or method, any critical or historical finding, any criticism of church polity which was in even mild dissonance with scholastic Ultramontanism was liable to be interpreted as Modernist.

Pascendi claimed that one of the symptoms of Modernism was a "dislike of the scholastic method."[2] Newman had displayed not so much a dislike of, as psychological and intellectual discomfort with, the scholastic method. His mind worked in a concrete, image-laden manner which was out of harmony with the deductive, logic-based, method of neo-scholasticism. His distinction between implicit and explicit reasoning is the heuristic key to much of his thought. The long reign of the syllogism in Roman Catholic theology had created an intellectual climate antipathetic to the working of some distinguished Christian minds, including Newman's. At many points during the second millenium of the Christian Church, Aristotle appeared to have been enshrined among the Apostles as a source of faith; for, as Tyrrell never tired of pointing out, as long as revelation was in practice identified with its theological expression, uniformity of method would be judged necessary to unity of faith.

When nineteenth-century Roman theology addressed itself to what it saw as the crucial problem of how to relate faith to reason in a way which would avoid the extremes of rationalism and fideism, it operated from premises incorporating primary and fundamental definitions of both faith *and reason* which to Newman's mind lacked subtlety and differentiation. As long as "reason" was understood as the operation of formal argument it could not, in his view, be satisfactorily related to faith, and attempts to do so would play into the hands either of the rationalists or of the Liberals. Neo-scholasticism secured the objectivity of belief at the expense of its moral dimension. Liberal theology secured its moral dimension at the expense of doctrinal objectivity. Newman therefore postulates the existence of a *tertium quid,* a mode of mental operation which "thrives upon the absence of causal relationships."[3] He consequently dethrones the syllogism as a guide to faith, having found it to be morally void, and replaces it with a procedure which can embrace "truth in the concrete."[4] This procedure is expedited by the illative sense, which "takes account of the uniqueness of each object and each experience. It comprehends love and desire, fear and guilt as relevant to the search for truth and does not dismiss them as potential distorters of our vision."[5] By neo-scholastic criteria this was unacceptably "subjective;" yet in spite of the subjectivity of his arguments Newman always seemed to arrive at impeccably orthodox and "objective" conclusions about doctrine. No wonder Rome did not quite know what to make of him. In the event, it refused to accept the extreme Ultramontane view of him as "the most dangerous man in England"; instead it gave him a red hat which probably did more than anything else to protect him from attack after his death.

Nevertheless the greatest posthumous danger to Newman's reputation for orthodoxy came from the very obvious enthusiasm of the Modernists for his writings. Admirers of Newman who wished to be adjudged orthodox by the current Roman criteria of orthodoxy had only one defense open to them, namely, to allege that the Modernists had twisted him to their own purposes. Bremond was the principal target here. Roger Haight argues convincingly that although Bremond may have exaggerated the role of conscience in Newman's thought, he did not falsify that thought in any essential respect. Haight's treatment of the question as a hermeneutical one is illuminating. "Newman's doctrines are to be understood as a function of his inner experience." This is an interesting application of Collingwood's theory of historical thinking. Bremond sought to enter Newman's mind and think Newman's thoughts. The result was a fascinating, if necessarily one-sided, interaction between two sets of concerns, Newman's and Bremond's. Bremond's well-known remark that "If Newman were born sixty years later, he would have written neither the *University Sermons,* nor the *Grammar*; he would have written *L'Action*" is a legitimate piece of hermeneutical extrapolation. It does not claim that *L'Action* was in any sense derived from Newman, only that it belongs to that alternative view of Catholic Christianity which Blondel himself recognized. It was, in fact, to Pascal and Augustine that the Blondelians looked back for historical validation of their most characteristic insights; but they could have found the same validation in Newman.

The common factor can be described in various ways. Its most salient features are its anti-rationalism, its opposition to logical procedures as means of reaching religious truth, its regard for that imaginative use of the mind which Pascal called the *esprit de finesse* and Newman the illative sense, and in general, its concern that an inner resonance should precede the acceptance and profession of religious truth. Newman referred to it as conscience; Blondel and Laberthonnière described it as immanence. It can be traced back to the role which Augustine gave to desire and the "affections" in the search for God. Because it has rarely if ever featured in official church documents, this alternative tradition has normally been consigned to the realm of the "mystical" and consequently denied a serious theological hearing in the Roman Catholic church. "Theology" was widely understood, by both integralists and Modernists, to apply only to scholastic modes of thought. Tyrrell frequently used the term "theology" in this sense. He, Blondel, and Newman all described themselves as not being theologians, meaning scholastics. Something is seriously wrong with received theology when some of the finest Christian minds of their age find it necessary to disclaim their status as theologians. In a way, it was a device for detaching themselves from the rigidities and limitations of mandatory scholasticism. It amounted to a polite refusal to employ the tactics prescribed by Rome while demonstrating that the game could be played by other, and more effective, tactics which were equally within the rule of faith. This might have mattered little had Rome not been disposed to disregard the distinction between tactics and rules. In effect what both Newman and the Modernists were saying was that while Rome had the authority to lay down the rules, it had no authority to prescribe the tactics.

Nicholas Lash has remarked with severity that "The question: Was Newman a modernist? is anachronistic and in the last analysis lacking in intellectual seriousness."[6] This observation is historically indisputable in so far as Modernism was a phenomenon belonging to a period which did not begin until after Newman's death. It would be anachronistic, for example, to describe Justin Martyr as a heretic by Nicene standards. It would not be anachronistic or frivolous to describe him as a binitarian whose views would be unacceptable if reproduced by a post-Nicene Christian. There is certainly a note of unreality in the debate over whether Newman was envisaged in *Pascendi* or not. Only in a church which appears to identify truth with the decrees of institutional authority has the question any meaning or logic. Posthumous and retrospective condemnations have a convoluted logic all their own. Two precedents come to mind: the case of Jansen's book *Augustinus* and Gregory XVI's strictures upon the sub-Kantian theological methodology of Georg Hermes.

Cornelius Jansen's *Augustinus* was published in 1640, two years after the author's death. Five propositions extracted from it were condemned by Innocent X in 1653.[7] Thus was born a new heresy which was immediately complicated by the distinction drawn by the defendants between *fait* and *droit*. The propositions, ran the defense, were heretical as stated (*droit*) but were not to be found in Jansen's book (*fait*); in short, Jansen was not a Jansenist. In 1656 Alexander VII, claiming authority over fact as well as doctrine, extended the condemnation from the Five Propositions to the whole book.[8]

Gregory XVI's condemnation of Georg Hermes in 1835, four years after Hermes' death, constituted an even more dangerous precedent. It was couched in startlingly hostile and hyperbolic language, and it gave great offense in Germany where Hermes was held in high esteem for his attempt to respond constructively to the Kantian critique. Several professors in the University of Bonn, following the precedent set in France during the Jansenist affair, accepted Gregory's condemnation as stated in the Brief *Dum acerbissimas* (26 September 1835),[9] but claimed that Hermes had never taught the condemned opinions. Hoping to secure a revocation of the condemnation, two German professors, Braun and Elvenich, actually journeyed to Rome, but to no avail. In 1847 Pius IX reiterated the condemnation in a letter to the archbishop of Cologne.[10]

If Rome had wished to condemn Newman in or around 1907, the condemnation would probably have proceeded on similar lines, and the Newmanians would presumably have been tempted to mount a similar defense. Ward's anxieties are chronicled elsewhere in this book. Tyrrell was openly contemptuous of Norris's letter to *The Times* in which the writer announced that he had it on "the highest authority that 'the genuine doctrine and spirit of Newman's Catholic teaching are not hit by the Encyclical.' "[11] Not for Tyrrell any compromising and timorous distinctions between *fait* and *droit*: "The agreement of Newman with the Encyclical is surely a matter to be settled by observation and not by oracle."[12] The point is obvious enough when one no longer has a special case to plead, a face to save, or a dilemma to meet. Theological condemnations are interpretative acts in the aggressive mode. In addition, they can resemble carpet-bombing which destroys acres of noncombatant housing in an attempt to eliminate a nest of real or imagined enemy activists. Ward's anxiety to have Newman cleared of posthumous complicity in the ideas condemned by *Pascendi* would merely have had the effect of distributing the obloquy elsewhere. Von Hügel pointed this out with perhaps excessive tact to Ward himself: "The thing would, to my mind, not be worth attempting, if it had to be restricted to Newman's case."[13] At any rate it is hard to avoid the conclusion that Ward was behaving less than honestly in seeking such an exculpation, since he was convinced "by observation and not by oracle" that Newman *was* "included." Ward's letter to Norris attempts a distinction between "condemnation" and "inclusion." Newman, wrote Ward, was not *condemned*, but "his chief positions are included in the exposition of Modernism which is condemned." It was just as well for Ward's integrity that he failed to secure a positive vetting of his hero. Ward was convinced by the evidence itself that Newman's thought could not be squared with *Pascendi* and he gave Willie Williams reluctant credit for seeing this and for having the conscience and courage to say it. The whole unhappy situation drove Ward to frenetic letter-writing. To Norris he wrote that Newman was not condemned. To the Duke of Norfolk he wrote that although he did "not believe that the Pope *meant* to condemn Newman," nevertheless the theology of *Pascendi* "condemned the modernists on certain points in terms which beyond question equally condemn Newman's theories."

Gary Lease shows that Rome had no *intention* of condemning Newman. He simply was not in the minds of those who drew up and issued the condemnation. Joseph Lemius, the principal draftsman of the "theoretical" portion of *Pascendi,* appears never to have read Newman. Raphael Merry del Val held him in respect and was disposed to quote him. Pius X himself wrote to congratulate Bishop O'Dwyer of Limerick on the latter's defense of Newman. "Included but not condemned" is one way of expressing the distinction between formal (intentional) and implicit (subjectively unintentional but objectively relevant) condemnation. Paul Sabatier, who had a keen ear for ecclesiastical gossip, writes that students in Rome were discouraged from reading Newman,[14] though in view of the fact that he had been a cardinal, the discouragement would no doubt have been discreet.

The predominant attitude of neo-scholastic orthodoxy toward Newman (on the part of those who had actually read him) was stated not by Rome but by two influential French theologians, Léonce de Grandmaison and Jules Lebreton, both of whom expressed serious dissatisfaction with Newman's "anti-intellectualism." Lebreton gave currency to the idea that Newman was a "psychologizer" rather than a theologian, and that his thought processes served to promote nominalism. De Grandmaison catches the neo-scholastic mood exactly in a lapidary sentence: "Newman is too original, too personal a thinker to be followed with safety."[15] "Unsafe" has been one of the weasel words in the vocabulary of neo-scholastic orthodoxy. It has normally been applied to writers who could not be received into the essentialist paradise. On the other hand they could not be condemned to the hell of heresy. They were therefore consigned to the limbo reserved for the "unsafe." Fortunately, history is the great liberator from such limbos. It is the jailers who are forgotten.

I have argued elsewhere that the imprecision and ambiguity of the word "Modernism" renders it virtually useless as an agreed theological currency.[16] The simplest answer to the question "Was Newman a Modernist?" is a denial that the question has any negotiable theological reference, or, as Lash puts it, any intellectual seriousness. Until Joseph Lemius emerged from his room with the draft of *Pascendi,* Rome had no firm speculative idea of, but only a passionate instinct about, what it wanted to condemn or how the condemnation should be framed. Lemius provided neo-scholastic orthodoxy with an antithetical system in its own image and likeness. Newman would have reacted with acute distaste to the fictional system depicted and condemned in the encyclical. It would have struck him as an extraordinary misalliance of liberal tenets on the one hand and scholastic method on the other, both equally at variance with his own elegant model of the "germination and maturation of some truth or apparent truth on a large mental field."[17]

The problem for all scholastic readers of Newman was how to relate his thought processes to their own. The question achieved a special relevance when certain Catholic scholars, shortly to be described as "Modernists," referred to him with approval. J. Bellamy, a seminary professor of open and scholarly, if cautious, dispositions, who was writing in the false dawn which marked the last years of Leo XIII's pontificate, made the observation: "Gratry [and] Newman were Catholic thinkers, sometimes admirable as negotiators (*brasseurs*) of ideas, rather than theologians" (again one notes the distinction between thinkers and theologians as a stratagem for dealing with nonscholastic theologians).[18] Bellamy was genuinely interested in the newer theories, for which his favorite epithet is "bold." Having briefly mentioned an article by Mgr. Mignot on "religious evolutionism," Bellamy continues: "The question was taken up again with still more audacity by a writer in the *Revue du clergé français.*" The writer was of course Loisy, using the pseudonym "Firmin."

> S'inspirant, disait-il, de la théorie formulée par Newman mais allant plus loin en réalité, le docte critique affirmait que les apôtres, après la mort du Sauveur, "n'étaient en possession ni d'une organisation définie, ni d'un symbole arrêté, ni d'un programme d'action religeuse ou de culte à instituer."[19]

"In short," Bellamy remarks, "our critic admits an objective growth in the deposit of revelation."[20] This theory is not to the taste of professional theologians, who continue firmly to maintain the principle of the objective immutability of the revealed deposit. Newman, according to Bellamy, had maintained that Catholic doctrine has journeyed through the ages "without undergoing any essential change."[21] Whatever one may think about the truth of this confident claim, it is at least witness to Bellamy's belief that the salient difference between Newman and Loisy is that the former does not hold with an "objective" change in the deposit, whereas the latter does. Even so, says Bellamy, Newman's theory "abounds in new insights (*vues*) and relatively bold ideas," and the really strange thing, he remarks perceptively, is that those insights and ideas did not cause a theological sensation. The reason would seem to be that "The moment had not yet come when the conception of Catholic doctrine as a living organism, which develops and grows ceaselessly over the ages, would come to be seen as one of the most important and fruitful insights of nineteenth century theological science."[22] There were, suggests Bellamy, dangers in this challenging and exciting insight, as the example of Günther's "rationalism" makes clear.

The invocation of Günther is interesting. Anton Günther wanted to make Christian faith responsible to the demands of reason, understood in the light of the Kantian critique. Pius IX's Brief *Eximiam tuam* of 1857 took Günther to task for deploying the distinction between faith and knowledge in such a way as to threaten the "perennial immutability of faith."[23] Was Newman's position vulnerable to the same charge? The similarities are real, though the respective preoccupations of the two men were different. Günther's distinction between *Vernunft* and *Verstand* has something in common with Newman's distinction between implicit and explicit reason. "Only *Vernunft*, intuitive intelligence, had access to the world of metaphysical reality. God's existence could not be established nor could his attributes be known through the discursive argumentation of *Verstand*."[24] Günther, however, wanted to convert the object of faith, delivered by historical revelation, into a systematically worked-out philosophy which would commend itself to educated post-Kantian man. Newman's concerns were quite different, and he was never in danger of meriting the accusation that he was a semi-rationalist. His very English preoccupation with imagination and its grasp of the concrete ensured that German Idealism would hold little fascination for him. But would Rome be able to appreciate this? Newman scholars have pointed to the difficulty of relating his theory of doctrinal development to his theory of religious inference and assent. If he had been condemned, either in life or posthumously, it would have been primarily on the grounds that his theory of development had threatened "the perennial immutability of faith." On this ground alone he was vulnerable to the sort of attack which had been brought to bear on Günther, mainly by Joseph Kleutgen. He was fortunate in that his enemies lacked the intellectual caliber of Günther's. Monsignor Talbot was not in the same league as Father Kleutgen.

If Rome had been seriously concerned about Newman's theory of development, it had a clear-cut opportunity to issue a warning at any point after 1847 when Newman, anxious to discover whether his theory accorded with Roman Catholic doctrine, cast it into Latin, tightened the argument, reduced it to its bare essentials, tried to give it some scholastic points of reference, and sent it off to Giovanni Perrone, the principal Roman theologian of the period. This paper was published for the first time in 1935, together with Perrone's comments, for which Newman had provided a margin.[25] Perrone's response was basically one less of disagreement than of noncomprehension. At certain points in the paper, however, he did express open disagreement. One of these occurs in chapter three, where Newman draws an analogy between personal and ecclesial growth in knowledge. The word of God needs time in order to be objectified in dogma, Newman wrote; just as the ideas which exist in a philosopher's mind take many years of reflection before they reach mature expression. In this respect, then, the word of God "est divina quaedam philosophia."[26] Perrone's verdict was forthright. Where Newman had written that the church could properly be said to be not fully aware (*conscia*) of what would later be expressed "in formam dogmaticam," Perrone commented: "Hoc dicere non auderem."[27] For Perrone any such growth would necessarily be a growth of the deposit *which is itself dogma.* "Verbum Dei *semper,* seu ex quo datum est transit in dogma, seu constituit objectum fidei nostrae."[28] The advent of heresy may, he adds, force the church to render explicit what she has always believed implicitly from the beginning.

Although Perrone observed despairingly that "Newman miscet et confundat omnia," he saw no reason for seeking Newman's condemnation as Kleutgen had sought Günther's—and this at the very time when Rome was disposed to issue condemnations liberally.[29]

Nothing Perrone had written caused Newman to alter his central insights. The reason is put tersely by Owen Chadwick: "Perrone had not convinced him because Newman was a historian and Perrone was not. Perrone had no notion of the difficulties created for the older form of the doctrine of tradition by modern historical research."[30] This was, of course, to be a crucial issue in the Modernist crisis. It was not so much a matter of historical information, important as this might be, as one of historical imagination, sense, and method. Newman's "great idea" enters into, and interacts with, history. It is designed *ab initio,* to do so as a living thing maintaining a living relationship with its changing environment. It must change in order to remain the same. Perrone lacked the sort of mind-set which would have enabled him to appreciate the value of this model. Perrone was accustomed to think in terms of, and work with, essences, which by definition do not, indeed cannot, change. Obtained by Aristotelian abstraction, essences achieve a timeless immobility which is basically Platonist. Blondel, though in radical disagreement with much of Loisy's argument in *L'Évangile et L'Église,* nevertheless appreciated the curious similarity between Harnack's liberal Protestant *fixisme* and that of the Catholic scholastics.[31] Harnack's "essence of Christianity" behaved in history in much the same way as the Catholic essentialist "deposit of faith."

In the end, it is the fact that the "idea" changes as a result of its symbiotic relationship with the mind (= church) which exposes Newman's theory to the criticism of scholastic orthodoxy. And Newman is quite unambiguous about the matter, making no alteration in 1878 to what he had written in 1845: ". . . an idea not only modifies, *but is modified*, or at least influenced, by the state of things in which it is carried out."[32] This observation deserves further scrutiny.

To describe Christianity as an "idea" is to employ a model. To use a model theologically is to proceed isomorphically: It is to deploy an argument on one level in the knowledge that its true and intended reference is to another, otherwise cognitively inaccessible, level. The theologian has control only over the model, never over the reality to which it refers. The theologian exercises scientific responsibility not only by recognizing that he or she is in fact working with and from a model (thus recognizing that religious language does not work in the same way as empirically based language), but also by taking care to show whence he or she is borrowing the model. A theological model ought to have the clarity of a good poetic metaphor, clearly etched, vivid, and, normally, limited to the context from which it is borrowed. While it may be legitimate for a poet "to hover between images," the theologian who seeks to do likewise ought to be fully aware of the specific images between which he proposes to hover. Failure in this respect destroys, or at least distorts, the isomorphic relationship between the image and its transcendent referent. (The classical doctrine of original sin is a good illustration of what happens when models are not hovered over, but grafted on to each other to form a misshapen image which simply loses its isomorphic possibilities because of linguistic dissonance springing from a disordered imagination.)[33]

The precise character and reference of Newman's "idea" has been the subject of much discussion and controversy. No one could deny its richness and vitality or its possibilities for what Loisy called *mouvement dans l'Église*. Newman calls it an *impression* made on the imagination. This impression has many aspects, i.e., it is subject to being viewed from many different perspectives; and it is this multiperspectival viewing which allows the idea to live in, and gain a grip upon, the mind. A great idea is infinitely rich in possibilities, for "there is no one aspect deep enough to exhaust the contents of a real idea, no one term or proposition which will serve to define it."[34] The theological problem here is that the argument is moving not on two but on *three* levels. The first level is that of individual psychology, the second is that of social psychology, and the third is of course the level of final reference, namely, the transcendent source of revelation and its relationship with the historically situated believer. There is therefore a *double* isomorphism: revelation enters the church as an idea enters society, which in turn resembles the making of an impression upon an individual mind. The basic model is the growth of a living thing and its relationship with its environment. The metaphor employed is inescapably biological and environmental. Newman's "idea" lives and grows in society in a fashion analogous to its life and growth in the individual mind. Therefore it changes, and such change constitutes *historical* perfection. In a higher world Platonic immutability may hold sway, but here below "to be perfect is to have changed often."

When, however, biological growth is translated into the model of substance or essence, progress from the *terminus a quo* to the *terminus ad quem* entails a substantial, or essential, change: the acorn and the oak are "essentially" ("substantially," "formally") different, however close their botanical relationship. Consequently one may say that as long as Christian doctrine was seen more or less exclusively in terms of essences, there could be no question of a biological model: essences do not grow. The essence of an oak tree is different from that of an acorn. Growth is a linear and cumulative model in fundamental dissonance with the static model of essence. Thus Newman's theory could get a fair hearing in the Catholic church only after the break with exclusive and mandatory essentialism. Now that this break has taken place, it is possible for Roman Catholics to approach Newman's methodology less edgily than the Modernists and their contemporaries were able to do.

Nicholas Lash in his examination of this aspect of Newman's theory of development has made a distinction between the "linear" or "cumulative" model and the "episodic" one.[35] George A. Lindbeck draws the same distinction under the rubric "developmental" and "situational."[36] Lindbeck makes it abundantly clear that only the situational model holds out any hope for ecumenical progress. Protestants are unlikely to be seduced by the poetic splendor of Newman's river which is "more equable, and purer, and stronger, when its bed has become deep, and broad, and full."[37] Protestants will continue to be impressed by the very image which Newman attempts to correct: "It is indeed sometimes said that the stream is clearest near the spring." After all, the Reformation was, for better or for worse, carried out on that assumption. Newman always insisted that the individual must grow in fidelity to conscience (i.e., in holiness) if he or she is to grow in the knowledge of God. Transpose that conviction to the arena of church

195

history and you find little reason to suppose that there has been corporate growth in fidelity to conscience or in the knowledge of God. Newman, Lash remarks, "never adequately considers this objection in the *Essay.*"[38] Neither did Vatican II.

It can hardly be denied that Newman has given Christian theology an endlessly fertile model with which to analyze and synthesize the problem of identity and change in the church's faith and in its successive formulations of the beliefs which arise out of that faith. Yet in spite of its very fertility— perhaps even because of it—the possibility of epistemological confusion and linguistic dissonance is undeniable. For all its fertility, the model has its limitiations. Its importance lies in its provision of a new perspective from which to view an old problem. Newman used it originally to account for a specific difficulty in his own life. The Modernists used it to tackle a different difficulty.

There are two extremes to be avoided in treating of the Modernists' debt to Newman. The first is that the Modernists were disciples of Newman *simpliciter*. Ernesto Buonaiuti came near to this extreme when, in his *Pelegrino di Roma,* he described Tyrrell as the "genuine heir—indeed one might say the eloquent and inspired reincarnation—of Newman."[39] The second extreme was stated by Werner Becker at the Newman Symposium held at Oriel College, Oxford, in 1966: "It is, of course, well known that the modernists at the turn of the century in England and France often referred to Newman, but it was to a Newman of their own invention."[40] This sweeping, unproven, and indeed antecedently improbable generalization is little more than just another—though particularly hyperbolic—expression of the need to placate the spirit of integralism which even as late as 1966 was still residual in the Catholic mind. Inasmuch as both Newman and the Modernists used nonscholastic concepts and language, the scholastics themselves were not slow to spot the similarities between them. Avoiding misleading generalizations about "the Modernists," however, let us come to instances. Loisy and Tyrrell were arguably the two Modernists most influenced by Newman's epistemology of faith and by his theory of doctrinal development, and it is instructive to consider how they approached and finally, each in his own way, transcended it—for better or for worse.

The ambiguity of Loisy's target in *L'Évangile et L'Église* has often been commented on. Poulat's suggestion that we should forget Harnack if we wish to understand Loisy[41] could, if adopted, lead us to overlook a very important element in Loisy's thought, an element on which Blondel felt able to congratulate Loisy, namely, the latter's exposure of the "fixisme" of Harnack "who is a scholastic in his own way."[42] Harnack's "essence of

Christianity" behaves in history much as the scholastic *depositum fidei* does: it pursues its course more or less autonomously and catalytically. The difference between the two is largely a matter of two different sets of theological spectacles. The scholastics see the *depositum* as something to be cherished and expounded to the world by a holy and Spirit-guided church: while Harnack sees essential Christianity struggling to protect itself from, and occasionally with brief success reasserting itself against, the corrupting influence of the cultural, including ecclesiastical, forms through which it has to pass.

Loisy saw and savored the irony of opposing Harnack with a "very Catholic,"[43] but very unscholastic, argument. The Christian vision and message (call it deposit or essence, as you will) had to enter as a living organism into a host which was itself a living organism. Newman's model of the multifaceted idea clearly suggests a symbiotic, not catalytic, relationship between the idea and *both* the mind which entertains it *and* the society which cherishes it. The symbiosis, however, cannot be unconditioned and unrestrained, for if it were, the resultant situation would be the very liberalism which Newman consistently repudiated: Something in the deposit remains unnegotiable. If its form changes, this can be only so that the content may remain the same. Loisy's use of the development model was far more "episodic" or "situational" than Newman's, and, as he remarks in the *Mémoires,* he was prepared to extend it to a far wider area (including the Bible) than Newman had done. In addition, whereas Newman had recognized the danger of corruption and had sought to provide diagnostic tests for discriminating between a true development and a corruption, Loisy gave the impression of being rather cavalier about the need for such discrimination, since for him both truth and corruption, being contextual, were destined to obsolescence and eventual replacement. As Loisy noted, Newman did not address himself to the problem which was central to the Modernists, i.e., the mode of contact between God's revelation and man in history. He was concerned with the behavior of revelation *after* it had been received rather than with the revelatory process itself.

When Loisy remarked that nothing is less Catholic than the cult of the formula, he was making a daring raid on the central stronghold of Catholic orthodoxy as it was then understood and proclaimed. He had just argued that revealed truths live preconceptually in ecclesiastical dogmas. Harnack claimed that Christianity has a timeless essence which can be detached from the Palestinian culture in which that essence was first expressed. Loisy chose to interpret this view not simply as static but also as characteristically

Protestant. Loisy therefore conjoins the church to the Gospel in a dynamic continuum. The church continues, prolongs, the Gospel in history. In fact the church provides the Gospel with an indispensable life-support system. Loisy thus gives the church a life or death role in embodying the Gospel through the ages. There is, of course, a price to be paid. The Catholic church of his age was trying to preserve an essence and at the same time to give itself a central role in the custodianship of that essence. Loisy in effect claimed that the neo-scholastic church had refused the keeping of a *live* body and substituted an enbalmed corpse. He was saying that if the church lays claim to the burden of Christianity, that burden must be a living one and must therefore be subject to change. This is precisely what Newman had claimed when he wrote that "to be perfect is to have changed often." You cannot have it both ways. If you want a timeless essence, you must settle for an inert deposit for which the church is no more than a conductor or security agent. If, on the other hand, you lay claim to the creative trusteeship of a living message, you must be prepared to concede that the message is subject in some way to modification by its passage through time. John XXIII and Vatican II attempted to meet the challenge by making a distinction between the substance of a doctrine and the manner of its formulation. This was a distinction which scholastic orthodoxy, trying to have the best of both worlds, utterly repudiated. A scholastically minded magisterium had custodianship of an immutable deposit and it allowed for its own historical contribution by an appeal to deductive theological procedures over which it claimed the right of absolute control: All was present in the original deposit; the church merely made deductive abstractions from the deposit and imposed these abstractions in the name of its own authority supported by Aristotelian logical procedures.

By converting Newman's subtle, multilayered model into a purely deductive one, the later neo-scholastics not merely denatured it but turned it into an instrument for widening the gap between scripture and tradition. This procedure allowed theologians to "deduce" further truths from the original deposit while claiming that the deposit remained intact and unchanged. These speculative deductions thus became subject to the judgment of the magisterium which, whenever it gave an authoritative definition of a speculatively derived theological position (e.g., the Marian dogmas), defined them as not merely true and binding on the Catholic conscience, but true and binding *because they are now declared to be part of the original deposit.* This is the controlling contention of all Protestant criticism of the Catholic approach to dogma. The whole system of logical deduction from an original deposit stands or falls on whether the logic is intrinsically compulsive or not. If in any particular instance it is intrinsically compulsive, precisely as logic, there is no need for authoritative pronouncements. If it is not, then the pronouncement is simply one of authority simultaneously declaring a *new* truth and denying its novelty by a concomitant declaration that the church has *always* believed it as belonging to the original deposit. The latter declaration is clearly open to straightforward *historical* examination—a point that Loisy and Tyrrell frequently made.

During the debate on *Dei Verbum* at Vatican II the "progressives" found themselves in opposition to *both* the scholastic conservatives *and* to the Protestant observers—for very different reasons. Article 9 of *Dei Verbum* was instrumental in ending the notorious two-source theory of revelation. The draftsmen wanted to give the fullest weight to the authority of scripture while at the same time asserting a Roman Catholic doctrine of tradition. Both scripture and tradition, "flowing from the same divine wellspring, in a certain way merge into a unity and tend towards the same end." Protestants like Oscar Cullmann saw a Trojan Horse here. The very attempt to give scripture a centrality within the Roman Catholic system seemed to Protestants to expose it to ecclesiastical control and innovation and thus to rob it of its transcendent authority over the church.

Newman had recognized that committal of the Christian "idea" to church and history involved *risk*, but, as he observed, without risk there is no life. The risk was the distortion of the original idea which he called corruption. The seven "tests," or "notes," are witness to his appreciation that the church might indeed "develop" the message in ways which were in dissonance with the primitive idea. The trouble about the tests is that they are so broad and abstract as to be virtually useless as actual criteria for a *concrete,* historically specifiable corruption. However, as Lash remarks, at least Newman recognized the problem. Loisy, on the other hand, is less concerned with the moral dimension of what is going on but instead remarks somewhat airily that truth changes with the passage of time.

At this point we must begin seriously to ask whether the term *change* has sufficient univocacy about it to make it a theologically negotiable currency without a great deal of philosophical qualification. The greatest danger here is confusion of areas or levels. We need to specify the area in which we are working: the epistemological (involving questions of "objectivity" and "subjectivity"), the metaphysical (involving questions of ontological transcendence), the historical (involving all the previous questions and adding further hermeneutical ones of its own), and the moral (involving conscience and its rights in relation to an extrinsic authority). There is potential dissonance between each of these areas and potential confusion in failing to distinguish between them while relating each to the other.

Tyrrell's attitude and debt to, together with his disenchantment with, Newman is something of a critical minefield.[44] Two facts, however, are clear if not indisputable. The first is that at a certain point in his life the *Grammar of Assent* "did effect a profound revolution in my way of thinking, in the year 1885, just when I had begun to feel the limits of scholasticism rather painfully."[45] The second fact is stated in the same letter: "I was formerly more of a Newmanite than I am now." Tyrrell quickly came to resent Ward's setting up of Newman as an object of para-orthodox loyalty. Tyrrell rightly saw that the texture and thrust of Newman's thought was profoundly antipathetic to neo-scholastic methodological orthodoxy. He therefore initially saw Newman in the same light as did the other Modernists, i.e., as a Catholic thinker whose approach to Christianity offered the possibility of a rapprochement with contemporary scientific and philosophical attitudes. Unlike Loisy, Tyrrell's complex intellectual honesty would not allow him simply to use Newman as a springboard to more advanced and developed theological positions and then to forget about him. Tyrrell's attitude to Newman was not unlike Barth's to Kierkegaard: one must go to school to him but one must then matriculate.[46] Newman scholars not unnaturally take a rather poor view of this attitude. Lash bluntly accuses Tyrrell of misunderstanding the *Essay* when he wrote that it "was undoubtedly written with one eye fixed on his scholastic critics, and with a view to dissemble the difference between their conception and his own as much as possible."[47] As it stands, Tyrrell's sentence lies wide open to Lash's criticism. The *first* edition of the *Essay* was obviously not written "with one eye fixed on his scholastic critics," and Tyrrell elsewhere shows his appreciation of the fact that if Newman's eyes were fixed anywhere, aside, that is, from the two absolute and luminously self-evident beings, himself and his Creator, it was upon his fellow Tractarians. But does not a textual comparison of the 1845 and 1878 editions, together with the Newman-Perrone Paper, give some support to Tyrrell's contention? Newman, after all, had entered a church in which the dominant conception of orthodoxy was inextricably bound up with scholastic forms of thought; and Tyrrell, finding himself in a somewhat similar situation, must have appreciated Newman's instinctive urge to commend his ideas in a fashion which would not have him antecedently ruled out of court. One can indeed quarrel with Tyrrell's choice of the word *dissemble*, which is gratuitous and uncritical. Newman knew that his mode of thought was uncongenial to the neo-scholastic mind, but since the neo-scholastics were in control of the statements of orthodoxy within the church he had joined, he had little choice but to establish as many bridgeheads as possible between his own thought and theirs. This is not "dissembling," it is plain common sense; and Tyrrell, in making the charge, was throwing stones in a glass house.

There is in Tyrrell's attitude to Newman an element of disillusionment which is unparalleled in the other Modernists. Tyrrell gives the impression of having invested heavily in Newman's thought and then of having discovered that the investment gave seriously inadequate returns. Loisy, on the other hand, got as much mileage as he could out of Newman and then passed insouciantly on. Newman, according to Tyrrell,

> had no quarrel but every sympathy with the dogmatic intransigence of scholastic theologians. What he questioned was the apologetic efficacy of their dialectical method, the prudence of accepting direct combat with rationalistic assailants on their own terms, instead of attacking their first principles and their whole theory of assent.[48]

If it is true that Tyrrell did experience disillusionment with Newman, it is highly likely that this disillusionment arose primarily out of the realization that Newman's "idea" was incompatible with his own conception of "prophetic experience."

In the last five years of his life Tyrrell arrived at a complex estimate of Newman's contribution to Christian theology. The Modernists, according to Tyrrell, took Newman's notion of an "idea" as a spiritual force or impetus "and turned [it] against much of that system in whose defence he had framed it."[49] Tyrrell's thesis is summarized in his introduction to Bremond's *The Mystery of Newman:* "Newman's incontestible abhorrence of doctrinal liberalism does not at once prove that he may not be the progenitor of it."[50]

John Coulson, in his fascinating study *Religion and Imagination,* writes of Tyrrell's "despair" over the prospect of achieving a critically acceptable relationship between faith as a response of the religious imagination and belief as the conceptual expression of that faith.

> Is there now, as the Modernists assumed, a radical and seemingly unbridgeable divide between, on the one hand, the metaphorical and symbolic language of imagination and faith and, on the other, the language of belief and conceptual formulation? Have the questions changed so radically as to invalidate Newman's grammar of imagination and belief?[51]

During the last four years of his life Tyrrell would have answered both questions with an affirmative. It is, however, difficult to estimate the extent to which his answers would have been determined by a change in his attitude to the intrinsic possibilities of doctrinal objectivity or merely by the temporarily limiting context of a pervasive and mandatory scholasticism which treated revelation as statement and nothing else. One has to appreciate Tyrrell's temperament in order to appreciate his theology. To use Newmanian terms, Tyrrell was so convinced that the scholastics had evacuated the real by their obsession with the notional (understood in a most restrictive way) that he deliberately played up the preconceptual and unthematized character of primal revelation. Stung by Lebreton's charge that he had reduced revelation to pure feeling, Tyrrell insisted that the original experience has a mental element which is susceptible of subsequent analysis.[52] Faith, however, is given, not to this analysis, but to revelation contained in the original *overall* experience. Where Tyrrell may have misread Newman can be seen in his apparent failure to appreciate the thrust of Newman's twofold analysis of the "idea" or impression made on the imagination. He may, however, be less culpable in this misreading than his critics allege owing to Newman's ambiguity on whether the "idea," notional *and real,* actually develops. In the *Grammar of Assent* Newman makes it clear that it is the notional element which is subject to development. In the last of the *University Sermons* he remarked that the development of the original idea "results in a series, or rather body of dogmatic statements, till what was at first an impression on the Imagination has become a system or creed in the Reason."[53]

Is the *original* impression on the imagination, however, itself subject to change in the course of its psychological and historical journey? Newman says that the "idea will in course of time expand into a multitude of ideas, and aspects of ideas, connected and harmonious with one another."[54] The model here has all the appearance of being the replication of cells, but, Newman immediately adds, these replicating ideas are "in themselves determinate *and immutable,* as is the objective fact itself which is thus represented." They are immutable—but they nonetheless replicate. Can Tyrrell be blamed for his impatience here?

Theological impressionism has much to commend it, but its logical limitations are disregarded at the theologian's peril. "There is," wrote Tyrrell to Ward, "no valid inference from analogues."[55] If a theologian

202

chooses a specific model, such as biological growth, he or she must accept *all* its relevant, if uncomfortable phenomenological implications. "Do we not forget that 'development' means death and decay as well as growth, that it means continuity only by way of reproduction in a new generation?"[56] To claim that the Christian idea changes in order to remain the same is a pertinent and arresting paradox. If, however, there is no valid inference from analogues, there is still less from paradoxes. Tyrrell's objection remains formidable: How can a paradox be translated into a dogma the expression of which claims to operate in a thoroughly rational manner? In short, Newman's model works well enough on a purely ecclesiological level: If one accepts Nicaea and Chalcedon, there appears to be no good reason for refusing Lateran IV and Trent. If, on the other hand, one recognizes, as Tyrrell did, that the problem begins in scripture itself as the record of an experience, then Newman's model opens up hermeneutical possibilities which Newman himself, with all his anti-liberal convictions, would have repudiated. Tyrrell saw this and said so.

Friedrich von Hügel saw it also but made less of it than Tyrrell. Von Hügel's debt to Newman, though very real, appears to have been less direct and less personally felt. Von Hügel was more concerned with the synchronic possibilities of Newman's model of the three offices of Christ, kingly, prophetical, and priestly, which von Hügel converted into the three elements of religion, the external, the intellectual, and the mystical, each corresponding to a stage in human psychological development.[57] He also borrowed Newman's distinction between the real and the notional and blended it with Leibniz's distinction between "dim Experience" and "reflex Knowledge."[58] The result of this blending was characteristically his own. "Dim Experience" constitutes the meetingplace of the Absolute with the contingent. Where Newman had been primarily concerned with the mechanics of human certitude, von Hügel was preoccupied with the mode of contact between God as absolute and man as contingent. What both men shared, in opposition to the scholastics, was an interest in the concrete, particularized fact of what happens when God approaches man. Where they differed was that von Hügel's difficulties stemmed from the objective, and Newman's from the subjective, reality of the revelatory instance. The similarity provides grounds for establishing a link between them. The difference is significant enough to inhibit one from claiming that the link was more than oblique and largely unconscious.

Writing to Ignatius Ryder after Newman's death, von Hügel spoke of his debt in a way which seems to epitomize the experience of others, the Modernists perhaps most of all.[59] In von Hügel's case Newman's influence began when he was still a boy reading *Loss and Gain* and receiving from it an indelible impression of "the intellectual might and grandeur of the Catholic position." With the passage of time, von Hügel made few explicit references to Newman and, as Michael de la Bedoyère has observed, "these few usually sound a critical note."[60] In his letter to Ryder, however, the Baron puts the matter in a somewhat different light: "I talk Newman even oftener than I know." He probably speaks for most of those who have ever gone to school to Newman when he writes:

> I suspect that this is the true explanation of the apparent disproportion between his magnificent endowments and their lavish use on the one hand and the tangible results on the other: that, in fact, the results have been and are too general and far-reaching, too secret and deep to be thus tangible and self-evident to a generation bathed in and penetrated by them.[61]

It is as good an assessment as any that might be made about the Modernists' debt to John Henry Newman.

NOTES

1. See T.M. Loome, *Liberal Catholicism, Reform Catholicism, Modernism: A Contribution to a New Orientation in Modernist Research* (Mainz: Matthias Grünewald, 1979), 24-5.

2. *Acta Sanctae Sedis* 40 (1907) 636-37.

3. T. Vargish, *Newman: The Contemplation of Mind* (Oxford: Clarendon Press, 1970), 52.

4. J.H. Newman, *An Essay In Aid of a Grammar of Assent,* (New York: Longmans, 1895), 279. Vargish, *Newman,* 67.

5. Vargish, *Newman,* 71.

6. N. Lash, *Newman on Development: The Search for an Explanation in History* (London: Sheed and Ward, 1975), 150.

7. Denzinger-Shönmetzer, *Enchiridion Symbolorum,* nos. 2001-2007.

8. DS 2010-2012.

9. DS 2738-2740.

10. J. Bellamy, *La théologie Catholique au XIXe siècle* (Paris: Beauchesne, 1904), 36.

11. M.J. Weaver, *Letters from a "Modernist": The Letters of George Tyrrell to Wilfrid Ward 1893-1908* (Shepherdstown WV: Patmos Press, 1981), 117n.

12. Ibid., 115-16.

13. L.F. Barmann, *Baron Friedrich von Hügel and the Modernist Crisis in England* (Cambridge: Cambridge University Press, 1972), 205.

14. P. Sabatier, *Les modernistes: Notes d'histoire religieuse contemporaine* (Paris: Fischbacher, 1909), 45. Sabatier had just written: "Que la bulle n'ait pas visé Newman, j'en suis tres sûr, pour la bonne raison que ses rédacteurs ignoraient Newman. Que ses idées ne soient pas atteintes par les condemnations, le dise qui veut, le dise qui peut" (Ibid., 44.).

15. Cited by B.D.Dupuy, "Newman's Influence in France," in J. Coulson and A.M. Allchin (eds), *The Rediscovery of Newman: An Oxford Symposium* (London: Sheed and Ward, 1967), 169.

16. G. Daly, *Transcendence and Immanence: A Study in Catholic Modernism and Integralism* (Oxford: Clarendon Press, 1980), 2-5.

17. J.H. Newman, *An Essay on the Development of Christian Doctrine* (1878), 38. In 1845 he had written "the germination, growth, and perfection of some living, that is, influential truth, or apparent truth, in the minds of men during a sufficient period." (Cameron edit. [London: Longmans//London: Penguin Books: 1974], 99.) Is there a shift of emphasis here, or does the 1878 version amount to no more than the stylistic conversion of a workaday sentence into one of Mozartian elegance?

18. J. Bellamy, *La théologie Catholique au XIXe siècle*, xl. Bellamy died before completing his book which was edited by J. V. Bainvel as one of a series published by the Institut Catholique of Paris under the general title *Bibliotèque de théologie historique*. The series included Joseph Turmel's *Histoire de la théologie positive depuis l'origine jusqu'au Concile de Trente* and F. Prat's *La théologie de saint Paul*.

19. Bellamy, *La théologie Catholique*, 130.

20. Ibid., 131.

21. Ibid., 124.

22. Ibid., 124.

23. DS 2829.

24. G.McCool, *Catholic Theology in the Nineteenth Century: The Quest for a Unitary Method* (New York: Seabury Press, 1977), 91.

25. T. Lynch (ed.), "The Newman-Perrone Paper on Development," *Gregorianum*, 16 (1935): 402-47.

26. Ibid., 413-14.

27. Ibid., 414.

28. Ibid., 413, emphasis added.

29. The period between 1846 and 1866 witnessed a stream of condemnations: Bonnetty, Günther, Baltzer, the Ontologists, Frohschammer, Ubaghs, and the Munich Congress of 1863. The *Syllabus of Errors* (1864) was a sort of grand finale at a fireworks display, with rockets and crackers going off in all directions.

30. O. Chadwick, *From Bossuet to Newman: The Idea of Doctrinal Development* (Cambridge: Cambridge University Press, 1957), 183.

31. H. Bernard-Maitre, "Un épisode significatif du modernisme: 'Histoire et dogme' de Maurice Blondel d'après les papiers inédits d'Alfred Loisy, 1897-1905)" *Recherches de science religieuse* 57 (1969): 58.

32. Newman, *Essay*, 1845 edit., 99; 1878 edit., 39 (italics added).

33. See G. Daly, "Theological Models in the Doctrine of Original Sin," *Heythrop Journal* 13 (1972): 121-42.

34. Newman, *Essay* (1878), 35.

35. Lash, *Newman on Development*, 57-60.

36. George A. Lindbeck, "The Problem of Doctrinal Development and Contemporary Protestant Theology," *Concilium* 1 (1967): 64-72.

37. Newman, *Essay* (1878), 40.

38. Lash, *Newman on Development*, 64.

39. E. Buonaiuti, *Pelegrino di Roma: La generazione dell'esodo* (ed. M. Niccoli, Bari:Laterza, 1964), 112.

206

40. W. Becker, "Newman's Influence in Germany," in *The Rediscovery of Newman,* 177.

41. E. Poulat, *Histoire, dogme et critique dans la crise moderniste* (Paris: Casterman, 1962), 61.

42. H. Bernard-Maitre, "Un épisode significatif du modernisme," 58.

43. A. Loisy, *Autour d'un petit livre* (Paris: Picard, 1903), 208.

44. See Loome, *Liberal Catholicism,* 17; and E. Leonard, *George Tyrrell and the Catholic Tradition* (London and New York: Paulist Press, 1982), 145 n. 38.

45. Letter to Raoul Gôut, in M.D. Petre, *Autobiography and Life of George Tyrrell* (London: Edward Arnold, 1912), 2:209.

46. K. Barth, *Fragments Grave and Gay* (London: Collins Fontana Library, 1971), 102-04.

47. G. Tyrrell, *Christianity at the Cross-Roads* (London: Longmans, 1909), 30; Lash, *Newman on Development,* 148.

48. G. Tyrrell, Introduction to H. Bremond, *The Mystery of Newman* (London, 1907), XV.

49. G. Tyrrell, *Christianity at the Cross-Roads,* 33.

50. P. XV.

51. J. Coulson, *Religion and Imagination: "In Aid of a Grammar of Assent"* (Oxford, Clarendon Press, 1981), 82.

52. G. Tyrrell, *Through Scylla and Charybdis: Or, the Old Theology and the New* (London: Longmans, 1907), 313.

53. D.M.MacKinnon and J.D. Holmes (eds), *Newman's University Sermons: Fifteen Sermons Preached before the University of Oxford 1826-43* (London: SPCK, 1970), 329.

54. Newman, *Essay* (1878), 55.

55. Petre, *Life of George Tyrrell* 2: 217.

56. Ibid., 220.

57. See J. Coulson, *Newman and the Common Tradition: A Study in the Language of Church and Society* (Oxford: Clarendon press, 1970), 175.

58. F. von Hügel, "Experience and Transcendence," *Dublin Review* 138 (1906), 358; *The Mystical Element of Religion* 2:338.

59. R.K. Browne, "Newman and von Hügel: A Record of an Early Meeting," *The Month* 212 (July 1961): 32-33.

60. M. de la Bedoyere, *The Life of Baron von Hügel* (London: Dent, 1951), 31.

61. Browne, "Newman and von Hügel"; ibid.,

SELECTED BIBLIOGRAPHY

Abercrombie, Nigel, *The Life and Work of Edmund Bishop* (London: Longmans, 1959).

Altholz, Josef L., *The Liberal Catholic Movement in England: The "Rambler" and its Contributors, 1848-1864* (London: Burns & Oates, 1962).

Artz, Johannes, "Entstehung und Auswirkungen von Newmans Theorie der Dogmenentwicklung," *Tübinger Theologische Quartalschrift* 148 (1968): 63-104, 167-222, also as the Introduction in Newman, *Ueber die Entwicklung der Glaubenslehre*, ix-lii, Ausgewählte Werke, 8 (Mainz: Grünewald, 1969).

————, "Newmans Kardinalat," *Theologie und Philosophie* 53 (1978): 220-47.

————, *Newman-Lexikon*, Ausgewählte Werke von John Henry Newman, 9 (Mainz: Grünewald, 1975).

Aubert, Roger, "Les étapes de l'influence du cardinal Newman. Un précurseur longtemps méconnu," in *Wissen Glauben Politik*, edited by W. Gruber, J. Ladrière and N. Leser (Graz: Styria, 1981).

Barmann, Lawrence, *Baron Friedrich von Hügel and the Modernist Crisis in England* (Cambridge: Cambridge University Press, 1972).

Barth, Karl, *Fragments Grave and Gay* (London: Collins Fontana Library, 1971).

Bellamy, J., *La theologie Catholique au XIX siecle* (Paris: Beauchesne, 1904).

Bernard-Maitre, H. "Un episode significatif du modernism: 'Histoire et dogme' de Maurice Blondel d'apres les papiers inedits d'Alfred Loisy, 1897-1905," *Recherches de science religieuse* 57 (1969): 49-74.

Blanchet, André, "L'Abbe Bremond: quelques traits pour un portrait futur," *Entretiens sur Henri Bremond*, edited by Maurice Nédoncelle and Jean Dagens (Paris: Mouton, 1967).

————, *Henri Bremond: 1865-1904* (Paris: Aubier Montaigne, 1975).

————, ed. *Henri Bremond-Maurice Blondel: Correspondance*, 3 vols. (Paris: Aubier Montaigne, 1970-1).

Bremond, André, "Henri Bremond," *Etudes* 217 (1933): 29-53.

Bremond, Henri, "Apologie pour les Newmanistes français," *Revue Pratique d'Apologétique* 3 (1907): 655-66.

————, "Autour de Newman," *Annales de Philosophie Chrétienne* 155 (1908): 337-69.

————, *Histoire littéraire du sentiment religieux en France* (Paris: Bloud et Gay, 1929-33).

————, *L'Inquiétude Religieuse,* vol. 1 (Paris: Perrin et Cie., 1901).

————, "Mémoire et Dévotion: Etude sur la psychologie religieuse de Newman," *Annales de Philosophie Chrétienne* 151 (1905): 259-70.

————, *Newman: Le Développement du Dogme Chrétien* (Paris: Librairie Bloud et Cie., 1904).

————, *Newman: Essai de biographie psychologique* (Paris: Bloud et Gay, 1906), translated by H.C. Corrance under the title *The Mystery of Newman* (London: Williams and Norgate, 1907).

————, ed. *Newman: la vie chrétienne* (Paris: Bloud et Gay, 1906).

————, *Newman,* vol. 2, *Psychologie de la foi* (Paris: Librairie Bloud et Cie., 1905).

————, "La Premiere Conversion de Newman," *Annales de Philosophie Chretiénne* 151 (1905): 160-79.

Briggs, Charles Augustus, "The Encyclical against Modernism," *The North American Review* 187 (February 1908): 204-5.

Browne, R.K. "Newman and von Hügel: A Record of an Early Meeting, *The Month,* N.S. 26 (1961): 24-33.

Buonaiuti, Ernesto, *Pelegrino di Roma: La generazione dell' esodo,* Ed. M. Niccoli (Bari: Laterza, 1964).

Burke, Ronald, "Loisy's Faith: Landshift in Catholic Thought," *The Journal of Religion* 60 (1980): 138-64.

Buschkühl, Matthias, *Die irische, schottische und römische Frage* (Sankt Ottilien: EOS Verlag, 1980).

Butler, Bishop B.C., "Newman and the Second Vatican Council," *The Rediscovery of Newman,* edited by John Coulson and A.M. Allchin (London: Sheed and Ward, 1967).

Chadwick, Owen, *From Bossuet to Newman: The Idea of Doctrinal Development* (Cambridge: Cambridge University Press, 1957).

————, *Newman* (New York: Oxford University Press, 1983).

————, *The Victorian Church*, 2 vols. (London: A. and C. Black, 1966-70).

Church, Richard W., *Occasional Papers*, vol. 2 (London: Macmillan, 1897).

Cockshut, A.O.J., *Truth to Life: The Art of Biography in the Nineteenth Century* (New York: Harcourt, Brace, Jovanovich, 1974).

Coulson, John, "Introduction," *On Consulting the Faithful in Matters of Doctrine* by John Henry Newman (London: G. Chapman, 1961).

————, *Newman and the Common Tradition* (Oxford: Clarendon Press, 1970).

————, and Allchin, A.M., editors, *The Rediscovery of Newman: An Oxford Symposium* (London: Sheed and Ward, 1967).

————, *Religion and Imagination: "In Aid of a Grammar of Assent"* (Oxford: Clarendon Press, 1981).

Cuthbert, Father, "Apologist of the Catholic Church," *Dublin Review* 159 (1916): 1-22.

Daly, Gabriel, "Theological Models in the Doctrine of Original Sin," *Heythrop Journal*, 13 (1972): 121-42.

————, *Transcendence and Immanence: A Study in Catholic Modernism and Integralism* (Oxford: Clarendon Press, 1980).

Darboy, Abbe G., "Comment y a-t-il progrès doctrinal dans le catholicisme?" *Correspondant* 23 (1848): 281-93.

Davis, Charles, " 'Fluent Benthamites and Muddled Coleridgians'—The Liberal and Conservative Traditions of Discourse," *Papers of the Nineteenth Century Theology Working Group*, edited by Garrett Green and Marilyn Chapin Massey (Berkeley, CA: The Graduate Theological Union, 1982).

DeLaura, David J., et al., *Victorian Prose: A Guide to Research* (New York: Modern Language Association, 1973).

Dessain, Charles Stephen, *John Henry Newman* (London: Thomas Nelson, 1966).

————, ed., *The Letters and Diaries of John Henry Newman*, 31 vols. (London and Oxford: Thomas Nelson and Son, and Oxford University Press, 1961-73).

Döllinger, Ignaz von, *Briefe und Erklärungen über die vatikanischen Dekrete* (Munich: C.H. Beck, 1890).

211

Fey, William R., *Faith and Doubt: The Unfolding of Newman's Thought on Certainty* (Shepherdstown, WV: Patmos Press, 1976).

Flanagan, Philip, "Introduction," *Newman against the Liberals*, edited by Michael Davies (New Rochelle: Arlington House, 1978).

Gadille, Jacques, et al., *Les catholiques libéraux au xixe siècle* (Grenoble: Presses universitaires de Grenoble, 1974).

Gilley, Sheridan, "Wilfrid Ward and His Life of Newman," *Journal of Ecclesiastical History* 29 (April 1978): 177-93.

Goodwin, Gregory, "Newman and the Matter of Reputation: The Contribution of the Letters and Diaries, 1845-1853," (Ph.D. diss., Vanderbilt University, 1981).

Grandmaison, Leonce de., *"L'Évangile et l'Église,"* *Etudes* 94 (1903): 155.

Harnack, Adolf von, *Lehrbuch der Dogmengeschichte,* vol 3 (Tübingen: J.C.B.Mohr, 1909).

Hastings, Adrian, ed., *Bishops and Writers: Aspects of the Evolution of Modern English Catholicism* (Wheathampstead: A. Clarke, 1977).

Hogarth, Henry, *Henri Bremond: The Life and Work of a Devout Humanist* (London: S.P.C.K., 1950).

Holland, Bernard, ed., *Baron Friedrich von Hügel: Selected Letters* (London: J.M.Dent and Sons Ltd., 1928).

Holmes, J. Derek. "Liberal Catholicism and Newman's *Letter to the Duke of Norfolk,"* *Clergy Review* 60 (1975): 498-511.

————, *More Roman than Rome: English Catholicism in the Nineteenth Century* (Shepherdstown, WV: Patmos Press, 1978).

————, "Newman and Mivart," *Clergy Review* 50 (1965): 852-67.

————"Newman's Attitude Towards Historical Criticism and Biblical Inspiration," *The Downside Review* 89 (1971): 22-37.

Hügel, Friedrich von, *The Mystical Element of Religion,* 2 vols. (London: J.M. Dent, 1908).

————, Nathan Söderblom and Friedrich Heiler, *Breifwechsel 1909-1931,* edited with commentary by Paul Misner (Paderborn: Verlag Bonifatius-Druckerei, 1981).

Kelly, E.E., "Newman, Wilfrid Ward and the Modernist Crisis," *Thought* 43 (1973): 508-19.

Kelly, James J., "Experience and Transcendence: An Introduction to the Religious Philosophy of Baron von Hügel," *The Downside Review* 99 (1981): 172-89.

————, *Baron Friedrich von Hügel's Philosophy of Religion* (Louvain: Louvain University Press, 1983).

Kraus, Franz Xaver, *Tagebücher,* edited by H. Schiel (Cologne: J.P. Bachem, 1957).

Lash, Nicholas, "Introduction," *Grammar of Assent* by John Henry Newman (Notre Dame: University of Notre Dame Press, 1979).

————, *Newman and Development: The Search for an Explanation in History* (Shepherdstown, WV: Patmos Press, 1975).

Lease, Gary, "Merry del Val and Tyrrell: A Modernist Struggle," *The Downside Review* 102 (1984): 133-56.

————, *Witness to the Faith* (Shannon: Irish University Press, 1971).

Lebreton, Jules, "Autour de Newman," *Revue Pratique d'Apologétique* 3 (1907): 488-504.

————, "Le primat de la conscience d'apres Newman," *Revue Pratique d'Apologétique* 3 (1907): 667-75.

Lee, G., "Newman's 'Probabilities,' " *The Ecclesiastical Review* 38 (1908): 528-41.

Leonard, Ellen, *George Tyrrell and the Catholic Tradition* (London and New York: Paulist Press, 1982).

Lindbeck, George A., "The Problem of Doctrinal Development and Contemporary Protestant Theology," *Concilium* 1 (1967): 64-72.

Loisy, Alfred, *Autour d'un petit livre* (Paris: Picard, 1903).

————, *Choses passées* (Paris: Emile Nourry, 1913).

————, *George Tyrrell et Henri Bremond* (Paris: Librairie Emile Nourry, 1936).

————, *Mémoires pour servir à l'histoire religieuses de notre temps,* 3 vols. (Paris: Emile Nourry, 1930-1).

————, *Un myth apologétique* (Paris: Emile Mourry, 1938.)

Loome, Thomas Michael, *Liberal Catholicism, Reform Catholicism, Modernism* (Mainz: Matthias-Grünewald, 1979).

Lynch, T., (ed.), "The Newman-Perrone Paper on Development," *Gregorianum* 16 (1935): 402-47.

McCool, Gerald A., *Catholic Theology in the Nineteenth Century: The Quest for a Unitary Method* (New York: Seabury Press, 1977).

MacDougall, Hugh A., *The Acton-Newman Relations: The Dilemma of Christian Liberalism* (New York: Fordham University Press, 1962).

McElrath, Damian et al., *Lord Acton: The Decisive Decade 1864-1874* (Louvain: Publications Universitaires, 1970).

Merry del Val, Raphael, *The Truth of Papal Claims* (London: Sands and Co., 1902).

Misner, Paul, "Newmanian Reflections on Religious Literacy," in *Foundations of Religious Literacy*, edited by John V. Apczynski (Chico, CA: Scholars Press, 1983).

————, "Newman's Concept of Revelation and the Development of Doctrine," *The Heythrop Journal* 11(1970): 32-47.

————, *Papacy and Development: Newman and the Primacy of the Pope*, Studies in the History of Christian Thought, vol. 15 (Leiden: E.J. Brill, 1976).

Nédoncelle, Maurice and Dagens, Jean, eds., *Entretiens sur Henri Bremond* (Paris: Editions Mouton, 1967).

Newman, John Henry, *Apologia pro Vita Sua*, ed., Martin J. Svaglic (Oxford: Clarendon Press, 1967).

————, *An Essay in Aid of a Grammar of Assent* (Westminster, MD: Christian Classics Inc., 1973). Rpt. of Uniform Edition.

————, *An Essay on the Development of Christian Doctrine* (Westminster, MD: Christian Classics, Inc., 1968), Rpt. of Uniform Edition (1878).

————, *The Idea of a University*, ed. Ian T. Ker (Oxford: Clarendon Press, 1976).

————, *A Letter Addressed to His Grace the Duke of Norfolk on the Occasion of Mr. Gladstone's Recent Expostulation*. In *Certain Difficulties Felt by Anglicans* (London: Longmans, Green,1876).

————, *The Letters and Diaries of John Henry Newman*, ed. C. Stephen Dessain, et al., 31 vols. (London and Oxford: Thomas Nelson and Sons and Clarendon Press, 1961-73).

————, *Newman's University Sermons*, Introductions by D.S. MacKinnon and J.S. Holmes (London: S.P.C.K., 1970).

————, *On Consulting the Faithful in Matters of Doctrine*, edited by John Coulson (New York: Sheed and Ward, 1962).

————, *On the Inspiration of Scripture,* edited by J. Derek Holmes and R. Murray (Washington, DC: Corpus Books, 1967).

————, *The Theological Papers of John Henry Newman on Biblical Inspiration and on Infallibility,* edited by J. Derek Holmes (Oxford: Clarendon Press, 1979).

————, *The Theological Papers of John Henry Newman on Faith and Certainty,* edited by Hugo M. de Achaval and J. Derek Holmes (Oxford: Clarendon Press, 1976).

————, *The Via Media of the Anglical Church,* 2 vols. (Westminster, MD: Christian Classics Inc., 1978). Rpt. of Uniform Edition.

O'Dwyer, Edward Thomas, *Cardinal Newman and the Encyclical Pascendi Dominici gregis* (London: Longmans, Green and Co., 1908).

Palmer, Roundell [Lord Selborne], *Memorials,* edited by Lady Sophia Palmer (London: Macmillan, 1896-8).

Petre, Maude, *Autobiography and Life of George Tyrrell,* 2 vols. (London: Edward Arnold, 1912).

————, ed., *George Tyrrell's Letters* (London: T. Fisher Unwin, 1920).

————, *Von Hügel and Tyrrell* (New York: E.P. Dutton, 1937).

Poulat, Emile, ed., *Alfred Loisy: sa vie, son oeuvre, par Albert Houtin et Felix Sartiaux* (Paris: Editions du Centre National de la Recherche Scientifique, 1960).

————, *Histoire, dogme et critique dans la crise moderniste* (Paris: Casterman, 1979).

————, *Modernistica* (Paris: Nouvelles Editions Latines, 1982).

Prickett, Stephen, *Romanticism and Religion: The Tradition of Coleridge and Wordsworth in the Victorian Church* (Cambridge: Cambridge University Press, 1976).

Prior, John, *Cardinal Newman and the Magisterium of the Church* (Rome: 1909).

Provencher, Normand, "Une tentative de renouvellement de l'herméneutique biblique: le modernisme d'Alfred Loisy," *Eglise et théologie* 7(1976): 341-66.

Przywara, Erich, "Zur Geschichte des 'modernistischen' Newman," *Stimmen der Zeit* 102 (1922): 443-51.

Purcell, Edmund, *The Life of Cardinal Manning,* 2 vols. (London: Macmillan, 1896).

215

Reardon, Bernard M.G., "Newman and the Catholic Modernists," *The Church Quarterly Review* 4 (1971): 50-60.

Rollman, Hans., "Holtzman, von Hügel and Modernism — 1," *The Downside Review* 97 (1979): 128-43.

Russell, H.P., "A Lesson from Newman," *The Ecclesiastical Review* 38 (1908): 514-28.

Sabatier, Paul, *Modernism* (New York: Charles Scribner's, 1908).

————, *Les modernistes: Notes d'histoire religieuse contemporaine* (Paris: Fischbacher, 1909).

Saisset, Emile, "De l'origine et de la formation du Christianisme, a l'occasion du livre de M. Newman," *La Liberté de penser* 12 (1848): 337-57.

Sanks, T. Howland, *Authority in the Church: A Study of Changing Paradigms* (Missoula, MT: Scholars Press, 1974).

Sarolea, Charles, *Cardinal Newman and his Influence on Religious Life and Thought* (Edinburgh: T. and T. Clark, 1908).

Schultenover, David, *George Tyrrell: In Search of Catholicism* (Shepherdstown, WV: Patmos Press, 1981).

Snider, Carlo, "Il Cardinalato di Newman," In *John Henry Newman: Saggio commemorativo nel Centenario del Cardinalato,* edited by M. K. Strolz (Rome: Gregorian University, 1979).

Tyrrell, George, *Christianity at the Cross-Roads* (London: Longmans, 1909).

————, "The Condemnation of Newman," *The Manchester Guardian,* 20 November 1907.

————, "Introduction," In *The Mystery of Newman* by Henri Bremond (London: Williams and Norgate, 1907).

————, " 'Newman through French Spectacles' — A Reply," *The Tablet* 108 (4 August 1906): 163-5.

————, "The Pope and Modernism," *The London Times,* 30 September and 1 October 1907.

————, *Through Scylla and Charybdis: Or, the Old Theology and the New* (London: Longmans, 1907).

Vargish, Thomas, *Newman: The Contemplation of Mind* (Oxford: Clarendon Press, 1980).

Vidler, Alec, *A Variety of Catholic Modernists* (Cambridge: Cambridge University Press, 1970).

Vieban, A., "Who are the Modernists of the Encyclical?" *The Ecclesiastical Review*, 38 (1908): 489-508.

Ward, Maisie, *Insurrection versus Resurrection* (New York: Sheed and Ward, 1937).

————, *The Wilfrid Wards and the Transition* (London: Sheed and Ward, 1934).

————, *Young Mr. Newman* (London: Sheed and Ward, 1948).

Ward, Wilfrid, "Catholic Apologetics: A Reply," *The Nineteenth Century* 45 (1899): 955-61.

————, "Doctores Ecclesiae," *The Pilot* 2 (1901): 774-6.

————, "*The Edinburgh Review* on Cardinal Newman," *The Ninetheenth Century* 72 (1912): 69-87.

————, "The Encyclical *Pascendi*," *The Dublin Review* 142 (1908): 1-10.

————"The Ethics of Religious Conformity," *The Quarterly Review* 189 (1899): 103-36.

————, *Last Lectures* (London: Longmans, Green 1918).

————, "Liberalism and Intransigence," *The Nineteenth Century* 47 (1900): 960-73.

————, *The Life and Times of Cardinal Wiseman*, 2 vols. (London: Longmans, 1897).

————, *The Life of John Henry Cardinal Newman*, 2 vols. (London: Longmans, Green, 1912).

————, "Newman through French Spectacles," *The Tablet* 108 (21 July 1906): 86-9.

————, "New Wine in Old Bottles," *The Nineteenth Century* 27 (1890): 942-56.

————, "Introduction," In *On the Scope and Nature of University Education* by John Henry Newman (London and New York: Everyman's Library, 1915).

————, "The Rigidity of Rome," *The Nineteenth Century* 38 (1895): 786-804.

————, "Two Views of Cardinal Newman," *The Dublin Review* 282 (1907): 1-15.

————, *William George Ward and the Catholic Revival* (London: Longmans, 1893).

Weaver, Mary Jo, "A Bibliography of the Published Works of Wilfrid Ward," *The Heythrop Journal* 20 (1979): 399-420.

————, "George Tyrrell and the Joint Pastoral Letter," *The Downside Review* 99 (1981): 18-39.

————, ed., *Letters from a "Modernist:" The Letters of George Tyrrell to Wilfrid Ward, 1893-1908* (Shepherdstown, WV: Patmos Press, 1981).

————, "Wilfrid Ward, George Tyrrell and the Meanings of Modernism," *The Downside Review* 96 (1978): 21-34.

Whyte, Alexander, *Newman: An Appreciation* (Edinburgh: Oliphant, Anderson and Ferrier, 1901).

Williams, William J., *Newman, Pascal, Loisy and the Catholic Church* (London: Francis Griffiths, 1906).

Yearley, Lee H., *The Ideas of Newman: Christianity and Human Religiosity* (University Park, PA: Pennsylvania State University Press, 1978).

Young, Urban, *Dominic of the Mother of God: The Life and Letters of the Venerable Fr. Dominic Barberi* (London: Burns, Oates and Washbourne, 1935).

Zenos [Franz Xaver Kraus], "Fluctus feri maris," (= centenarbetrachtungen V) *Beilage zur Allgemeinen Zeitung* 75 (Munich: 1 April 1901).

CONTRIBUTORS

PAUL MISNER, associate professor of theology at Marquette University, has published a book on Newman as well as an edition of letters of Baron von Hügel (in German). He is currently working on a history of Catholic social thought.

MARY JO WEAVER, associate professor of religious studies at Indiana University, has published articles on Wilfrid Ward in *The Downside Review, The Heythrop Journal*, and *Recusant History*. Her book, *Letters from a "Modernist"* (1981) is an edition of previously unknown letters from George Tyrrell to Wilfrid Ward.

NADIA LAHUTSKY is an assistant professor of religion-studies at Texas Christian University, Fort Worth, Texas, where she teaches Introduction to Religion-Studies, Church History, Contemporary Catholicism and Women's Studies. She received her doctorate from Vanderbilt University after completing a dissertation on Wilfrid Ward.

JOHN D. ROOT is associate professor of history and chairman of the Department of Humanities at the Illinois Institute of Technology. His investigations of British intellectual and religious history have appeared in such journals as *The Catholic Historical Review, Victorian Studies, The Harvard Theological Review* and *The Downside Review.*

NICHOLAS SAGOVSKY is vice-principal of the Episcopal Theological College, Edinburgh, where he teaches doctrine. He has published *Between Two Worlds: George Tyrrell's Relationship to the Thought of Matthew Arnold* (1983) and is presently working on a biography of George Tyrrell.

ROGER HAIGHT, S.J., is an associate professor of systematic and historical theology at Regis College of the Toronto School of Theology. His essays on Modernism include an essay on Bondel, Laberthonnière and Le Roy in *Theological Studies* (1974), and one on Edouard Le Roy in *Science et Espirit* (1983).

219

RONALD BURKE, professor of religion at the University of Nebraska, Omaha, has published on Modernism and more recent Catholic thought in *The Journal of Religion, Theological Studies, The Downside Review, JAAR,* and other places. He founded the Roman Catholic Modernism Group in the American Academy of Religion in 1976.

GARY LEASE, currently professor of history of consciousness at the University of California, Santa Cruz, is a cultural historian who specializes in the history of religions. His main areas of concentration are Hellenistic religions, including nascent Christianity, and 19th- and 20th-century European religious thought, in particular, the inter-relationship of the political and religious orders.

GABRIEL DALY is an Augustinian who teaches systematic and historical theology in Dublin at Milltown Institute and also at Trinity College and the Irish School of Ecumenics. He is chairman of the Irish Theological Association. His books include *Transcendence and Immanence* and *Asking the Father: A Study of the Prayer of Petition.*

INDEX

Acton, Lord, 5, 8, 60-61, 62
Apologia pro Vita Sua, 5, 6, 8-9, 10, 11, 12, 14, 16, 18, 48, 97, 98, 164, 169, 173, 174
Aquinas, Thomas, 30, 98-99

Bacchus, Joseph, 55
Bellasis, Edward, 50, 51
Bellasis, Henry, 50
Bellasis, Richard, 50-59
Birmington Oratory, 47-60
Blondel, Maurice, 20, 71, 120, 123, 125, 128, 130-31, 187, 193
Bremond, Henri, 16, 28, 81-82, 110, 140, 145, 168, 169-70, 173; context of interpretation of Newman, 120-21; method of interpreting Newman, 121-22; portrayal of Newman, 123-32, 166, 167, 187

Difficulties of Anglicans, 167
Döllinger, J. J. Ignaz von, 61-63, 161

An Essay in Aid of a Grammar of Assent, 12, 14-16, 21, 84, 97, 98, 99, 101, 102, 109, 123, 124, 125, 126, 130, 167, 168, 172, 200, 202
An Essay on the Development of Christian Doctrine, 12-14, 16, 73, 77, 84, 97, 98, 101, 108, 109, 124, 140, 141, 161, 167, 168, 169, 172

Hermes, Georg, 188-89
Home and Foreign Review, 8, 60, 62

Hügel, Friedrich von, 10, 16, 17, 19-19-20, 28, 31, 34, 35, 38, 56, 64, 70, 71-72, 73, 74, 86, 203-204

Idea of a University, 7

Jansen, Cornelius, 30, 56, 188
Jansenists, 31, 188
Joint Pastoral Letter (1901), 30, 36, 104-105

Lebreton, Jules, 129, 190, 202
Lectures on the Prophetical Office, 12, 16-17
Leo XIII, 11, 17, 19, 72, 163, 166, 174, 175, 191
Letter to the Duke of Norfolk, 10, 16, 48, 97, 109, 172
Liberal Catholicism, 4-6, 11, 21, 60, 71-72, 83, 104, 186
Loisy, Alfred Firmin, 13, 37, 38, 56, 71, 74, 78, 79-80, 110, 119, 120, 167-68, 169, 196, 201; compared to Newman, 139-41, 151; criticized Newman, 142; early life of, 142-145; *Essais* of, 145-51; faith of, 143-44, 147-51, 152-53; familiarity with Newman's writings, 141, 144; idea of inspiration, 142-43; idea of revelation, 142, 147-79, 151, 152; influenced by Newman, 144-45, 147, 152

McIntyre, John, 55
Manning, Henry Edward, 7, 9, 10, 20, 48, 62, 162-63

221

Merry del Val, Raphael, 82-83, 164, 176, 190

Modernism, 3, 20, 28, 35-38, 120-21; and Newman, 12-16, 29-31, 51-53, 55-57, 82-85, 97, 108-110, 123, 128-32, 163-76, 185-204

Munich Brief, 62

Neville, William, 31, 47, 50, 51

Newman, John Henry: associated with Modernism, 12-16, 29-31, 51-53, 55-57, 82-86, 97, 108-111, 123, 128-32, 163-76, 185-204; attitude toward inspiration of scripture, 17-20; attitude toward papal authority, 5, 9-10, 173-74, 175; Bremond's, 119, 123-32; compared to Loisy, 79-81, 139-42, 144-47, 151-53; conservativism of, 3-4; converted to Catholicism, 161-62; "Liberal Catholicism" of, 5-11, 20-21, 37, 60-61, 162-76; on education, 7, 58-59, 62; principles of, 13; Tyrrell's debt to, 97-111; Ward's interpretation of, 27-28, 58-64, 164; Williams's representation of, 75-80. *See also names of individual works*

Norris, John, 50, 51, 53-54, 56, 83-85, 171, 189

O'Dwyer, Edward, 37, 52, 54, 173-74, 190

"On Consulting the Faithful in Matters of Doctrine," 7, 162

"On the Inspiration of Scripture," 18

Oxford Movement, 5, 6, 161, 166

Papalism. *See* Ultramontanism

Pascendi dominici gregis, 28, 29-30, 31, 33, 36, 37, 38, 51-53, 64, 82-86, 87, 97, 109, 164, 165, 168-75, 185-86, 188, 189-90

Pius IX, 5, 30, 62, 163, 166, 189, 192

Pius X, 82, 84, 174, 175, 190

Providentissimus Deus, 19, 69

Rahner, Karl, 151-52

Rambler, 8, 60-61, 162

Simpson, Richard, 60-61

Synthetic Society, 70-71

Talbot, Edmund, 53, 54, 56-57

Talbot, George, 11, 162, 192

Tyrrell, George, 16, 19, 30, 35, 37, 56, 70, 71, 72, 74-75, 79, 80, 81, 82, 83, 84, 86-87, 167, 168, 169-72, 186, 187-88, 189; debt to Newman, 13, 97-103, 196; departure from Newman's thought, 103-111, 200-203

Ullathorne, William Bernard, 7

Ultramontanism, 5, 9, 10, 17, 21, 185, 186

University Sermons, 12, 14, 16, 32, 97, 98, 107, 123, 124, 130, 187, 202

Vatican Council, First, 9-10, 17, 18-19

Vatican Council, Second, 151, 175, 185, 196, 198-99

Vaughan, John, 9, 70, 84, 171-72

Ward, Wilfrid, 10, 16, 17, 19, 72, 74, 98, 100, 122, 164; applied Newman to own time, 34-38, 73, 107; as biographer, 27; difficulty of assignment to Newman biography, 47-50; difficulties in writing Newman biography, 50-57; founder of Synthetic Society, 70; interpretor of Newman, 27-31, 32-34, 58-64; life and beliefs of, 27-28; reaction to *Pascendi*, 84-86,

222

171, 189-90; reaction to Williams's book on Newman, 80-81

Ward, William George, 7, 9, 10, 16, 20, 34, 40, 62, 100

Williams, J. Herbert, 73-74

Williams, William John, 30, 189; argument with J. Herbert Williams, 73; critical reaction to work on Newman, 80-82; early life of, 69-70; later years, 86-88; member of Rota, 72; member of Synthetic Society, 70-71; reaction to *Pascendi*, 82-86, 171; work on Newman, 73-80

Wiseman, Nicholas, 7, 58-59; subject of biography by Wilfrid Ward, 27, 49, 50